PRAISE FOR

TO STOP A WARLORD

"Sister Shannon's compelling and inspiring book, *To Stop a Warlord*, beautifully moves each of us to take action to help the most vulnerable among us."

—ARCHBISHOP EMERITUS DESMOND TUTU

"How far would you go to stop a murderous Ugandan warlord who had turned thousands of children into soldiers? As the head of a human rights foundation, Shannon Sedgwick Davis did something unprecedented: She hired private military contractors to train an army to stop him. This is an extraordinary memoir by an extraordinary leader—it's impossible to read without feeling moved to do more to help those with less."

—ADAM GRANT, *New York Times* bestselling author of *Originals* and *Give and Take*

"Buckle up—this book is about to make you feel delightfully uncomfortable and incredibly motivated to stop waiting for permission and go live your life."

—BOB GOFF, Honorary Consul, Republic of Uganda, and author of the *New York Times* bestsellers *Love Does* and *Everybody Always*

"In this remarkable book, Shannon Sedgwick Davis proves what can be achieved when you have the courage and determination to end suffering. Her story reminds us that we have more in common than we suspect, and more power than we believe."

—PRESIDENT JIMMY CARTER

"Shannon Sedgwick Davis is a mom, a lawyer, the leader of a powerful foundation, but most of all, she is someone deeply committed to justice for all. Her captivating story takes the reader on an adventure like no other, one that challenges us to rethink how we make change in the world."

—SIR RICHARD BRANSON, philanthropist
and chairman of the Virgin Group

"When I met Shannon ten years ago, I knew I had much to learn from this powerful, wise, and unstoppable person. Since then, she's been a role model for me, and an unwavering guiding force in my life. She's a businesswoman who leads with her heart, every decision she makes is ethically informed, and she walks through life with compassion and grace. Shannon's story about her tireless pursuit of justice is not only required reading for today's activists, but is also a way for readers to experience her the way I am lucky enough to—as a friend."

—KRISTEN BELL

"Shannon Sedgwick Davis imagined, planned, and launched a brilliant, courageous effort that empowered local African heroes to defeat one of the world's most brutal and evil terrorist organizations. Even more stunning, she and her team helped win the peace. One of the most remarkable leaders I've ever encountered, Shannon proves what a citizen can do. Now, she has shared her story in a superb book—a blend of grand vision, bold decisions, gritty operations, wrenching heartbreak, and enduring inspiration. She writes like she leads—with modesty in herself, unrelenting dedication to the mission, and hope for humanity."

—AMBASSADOR HENRY A. CRUMPTON, former U.S.
Coordinator for Counterterrorism, and author of the
New York Times bestseller *The Art of Intelligence*

"I have always admired Shannon Sedgwick Davis's deep compassion, relentless determination, motherly protective instinct, and steadfast courage. And then I read *To Stop a Warlord*, a beautifully written memoir, and smiled knowing that her story will inspire so many more to follow in her footsteps."

—BLAKE MYCOSKIE, Founder and Chief Shoe Giver, TOMS

"I have met Joseph Kony face-to-face and spent years trying to convince him to peacefully surrender. As a Ugandan from the LRA-affected areas and a mother myself, I found this book truly remarkable and inspiring. It shows how we can make a change outside our backyards in a meaningful and culturally appropriate way."

—BETTY BIGOMBE, Senior Director for Fragility, Conflict, and Violence at the World Bank, Chief Mediator for the peace initiative with the Lord's Resistance Army, 1994–2005

"A fast-paced and intense geopolitical narrative."

—*Publishers Weekly*

"[Sedgwick] Davis's story has all the makings of a great thriller. The author shares her insight as a young Christian mother as well as a lawyer and peace advocate. The story is filled with adventure, unexpected turns, and heart-wrenching moments and is capped by an unexpected but credible ending."

—*Library Journal* (starred review)

TO STOP
A WARLORD

TO STOP
A WARLORD

MY STORY OF JUSTICE, GRACE,
AND THE FIGHT FOR PEACE

Shannon Sedgwick Davis

RANDOM HOUSE · NEW YORK

2020 Random House Trade Paperback Edition

Published in the United States by Random House, an imprint and division of
Penguin Random House LLC, New York.

RANDOM HOUSE and the HOUSE colophon are registered trademarks
of Penguin Random House LLC.

Originally published in hardcover and in slightly different form in the
United States by Spiegel & Grau, an imprint of Random House,
a division of Penguin Random House LLC, in 2019.

LIBRARY OF CONGRESS CATALOGING-IN-PUBLICATION DATA
Names: Davis, Shannon Sedgwick, author.
Title: To stop a warlord: my story of justice, grace, and the fight for peace /
Shannon Sedgwick Davis.
Description: | New York: Spiegel & Grau, [2019]
Identifiers: LCCN 2018024393 | ISBN 9780812985863 (trade paperback) |
ISBN 9780812995930 (ebook)
Subjects: LCSH: Davis, Shannon Sedgwick. | Human rights workers—Uganda—Biography.
| Lord's Resistance Army. | Military assistance—Uganda—History—21st century. |
Special forces (Military science)—Uganda—Training of. | STTEP (Private military
company)—History. | Human rights workers—United States—Biography. |
Military assistance, American—History—21st century. | Insurgency—
Uganda. | Uganda—History—1979– | LCGFT: Autobiographies.
Classification: LCC DT433.287.D38 A3 2019 | DDC 967.6104/4092 [B]—dc23
LC record available at https://lccn.loc.gov/2018024393

Printed in the United States of America on acid-free paper

randomhousebooks.com

2 4 6 8 9 7 5 3 1

Book design by Jo Anne Metsch

For Laren—this mission was one of the greatest privileges of my life—thank you

For my boys—you are my whole heart

CONTENTS

FOREWORD BY HOWARD G. BUFFETT   xi

INTENTIONS   xv

MAP   xvii

PART ONE   1

1. To Stop a Warlord   3

Who Do You Love the Most?—David Ocitti   9

2. Protection Urgently Needed   21
3. Band-Aids on Bullet Holes   26
4. A Thousand Haystacks   31
5. A Mother's Wish   37
6. Makombo   40

You Could Be Next—David Ocitti   47

7. Training and Communications   52
8. The Ones We Were Waiting For   55

Panga—David Ocitti   60

9. Zebras   63
10. Red Tape and River Rafts   67
11. A Close Call   72

12. Red Zone   78

13. Leather Shoes and Radios   83

   There Is a Time—David Ocitti   89

14. Iron Lady from Texas   95

15. Non-negotiables   101

16. Al Dente   104

17. Impossible Terms   106

18. Drone   109

   The Face of God—David Ocitti   111

19. Black and White   113

PART TWO   119

20. In at Half   121

   A Dirty Path—David Ocitti   123

21. Impossible Cause   125

22. Use the Force   129

23. Operation Viper   131

24. Flight Manifest   134

   It Was You—David Ocitti   138

25. False Ridge   140

26. Camp Bondo   143

27. Dance for Saint Jude   152

28. Not in Our Interests   156

29. Contact   161

30. Command, Man Down   163

31. Crocodiles and Killer Bees   167

   Peace Club—David Ocitti   171

32. Father, Daughter   174

33. Jamaled 176
34. Called Out 179
35. The Farmer 182

Gulu University—David Ocitti 188

36. Coined 191
37. *Kony 2012* 193
38. Otukene Means Grace 198
39. Big Fish 201
40. Peanut Butter and Jelly Sandwich 209

Roadie—David Ocitti 215

41. Tracking White Ant 218
42. Okello's Teeth 227
43. Binany's GPS 233
44. Operation Merlin 236
45. What Is Good 245

PART THREE 247

46. Cut the Snake off the Head 249
47. Odhiambo the Butcher 256

History Checks In—David Ocitti 261

48. Blue-Eyed Acholi 263

Five-Piece Suit—David Ocitti 266

49. Let Your Heart Speak to You 269
50. A Son Never Forgets 273
51. Brother, You Are Home 276

The Bitter Root—David Ocitti 279

52. Grace's Sun 284
53. He Calls Himself Ali 287

CONTENTS

So It Can End—David Ocitti   290

54. Evil Has Taught Me the Most   293

EPILOGUE   299

ACKNOWLEDGMENTS   305

TIMELINE   313

GLOSSARY OF TERMS   317

HOW YOU CAN HELP   321

FOREWORD

by Howard G. Buffett

More than two decades of working on food security in Africa has taught me that where there is hunger, rule of law is often absent. In January 2012 that reality brought me back to the historically unstable and violent region of eastern Democratic Republic of Congo (DRC), where dozens of armed groups operate with impunity. Among the armed groups active in the DRC and several neighboring countries was the Lord's Resistance Army (LRA), and its sadistic leader Joseph Kony. The LRA would attack villages, steal food, kill adults, kidnap boys to serve in their army, and force girls to serve as sex slaves. It was on this trip that I first met Shannon Sedgwick Davis, who was involved in the effort to find and capture Kony.

We spent most of our time on the trip talking about her work combatting Kony and the LRA. Shannon had supported the development of a radio network designed to track the LRA and warn local villagers of attacks. I was impressed with her fearless intellect and commanding presence. She doesn't take no for an answer. I realized we shared a desire to help the world's most vulnerable, and also a willingness to take risks and engage in unconventional approaches to solve tough problems.

Soon after that trip, Shannon came to visit me in Decatur, Illinois, where my Foundation is based. This time, she showed me a video of Ugandan troops she was helping to train to rescue LRA victims and dismantle Kony's army. In the video, generals from the Uganda People's Defense Force stand up to thank Shannon. I know enough about generals to know that any praise directed her way must have been well earned. I instantly knew I wanted to be part of the operation. In fact, I told her, "You better not do this without me."

That began a unique partnership that continues today. Her specific need at the time was funding for a helicopter, but it didn't take me long to also offer funding for dog tracking teams. I am used to people asking me for money for good causes—but this was different. Shannon was all in. She was going there at great personal risk, she was spending her foundation's dollars on the effort, and she had put together a team of highly skilled people who were making incredible personal sacrifices on the ground.

I've lost track of how many trips we made together to South Sudan, the Central African Republic, Uganda, Rwanda, and the DRC. We've been detained in Congo, once thought we were accidentally landing on a rebel-controlled runway, got caught in a thunderstorm in a Cessna over the jungles of Uganda, and, as you'll read about in this book, shared a sandwich with a warlord in the Central African Republic. Shannon understands the importance of showing up, the value of working with local leadership, of assembling complementary resources to tackle the toughest problems, and she navigates personal dynamics like few others can—whether it be comforting a two-year-old LRA victim or persuading senior military officials from Uganda and the United States to work together. She will humbly downplay her role in this story, but as I witnessed firsthand, the effort to dismantle Kony's army was a team effort that never would have achieved so much success without her.

The Howard G. Buffett Foundation has made more than $1.2 billion in grants since 1999, and I assure you it is rare to find partners like Shannon and Bridgeway Foundation. In fact, I would say that there is no one out there doing the kind of work that Shannon is doing to address some of the worst humanitarian crises on the planet. Shannon will always be the first person I call when I want to accomplish some-

thing important and difficult in Africa. There are fewer people suffering in the world today because of Shannon.

This is an important book. It will force you to confront the reality
of atrocities committed in faraway places against innocent men,
women, and children who deserve to live with basic dignity and respect. I hope you will feel good knowing there are people like Shannon
on the front lines—working to knit together improbable collabora-
tions between organizations trying to reduce violence and conflict in
the world.

INTENTIONS

I wrestled incessantly with whether or not to tell this story. In some ways, the decade-long journey felt too sacred for paper.

In our shared efforts to help protect those vulnerable to Joseph Kony's violence in Central Africa, I worked with incredible souls, people who were united in giving their all to push humanity forward and past some terrifying events. I feel honored and humbled to have met so many of these heroes along the way.

Some of those involved in this story remain in positions of government or have profiles that could be affected by their appearance in this book. I've changed several names in order to protect these people. (All pseudonyms are denoted with an asterisk at first introduction.) Certain details of sensitive operations have been omitted. Although I seek to honor all of the participants' unique perspectives and contributions, this story is by necessity my account, describing experiences from my perspective. Given the nature of military operations, we didn't always have full visibility of every dynamic at play, and the story is limited to my perspective and understanding of the events that unfolded. For times I was not present, I relied heavily on the recollections and stories that were relayed to me. I did my best to corroborate each of these stories but due to the long time that had passed, exact details and dates could not always be confirmed.

More than anything, I hope this book serves as an encouragement to engage more deeply in issues of injustice in the world, to look at the problems around us and seek creative solutions. I hope it adequately honors local heroes on the ground and encourages more support of locally driven solutions in areas of poverty and conflict. I hope it inspires deep listening, lively discussion, and thoughtful action as we strive toward a world with more justice, accountability, and love.

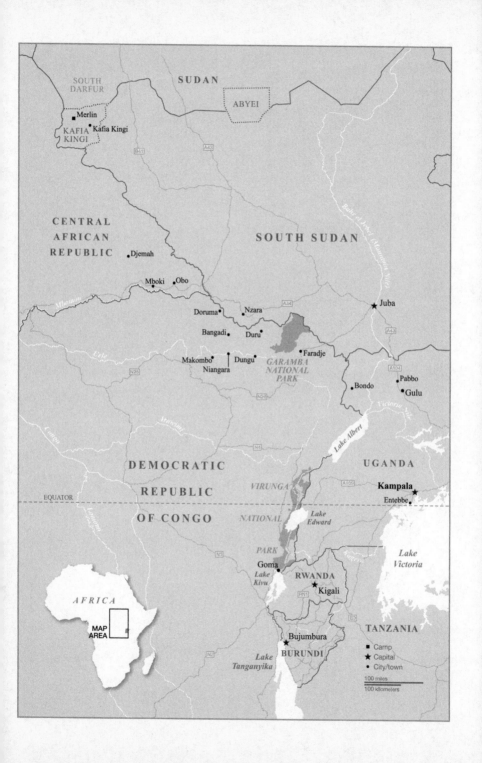

PART ONE

We are caught in an inescapable
network of mutuality, tied in a
single garment of destiny.
Whatever affects one directly,
affects all indirectly.

—MARTIN LUTHER KING, JR.

TO STOP A WARLORD

IT WAS LONG after midnight in San Antonio, Texas, when the phone rang. Brody, my four-year-old, had crawled in beside me an hour or two before and was taking up most of the bed. I never sleep deeply anymore, even at home, even in the middle of the night. When I heard my cellphone ring I was quick, pulling on my robe, heading for the back porch where I took my early morning calls from the field. The alarm on the back door beeped as I crossed into the night. Steps away from my sleeping husband and sons, I suddenly felt as distant from them as I did during my trips to Central Africa, where I slept alone in a tent, surrounded by the snoring of hundreds of men, where being so far from my family was a physical ache in my chest.

Laren Poole's voice came through the static of his satellite phone. Laren managed the operations of our mission in the field. His voice rippled with urgency as he spoke the words, the coded phrase we had devised should a moment like this ever arise.

"Boss," he said, "it's time to bet the farm."

My heart leapt and my stomach dropped, some combination of excitement and dread, my mind whirring with the additional resources we'd need to pull together in support of a targeted operation, an unconventional collaboration between the Ugandan military, US Special Forces, humanitarian organizations, and the Bridgeway Foundation, the organization I run. Our cobbled-together alliance of private and public, military and humanitarian organizations was piloting a new way of trying to stop mass atrocities, and Laren's words were the signal that it was time to go all in on our mission to catch Joseph Kony.

It was 2013, and by that point Joseph Kony and his Lord's Resistance Army (LRA) had terrorized the citizens of four countries in Africa for more than twenty-five years. The numbers were staggering: more than a hundred thousand dead. At least thirty thousand children abducted and forced to become soldiers or sex slaves. At the height of the conflict, ninety percent of the northern Ugandan population—almost two million innocent civilians—were forcefully displaced and put under curfew by the Ugandan military in their attempts to counter the LRA. Government troops denied civilians access to their land and they were crowded into squalid camps, caught in the midst of a brutal war. Even those devastating figures don't fully describe the suffering unleashed by the LRA. Their violence was especially brutal, often worse than I'd seen elsewhere in my human rights work. Kony and his army were setting a bar for evil in our world and kept raising it. In 2005, when the International Criminal Court in The Hague issued its first-ever arrest warrants, indictments were handed down against Joseph Kony and four other LRA leaders for war crimes and crimes against humanity. Three of five indictees, including Kony, were still at large, and the violence against the innocent had only worsened.

For a decade Kony had been like a ghost, invisible except in the stories of those who had escaped from his army or survived LRA attacks. Over the last five years, all the information our shared mission had gathered had made us fairly certain we knew the general area in which he was hiding. But pinpointing his exact location in that terrain was nearly impossible. On bad days, I'd often wondered whether our hope of capturing him and bringing him to justice was nothing more than a moonshot. But now, our target had materialized clearly in our sights: Kony's nerve center in Kafia Kingi (K2), on disputed land between Sudan and South Sudan, had been identified.

Now, if we worked quickly, if our allies were skilled, and if we were lucky, Kony's reign of terror might finally come to an end. Laren and I couldn't talk specifics over the satellite phone; it wasn't secure. It would be another week before he could brief me on the new intelligence that had bolstered his confidence that this time we could catch Kony.

I sat on the back porch, watching the sun start to rise. I had waited for this moment for almost three years, yet the surge of excitement and enthusiasm was muted by exhaustion. I was tired. And alone. Laren, my sounding board and partner in the operation, was half a world away and not around to answer the many questions racing through my mind. And I was all too aware that history was not on our side. One of the last times there had been confirmation of Kony's hideout was in 2008, when Ugandan, Congolese, and southern Sudanese forces, with advisement from the US military, had launched a joint assault on the LRA camp. The operation had failed, reportedly due to leaked intelligence, bad weather, poor coordination, and resentments among the collaborating armies. Kony and his soldiers had scattered, breaking into small, mobile groups that were able to weave back and forth across borders and evade capture. The failed operation had made it more difficult to combat the LRA, and it had been devastating for civilians: in the weeks that followed, close to a thousand people were killed in a series of bloody reprisal attacks in northeastern Congo and southern Sudan.

If this opportunity was missed, Kony would likely slip off the edge of the Earth again, taking his army and hostages with him and perhaps leaving a trail of destruction in his wake. We weren't only betting the resources and partnerships it had taken us most of a decade to cultivate. Also at stake were the lives of women and children held captive in Kony's K2 camp and the civilians who might become victims of his vengeance.

And yet, what if we succeeded? What if we could bring Kony out in custody? Perhaps the tens of thousands of children in South Sudan, the Central African Republic, and the Democratic Republic of Congo would be a little safer. Fewer girls would be used as sex slaves. Fewer boys would be forced to kill.

I had been chilly in my robe and slippers when I first came outside, but now the morning air was growing warmer, the pale early light revealing a thick yellow blanket of mountain cedar pollen that had settled on the grass overnight. A light came on in the house, and I could see Sam and the boys shuffle into the kitchen. I watched them for a moment—Sam in sweatpants and a Captain America T-shirt, pouring bowls of cereal; Connor and Brody in their cotton-print jammies, grabbing their Lego spaceships from the coffee table, flying them through the air.

"Mommy!" they called, smiles bright, as I came back into the house.

When I landed in Entebbe, Uganda, a few days before the Kafia Kingi (K2) mission was to begin, the heat was so intense I could see it, a bright glare coming off the tarmac. If this were a routine visit, after going through Immigration and Customs and a few hours' wait, I'd head back out to the tarmac, climb into our nine-seat Cessna Caravan plane crowded with drums of jet fuel, and fly four and a half hours north to our forward operations base. I'd put on headphones and listen to music, hoping to block out engine noise and turbulence, trying not to obsess over my worries. I am a peacemaker, a human rights activist. And here I was, in the middle of a military operation.

But this wasn't a routine visit.

I passed my visa documents to the immigration official and stopped in the bathroom to put myself together after twenty-four hours of travel. I pulled my blond hair back under a headscarf to keep the fine strands from sticking to my face and put on a pair of sunglasses. Of all the thousands of people I interacted with in my work in Central Africa, in my meetings at the highest levels of military and government groups, I was almost always the only woman. I pinched my cheeks to wake up and to move some color back into my face. I pulled my backpack on and made my way out to the line of taxis at the curb.

On the drive to the US Special Forces compound in Entebbe, I reviewed the operation that had been diagrammed on paper and rehearsed in the field for over a month. Five Mi-17 helicopters—two from the Ugandan military, one provided by Bridgeway, and two more we had agreed to charter from a contractor in Entebbe—were ready to carry sixty Ugandan special operations soldiers from their forward base in Obo, Central African Republic, to a location on the other side of a ridge from Kony's suspected hideout. To move quickly, to avoid detection, the soldiers would split into nimble splinter groups, each equipped with a satellite phone. They would put on night vision goggles and cross a mountain range and then semi-arid savanna, traveling only under the protection of darkness over the course of two successive nights. And when dawn broke they would attempt to catch Kony.

US Special Forces Commander Paul Korbel* met me at the gate to the compound. As we walked together, the soldiers looked up from their work. They always treated me with respect, but I couldn't escape the feeling that they thought of me as a trespasser in their domain, a humanitarian civilian who didn't belong behind the scenes of a military operation.

Commander Korbel wiped sweat from his forehead and grinned. "We've got our eyes on K2," he said. "We estimate between forty and sixty combatants in the camp. A hundred and twenty-five women and children."

"They're still there?"

"Looks like it, with smoking fires."

Military personnel understandably tend to undersell success and downplay certainty. Even so, I couldn't help myself from asking, "Is this going to work?"

"We've got a shot," he said.

Okay, it was only a shot. But it was the best chance we were likely ever to have. I wanted to say, *That's enough for me.* But of course we all wanted more than a shot: we wanted to stop the LRA. We wanted the man who had led the kidnapping of more than thirty thousand children to be brought to justice. We wanted every mother in Central Africa—in the world—to have the right that I have, the right to put her children to sleep at night and trust that in the morning they will still be there. To shatter the lie that we are powerless against violence and evil. To remember that in the face of monumental darkness, there is no limit to what we can do for each other, there is no fence around the human heart. I traced my finger over the Saint Jude pendant I'd been wearing since we began this mission. Saint Jude, the patron saint of lost and impossible causes. The contours of the pendant had become like Braille to me. We would get him this time. I felt sure.

WHO DO YOU LOVE THE MOST?

David Ocitti

WE BECAME INVOLVED in the mission because of people like David Ocitti. Many years later, when David told me his story, I would be humbled and inspired all over again by the courage and resilience of the countless people impacted by the LRA, whose leadership made it possible for all of us to take action—and whose experiences made it imperative.

David was born in northern Uganda in 1986, the same year that hostilities intensified between northern and southern Uganda. Life wasn't secure or peaceful. But growing up with his large extended family—his parents and siblings, grandmother, uncles and aunties, and many young cousins—and playing within the circle of mud-walled, thatch-roofed homes that made up their family homestead, David felt protected. He knew the elders would keep them safe. He thought the war outside couldn't break through.

His earliest memories were of safety and love. He would watch his mother prepare meals and tend to his younger sister and stepbrothers, caring for them the way she had cared for him: breastfeeding him till he was two, tying him on her back till he was three, singing to him in Acholi, their native tongue: *Little baby, don't cry again, Mommy loves you, she's going to cook for you, she's going to get you what you need.*

Love was her food, practical, nurturing. Love was her face, long like his, her high cheekbones, her eyes as peaceful and watchful as a cat's.

And love was his grandmother, the wrinkles that spread across her face like ripples over still water. *Kara konyo,* she called him. Helpful one.

And love was his father. David's biological father had died when he was only three. His stepfather, full of jokes and laughter, always smiling, was the man he considered his father. While David's mother's sense of humor was quiet, reserved for the people she knew best, his father was outwardly jovial. The only time he scolded any of the children was for eating alone. "Everything you have is to be shared," he would say. He was full of lessons. He would make David eat peppers so spicy his entire mouth would feel like it was exploding. "Hold your ground," his father would say. "In less than a minute it will cool off." And no matter how badly it burned, how intense the discomfort, the heat would always ease and fade. "It's the same with difficulty," his father said. "Nothing is permanent. Your body will react appropriately when you give it time to understand."

David's hometown, Pabbo, was a small village and trading center north of Gulu, the most populous city in northern Uganda. Only three roads passed by his homestead. One led to the village well, a pool formed and filled by a channel dug beside a rushing creek. The second road led to the garden, where each family farmed a plot of crops for subsistence and trade. And the third led to the trading center. Whenever he saw someone passing his family's homestead, David instantly knew where the person was going or where he had been.

Life followed predictable rhythms. The whole family woke at sunrise, earlier during the hot dry seasons. David would wash his face, then take a hoe and follow his parents to the family farm. Late morning, when the sun was high and the heat growing fierce, they would return home to sweep and clean the packed earth of the homestead, clearing the ground of leaves, insects, debris blown in by the wind. Everyone helped sweep. It was the best way to prevent infestations. And it was a cultural value. "Don't judge a man's success by his clothes," his grandmother would say. "A fancy suit means nothing. Go home and see the state of his homestead. A large, clean homestead—that signals a real man."

After the homestead was clean, the children would bathe in the river while their mother cooked lunch—cassava and beans, sorghum bread. His mother had the biggest pot, he thought—always full, brimming with enough to feed anyone who was hungry. After the meal, the whole family rested through the hottest part of the day. The children were free to nap, or climb one of the two dozen mango trees on their homestead, or play soccer in the empty space at the center of the circle of homes. The children made their own balls from plastic bags and pieces of cloth bound together with twine or thin branches, competing to see who could make the longest-lasting ball.

When the day was beginning to cool off, they would all return to the garden to move the weeds and branches they'd cleared away that morning. As the sun went down, they would walk back to their homestead, the boys gathering firewood on the way. Again they swept the homestead, and while the girls helped the women prepare the evening meal, the boys would finish gathering wood and build the *wang-oo,* the bonfire where the whole family sat together each night. They would set down a mat and eat dinner by the fire. The elders would sip *waragi,* potent distilled cassava, and the stories would begin. They would talk late into the night, the stars bright overhead, the air chilled, the fire warm.

"Back in the day," his grandmother would begin, telling a favorite story, "the men used to hunt without flashlights. They had to know how to find their way home in the dark. The smart hunter knew how to search the night sky for *latwok,* the brightest star. But the foolish hunter forgot about what was right above him, and stayed lost in the dark night."

David had been taught that latwok was the first star to come out at night. When they were walking back home before sunset, he and the other children would see who could spot it first.

"Don't be a foolish hunter," his grandmother continued. "If you're smart, you know its position in the sky. If you follow the star, it will always guide you back."

It was easy to identify latwok at sunset. But now, the sky was full of bright stars. Each time David thought he had found the brightest one, a different star would flicker and shine, appearing even brighter. "How can you be sure you are following the right one?" he asked.

"Latwok is distinct among the many stars," she replied. "If you think you've found the brightest one, keep an eye on it. If it's really latwok, it will keep changing color, showing you many shades as you focus on it."

When David grew sleepy, one of his parents would lift him up or take his hand and lead him into the small, dark house. They'd lay him down on a mat, cover him with a light blanket. Sometimes his uncle would kneel beside him and play the *lukeme,* the thumb piano he had built just for David. He would sleep to the throb of the lukeme, to the murmur of his family all around. In the dry season, they would often carry the mats and blankets outside and the children would fall asleep while the elders talked, the whole family resting all night together by the glowing embers.

The seasons came, unbroken. In May, the mangoes ripened. Children climbed high into the trees to shake down the fruit, their faces stained orange from eating so much, the sweet juice gushing down their chins and necks and chests and then drying, turning their shirts as stiff and hard as wood. Trouble Month, they called it. All through the village, children went around with casts on their arms or legs from climbing too high in search of fruit. David, too, fell once or twice. Fear seized his stomach on the way down, then the rush of laughter when he found he wasn't hurt after all.

In October, Independence Day came and went without much fanfare. Everyone in the village was saving every penny, every bit of food, for the weeklong Christmas celebration, the culmination of family and community life, a constant feast that ran from Christmas Eve till New Year's Day.

So the annual rituals came and went, but all around them, there was the ever-present war. It was a new manifestation of an old conflict, a hundred-year-old struggle that began in 1894 when British colonizers came to the Nile and invented a nation. Ignoring the tribal sovereignty of the many kingdoms and chiefdoms in the region, the British had hemmed more than a dozen culturally and linguistically distinct groups into a single protectorate.

Then they began systematically dividing the same groups they had artificially and arbitrarily unified. The Baganda people in the south—for whom Uganda was named, and whose king was made the de facto leader—were elevated into social and political elites. But the Acholi in the north were marginalized and stigmatized, their labor and military conscription used to further the south's dominance.

The cycles of revenge and mistrust between north and south continued after Uganda achieved independence in 1962. Disputed elections, military coups, and bloody dictatorships dominated Uganda's early years of statehood. David's life began in a country that had been mired for decades in political turmoil and violence, where leaders often seized—and kept—power by force.

The threat of violence was so normalized that David had no way to understand how destructive the war was. He just knew that sometimes he'd hear gunshots and see everyone around him start to shake. When he saw others running, he had to run, too. Sometimes they hid all day in the bush in broad daylight, the screen of leaves safer than the thick mud walls of home. He grew used to the fear, so steady and constant it felt normal to go about daily life with a mental tremble. Yet he didn't really understand what it was he was afraid of.

"What's that sound?" he asked his grandmother once as they huddled together in the bush, a hot wind rustling the leaves. Around them, the quick flit of bird wings. Farther away, a groaning sound.

"It's our neighbors, kara konyo," his grandmother said. "They are crying."

"Why are they crying?"

"Because the LRA have come and are killing people. When they kill it is painful."

The group that became the Lord's Resistance Army formed around the time David was born, ostensibly aimed to protect the north. Its leader, Joseph Kony, was an ethnic Acholi like David, born in Odek, northern Uganda, in the early 1960s, also the first years of Ugandan independence. The son of subsistence farmers, Kony grew up amid chronic poverty and the political marginalization of his people—and then the ruthless violence of dictator Idi Amin's regime.

Early in his life Kony's aspirations seemed more spiritual than militaristic. He served as an altar boy in the Catholic Church where his father was a lay apostle, and when he was fifteen, he dropped out of school and apprenticed with a local witch doctor, learning to be a healer and spirit medium. He became a trusted spiritual adviser in his community, especially to rebel soldiers hiding out in the north, waiting for an opportunity to free Uganda from the disputed rulers and repressive regimes that followed Idi Amin's reign.

When Kony was in his early twenties there was another coup—this time staged by a northern general, a fellow Acholi. When General Tito Okello ascended to power, long-standing grievances among Acholi in the north seemed vindicated. But just six months later, in January 1986, Yoweri Museveni, one of the commanders who had helped oust Idi Amin, led his National Resistance Army to topple Okello's Acholi-dominated government, despite having signed a peace deal with Okello the month before. Museveni became the new president of Uganda, and his forces took control of northern Uganda in sometimes brutal fashion. Museveni's decision to undermine the peace agreement, Okello's swift fall from power, and the Acholi's ensuing suffering, recatalyzed northern bitterness and rage.

A militaristic and spiritual group rose to oppose Museveni. Led by spirit medium Alice Auma "Lakwena," the Holy Spirit Movement unified the various rebel fighters in the north. More than an army, the group used mystical practices to protect its members and to cleanse and purify them. Lakwena promised her soldiers freedom from political persecution—and freedom from guilt. Before battle the soldiers rubbed themselves with shea butter, sang hymns, doused the ground with holy water to protect themselves from enemies' bullets, and flung rocks they believed would explode like bombs. In November 1987, the Holy Spirit Mobile Forces very nearly succeeded in toppling Museveni's government. But in the end Museveni's forces defeated them just sixty miles outside of Kampala, the capital.

Lakwena went into exile and Joseph Kony, who was already known and trusted by the rebel fighters, recruited her former soldiers to build the Lord's Resistance Army, adopting many of Lakwena's mystical practices along with her military ambitions. Kony used his charisma and status as a spiritual leader to galvanize an army of thousands of combatants intent on overthrowing Museveni and protecting the Acholi from the retributive violence they expected as punishment for Lakwena's nearly successful coup. For the first eight years of David's life, the war that raged around him was between north and south, between the LRA and Museveni's army.

But by 1994, the civil war had all but fizzled out. Northerners, exhausted by decades of violence, were ready to embrace peace. The LRA had long since lost most of its local support, and Kony's forces were dwindling. This is when Kony began abducting Acholi children—his own people—to fill the ranks of his flagging army. The LRA, which had been created to protect the north, began attacking its own.

Life in Pabbo began to change. By the time David was ten, the children, even those as young as two or three years old, had to spend days at a time in the bush to avoid abduction by the LRA. They hid alone, without their elders near. Their parents would sneak into the bush to bring them food, warning them not to make a sound, not even a footprint, as they moved to their next hideout.

As life grew more dangerous, Pabbo became the biggest of more than two hundred displacement camps created in northern Uganda to house the nearly two million people driven from their homes by the ongoing war. As many as sixty-seven thousand people came to live in Pabbo, where circular mud huts were crowded together so closely that the grass-thatched roofs often touched. Narrow dirt paths—dusty or muddy depending on the season—wound between the thousands of huts. The camp was patrolled by Ugandan military troops and a curfew imposed—residents had to wait until nine or ten in the morning to leave the camp to farm, trade, or go to school, and they had to return no later than five in the evening. Surrounding the camp were green cornfields and farmland, fast rivers, mountains that rose in the distance, and all around, as far as the eye could see, an ocean of six-foot-high grass and brush, tall and thick enough that an entire army could tread through it undetected.

Constant war had eroded the school system in northern Uganda, but David was determined to keep up his studies. He began attending a school in a nearby village, paying for his uniform and supplies by doing odd jobs, sleeping away from home in the dormitories set up for students who had too far and too dangerous a path to travel each day between home and school. To be out late in the evening or in the early morning was to risk being abducted by rebels—or to risk being mistaken for one.

In January 2002, when he was sixteen, he came back home to Pabbo on a short holiday. He planned to spend his time earning enough to pay for the next term of school. Late at night his first night at home, he was fast asleep on a thin mat in his family's mud hut when he heard shouting from outside. Someone banged on the door.

"Open up, don't try to run," the man outside shouted in Acholi.

At first, David was more disoriented than scared. He stumbled out into the dark with his two younger stepbrothers. A rebel fighter in dirty fatigues pointed them toward a large group of children and teenagers gathered in an open area, flanked by armed rebels. Just then, his uncle's house went up in flames. He heard the crackle of fire all over the camp. The air thickened with smoke. Adults were being rounded up nearby.

When all of the huts in David's section of the camp had been emptied, a commander moved among the children, shoving them, shouting questions. "Where's your brother? Where's your sister?" Siblings were pushed together in clusters. Nearby, men were being shoved into one group, women into another.

David and his brothers huddled together, trying to keep track of their parents in the commotion. A commander approached them. His uniform was tattered, his hair in dreadlocks. He waved his bayonet at them. David held his brothers close. He was tall enough to look the rebel in the eye. He wanted to bow his head, to stare at the ground, to look anywhere but into the commander's fierce eyes, but he couldn't look away.

"Where's your father?" the commander barked at David.

David nodded toward the nearby group of men. He could recognize his father even at a distance, even in the dark, the calm and steady way he held himself. He could feel his father's protectiveness, his fearlessness and commitment. David tried to gather his father's strength into himself, to become a shelter for his brothers.

"Where's your mother?" the commander demanded, shoving the bayonet toward David's face. He saw her, arms crossed over her chest, eyes fixed on him and his brothers. She was a protector, too. After David's biological father had died, one of his uncles had demanded to "inherit" his mother as a wife. She had refused. She had faced his anger, and worse, to protect against a forced marriage, to keep her children from having to leave their home. David felt his parents' eyes on him now like a shield. He squeezed his arms around his brothers' shoulders.

"Who do you love the most?" the commander shouted at David. "Your mother or your father?"

An absurd question. David shook his head.

"Answer me!" Spit flew out of the commander's mouth when he yelled. "Who do you love the most?"

David could feel his brothers shiver against him. "I love them both the same."

"You have to choose!" The commander was so close David could smell his sweat, the stench of his uniform. He could see the dark sheen of his gun, the hands that gripped it. They were thin hands. Dirty and calloused, but young and bony. "Answer me! Who do you love the most?"

David knew he had to answer. But his tongue felt stuck, his mind tangled. He looked at his father and mother in turn. He had to speak a name. But he couldn't find an answer.

"Who do you love the most?" the commander shouted again. "Answer me now or I'll shoot!"

His brothers had begun to cry. David felt the burn of a pepper filling his mouth. A heat so intense it felt lethal. He squeezed his brothers' shoulders again. "My father," he said, choking on the words.

The commander signaled to one of the rebels guarding the group of men and then moved to another group of siblings, demanding, "Who do you love the most? Who do you love the most?" "My father," David heard many answer. The rebels brought the fathers to stand before their children in a ragged line, and then surrounded them, holding large sticks, chunks of wood. At some unknown signal, the rebels threw themselves at the fathers, beating them. The sound of wood against flesh was low and deep. Then the sharper crack of clubs on skulls. The fathers moaned and one by one they dropped to the earth. David's father was the last to fall. The LRA didn't stop beating them until all of the fathers were dead.

David's father lay with his face in the dirt. Blood stained the ground. David's brothers were crying, but David couldn't cry. He felt overcome by heaviness, as though someone had rolled a boulder onto his chest. His breath came in little gasps. He searched the crowd of bystanders for his mother but she wasn't there. While the fathers were being killed the other adults had been taken away. His parents were gone. David and his brothers were forced to march out into the dark with the other abductees. His feet stumbled over the uneven earth in the night.

2

PROTECTION
URGENTLY NEEDED

"WHEN ARE WE going to give him back?" my three-year-old son Connor asked.

"Shhhh," I murmured, rocking the newborn baby in my arms. Sam was in our bedroom, trying to squeeze in a few hours of studying before his evening law school class. It was January 2009 and by then Brody was a month old, and time felt blurry, measured not in grant assessments, board meetings, and international travel itineraries, but in the too-brief stretches when my newborn son's colic subsided long enough to allow him (and me) to sleep. My words were a feeble attempt to soothe all of us: the tired baby, Connor's frustration over Brody's constant demands on my attention, my own fear that my love—which I knew to be endless—somehow wasn't enough to meet both of my boys' needs.

I had chosen motherhood. I had no ambivalence about becoming a mom. And even my strong desire to experience this kind of human love had not prepared me for the profound and total merging of myself with another. The call to love and mother them was like the call to life—something no less precious because I did it automatically, without questioning.

"Mommy," Connor demanded, "answer me."

I looked at Brody's round cheeks and scrunched-up nose, his bald head, the way his face twitched as he struggled to sleep. "Baby Brody's here to stay, my love," I said. "He does cry a lot. He can be really loud and he makes Mommy really tired, too. But he won't always be a baby. One day he'll be a boy like you. He will love you and want to be your friend. You might even find that he's pretty fun to play with."

Connor eyed me skeptically and returned to sorting his plastic safari animals by color and size.

Brody asleep at last in my arms, I dug my phone out of the couch cushions and scrolled through work emails, looking for any new reports from the organizations funded by Bridgeway. When I had joined Bridgeway a year and a half earlier, when Connor was going on two and Sam and I were starting to try for a second child, I had done my best to keep clear boundaries between my work and family life. But I quickly learned that I just don't operate that way. This work and my family would always be present, daily.

At Bridgeway, I managed a global portfolio of grants aimed at helping people around the world stop, prevent, and recover from mass atrocities. Now I scanned my in-box, particularly eager to see if there were any new developments from Sudan, where we were keeping an eye on the crisis in Darfur. My quick review didn't reveal any news from Sudan, but I did notice a post from Human Rights Watch, written by Ida Sawyer, a lead researcher in Uganda and Central Africa, whose position Bridgeway had been funding in response to the LRA's ongoing violence in the region.

In 2006, the Ugandan military, the Uganda People's Defense Force (UPDF), had succeeded in driving the LRA out of Uganda and into southern Sudan (they eventually took refuge in the Democratic Republic of Congo), and the Ugandan government entered into peace talks with Kony. We had believed that the LRA would soon be dismantled. But the LRA threat hadn't diminished. Far from it. Still intent on overthrowing the Ugandan government, Kony had set up his new headquarters near Garamba National Park in northeastern Congo, where Ugandan troops weren't allowed to pursue him, and in the two years that the peace talks had dragged on and ultimately failed, his army had rested, regrouped, and rearmed. By 2008 the LRA's violence against civilians was reaching new extremes and had spread not only to Congo, but also to the remote corners of southeastern Central African Republic and southern Sudan.

When I saw the headline of Ida's report, my heart sank: "LRA Slaughters 620 in 'Christmas Massacres,' Protection Urgently Needed as Killings Continue." A lump formed in my throat as I read on. Joseph Kony's army had murdered hundreds of innocent people and abducted more than 160 children in a string of bloody reprisal massacres after a failed assault on an LRA camp in the Democratic Republic of Congo, near the border with southern Sudan.

On December 14, 2008, just three days before Brody's birth, the Ugandan military and its partners had launched Operation Lightning Thunder, a joint effort between the armies of Uganda, the Democratic Republic of Congo, and southern Sudan, and supported by a number of US military advisers whom, in the last weeks of his presidency, President George W. Bush had assigned to provide logistics, communications, and intelligence.

But, as I read in Ida's report, the mission was riddled with flaws and mishaps. The attack helicopters that had been sent ahead of the ground forces were delayed by bad weather. By the time they bombed the compound, Kony, apparently tipped off to the attack, had already fled with his top commanders. There might still have been a chance to capture them, but the ground troops meant to pursue any LRA members who fled after the aerial assault were hampered by transport problems, and also arrived late—seventy-two hours late. Worst of all, the troops delegated to protect civilians in the region *never appeared at all*.

On the upside, the operation had succeeded in destroying the LRA central camp and forcing Kony and the other leaders into hiding. But this actually made them harder to pursue. The LRA splintered into small groups, a multitude of tiny armies hiding within an area that spanned three countries, a region roughly the size of California. In trying to mitigate the threat of the LRA, the intervention had only made them more dangerous.

And then the LRA retaliated.

On Christmas Eve and Christmas day, LRA rebels committed horrific murders. In town after town across northeastern Congo, invisible to most of the world, the LRA went on a killing spree. One of the first attacks occurred in Batande, a small village about a mile from the Sudanese border. A close-knit community, the whole town had gathered to share a feast after Christmas services at the Protestant church. A seventy-two-year-old man arriving late for the festivities was on a footpath leading to the church when the LRA attacked. I held my breath as I read his account of the massacre:

> The LRA surrounded all the people and began to tie them up with cords, rubber strips from bicycle tires, and cloth from women's skirts, which they tore into strips. I saw them tie up my wife, my children, and my grandchildren. I was powerless to help them.
>
> After tying them up, they tore off their clothes and put them facedown on the ground. Then they started to hit them one by one on the head with large sticks. They crushed their skulls till their brains came out. They were quick at killing. It did not take them very long and they said nothing while they were doing it.
>
> I slipped away and went to my home, where I sat trembling all over. That night I heard the LRA celebrating. They ate the food the women had prepared and drank the beer. Then they slept there among the bodies of those they had killed.
>
> The next morning, they left and I went to try to find my wife. There were bodies everywhere. I could not find my wife. It was only after a few days that I found her just beyond the stream. Her skull had been crushed like the others. Her body was already decomposing so I had to bury her where she was killed in a mass grave with other women and children.

In town after town throughout this region of northeastern Congo, in the Doruma area near southern Sudan and the Faradje area 180 miles to the east, it was the same. The LRA attacked people gathered for Christmas feasts, concerts, and services, tying up the men and raping women and children before crushing their skulls. They shot off the legs of children. They took girls away into the bush on a rope. They tried to twist off the heads of two three-year-old girls.

With more than sixteen thousand United Nations peacekeepers stationed in Congo, only two hundred were deployed in LRA-affected areas. In the Haut-Uele district of northeastern Congo where the massacres occurred, fifty villages were attacked in the space of two days, with zero protection from the international community. A terrible tragedy had occurred in response to a failed intervention.

As I read the final troubling paragraphs of Ida's report, Brody stirred in my arms and began to cry. I held his tiny body against my chest, gently patting his back. His fragility overwhelmed me sometimes. I hated not knowing what was making him hurt, not knowing how to help him feel better. Brody struggled and cried in my arms. Connor looked up from his animals, waiting for my response.

3

BAND-AIDS ON BULLET HOLES

"HOW DEEP ARE the cutbacks?" my board member Ann asked one afternoon a few months after the massacres in Congo.

"They're deep," said John, her husband and fellow board member. John had founded Bridgeway Capital Management, an investment firm that donates half of its profits through the work of the Bridgeway Foundation. John leaned in as he spoke. The low sun slashed through the blinds of our meeting room, framing his head in gold. The mood in the room was somber. But John seemed to gather the light.

He was one of the most intentional people I had met, and came from a line of powerful women and extraordinary, open-minded parents. His grandmother was a suffragette; his father prioritized integrity above all else in business; and his mother crossed social barriers her entire life: she was the first woman ever to earn a PhD in religion at Rice University. John's parents encouraged him to make his own choices about how he engaged with the world. He'd founded an investment company with the mission of preventing genocide because he couldn't ignore the responsibility inherent in privilege, and refused to look at the world through protective lenses. He faced the hard truths directly, and he had a way of bringing life and light into the toughest situations.

Even now, as he delivered difficult news to the Bridgeway Foundation board members, I could sense him trying to reframe the losses and costs of the current recession as an opportunity.

"We're going to give less, and that's going to hurt," he said. "It's also an invitation: to make the dollars we *can* give count the very most. To be completely clear and united about the work we do."

I felt a wave of dread. On the table in front of me was the binder in which I kept a printout of our current grant portfolio, a roster of urgent and highly worthy causes. And now we would be supporting fewer of them. We needed to be doing more, not less.

Bridgeway was built on the conviction that human security is a right that you're born into, no matter where. Whether you're a native of San Antonio, Texas, or Batande, Democratic Republic of Congo, it is your right to live free from fear, free from being terrorized, free from being raped, free from being abducted, free from having your kids stolen.

But the right to human security is not equally protected in the world. When the global community fails to preserve security it affects the poorest of the poor disproportionately. People at the bottom of the development spectrum. The most isolated. The ones who go about their days working hard to make sure their kids have enough to eat and that they can go to sleep under a peaceful sky. The people most threatened by oppressive groups like the LRA. These are the people whose human right to security is routinely violated because the conflicts that threaten the innocent often don't threaten Western interests.

My eyes were first opened to the complexity of global systems of injustice when I was in my second year of law school at Baylor University in Waco, Texas. In August 1999, there was a devastating earthquake in Turkey. At least seventeen thousand people died, and half a million were left homeless. The following spring, my church in Waco sponsored a one-week mission trip to provide relief near Istanbul. When we arrived, it was clear that a quick drop-in visit wasn't going to go very far in helping people. The needs were tremendous, and the people doing day-to-day relief work were too few—and too exhausted. I had very little flexibility in my law school program, but when I returned home I asked my professors if I could interrupt my studies to go back to Turkey for another few weeks to support the relief efforts. To my surprise, they agreed.

For several weeks, I ferried across the Bosporus Strait each morning to the side of Istanbul where the earthquake damage was most severe, and crossed back across the water in the evening to sleep. At the ferry crossing, children flocked, selling small items, begging for money. The first morning I crossed, one boy in particular caught my attention. He wore a blue sweatshirt and carried a yellow plastic bag filled with packages of tissues he was selling, little plastic-wrapped pouches meant to go in a pocket or purse. When he grinned, I could see that he had recently lost his top two front teeth. His name was Pilar. He was six years old. I asked him how much for a package of tissues and gave him the money, but told him to keep the tissues so he could sell them to someone else. As I boarded the ferry, I saw a bigger boy come and take his money away. I decided that when I came back across that night, I would be smarter. I would give Pilar food instead of money. That evening, I looked for him and bought him a toasted cheese sandwich. As I walked away I noticed that when he started to take a bite, an older child ran by and snatched it from him. The next day, I bought him another sandwich and a Coke to drink, but this time I sat with him until he had finished his meal. That became our routine each morning when I waited to board the ferry, and each evening when I returned. It was a lesson in presence, in the importance of just being there—to witness, to become aware, to attune to the culture and the strength all around, to learn and absorb without reactively trying to fix something you don't yet understand, or misapprehending your power or role. Often we look to the easiest ways to help—give money, give food—but presence is also an aspect of giving.

One evening I came home later than usual, after dark, and looked for Pilar. Usually he waited right near the platform and ran up to me, eager to eat and share smiles, but this time I couldn't find him. I wandered around in the dark, searching for him. And then I saw him. He was under a tree, asleep, using his yellow plastic bag full of tissue packages as a pillow. That's when it struck me: he was a street child. I couldn't believe how utterly naïve I'd been. For the rest of my stay, I began talking to the homeless children, and asking the humanitarian workers I met about Pilar and the many other homeless kids. I learned how dire their situation was. In order not to starve, they were forced to pay off corrupt adults, selling small items to tourists, handing over all of the profit. Many children resorted to sniffing glue—in fact, many were forced to so they could be doped into addiction and compliance. I had come to Turkey to assist with disaster relief, but in trying to do something small to fill one extreme need, I became aware of a deeper—and perpetual, chronic—injustice. I realized how important it is for every person to take responsibility for what happens in the world—and at the same time, how easy it is to discharge our guilt, to do something superficial and think we're helping in a way that matters. There was nothing wrong in giving money and sandwiches to a little boy. But the larger system of injustice in which he was trapped was allowed to perpetuate.

My work and my passion have taught me it is possible—and necessary—to stand with others to protect the basic rights of freedom withheld from those trapped by systemic injustice or caught in the middle of conflicts like the LRA's long-running war. To stand for something bigger than oneself, bigger than philanthropy, bigger even than a nation. To come together to stand for justice, and the belief that we are all equal, regardless of where we live. To live with the unshakable certainty that everything we do today matters forever, and that we must use our own freedom to enhance the freedom of others.

I passionately believe in Bridgeway's mission statement, which says in part: *to prevent oppression, genocide, and human rights abuses throughout the world.* As I sat in the quiet boardroom that afternoon, it hit me. Since its inception, Bridgeway Capital Management had been committed to creating a world without genocide and stopping crimes against humanity. Meanwhile, Kony was brutally killing entire communities. And what was the humanitarian community—what were we—really doing to stop him?

My words tumbled out into the silence. "We're not being true to our mission statement."

John looked at me intently. This was one of the ways John was exceptional: never being judgmental and always being curious.

"We say *a world without genocide.* But we're not preventing mass atrocities. We're picking up the pieces and patching up victims in the wake of violence. It's like we're just putting Band-Aids on bullet holes."

Our grant partners in Central Africa and all over the world were of course doing incredibly important work—researching ongoing violence, performing analysis, making policy recommendations, creating campaigns to motivate political leaders to prioritize ending crises. But generating reports about a conflict wasn't really *stopping* a conflict.

"It's not enough," I said. "It's not enough for the kids who are being threatened. It's not enough for the moms trying to keep their kids safe."

"Yes," John said. It was his most-used word, a word that signaled his intense engagement as much as his agreement. "What are you proposing?"

"We need to either change our mission statement, or do what we say we're doing."

I wanted to test what it would look like to try to actually stop a conflict. And—because of the way children were being used in the conflict, because it was Africa's longest-running war, because no one in the international community seemed to be taking action—I thought we should start with the LRA.

4

A THOUSAND HAYSTACKS

ON PAPER, THE LRA conflict should have been a relatively straightforward problem to solve. In terms of mass atrocities, it was low-hanging fruit. There seemed to be global consensus that the LRA was in the wrong. Unlike in Sudan, where the head of state was actually inciting the violence, the LRA was not a state actor. A country didn't have to declare war on another country to intervene against the LRA. The LRA had no country. Unlike our conflict resolution work in the Middle East, where building lasting peace depended on mending tattered and nuanced relationships among many players and navigating historical tensions as well as current hostilities in which it wasn't always clear which groups were perpetrators and which were victims, counter-LRA work was relatively clear-cut. And unlike our postgenocide reconciliation work in Rwanda, the LRA conflict was happening now. It needed to end.

But it wasn't that simple.

In September 2009, a few months after the board meeting when we'd decided to focus on solutions to the LRA problem, I sat on a plastic chair in Ida Sawyer's Human Rights Watch office in Goma with its bare cement walls. Diesel fumes and the smell of charcoal fires pressed in through the open window. So did the sounds of the streets—the rumble of traffic, music cranked up through car stereos and speakers in street stalls. Goma, the Democratic Republic of Congo's eastern capital, was a vibrant and hectic city. Ida was a point of calm amid the motion and noise.

"There's good news and bad news," she said. Ida spoke softly, but she was a fierce advocate and brilliant researcher. She wore brown oval glasses and had a metamorphic ability, as comfortable in a rain jacket in Congo as she was wearing a suit to brief the US Congress. Her face, usually serious and studious, would sometimes flash into the brightest smile.

In the years that we had worked together, Ida had impressed me with her unflinching frankness, even when the truth was profoundly upsetting and devastating. At the same time she reported what was happening in a direct and unemotional way, she developed warm relationships with the community members whose human rights she was there to promote. Everywhere I went, people had an obvious affection for her. Ida's plain speaking was not a sign of her detachment but of the opposite: her stalwart belief that constantly searching for and reporting the truth gave her the best chance to help.

She was one person doing the work of many, many people. Congo is a huge and hugely troubled country. Many armed groups routinely terrorized civilians in the eastern region where Ida was the lead researcher. There wasn't time for her to fall apart in a crisis. She had to keep going.

"Bad news first," I said. All summer I'd been following statements issued by military chiefs of staff from Congo, Uganda, and the Central African Republic that said the LRA had been "dramatically reduced," that the LRA combatants were "fighting for their survival." But I knew that the view from the rooms where policy was made didn't always match the truth on the ground.

"This has been one of the bloodiest years in recent history of the LRA," Ida said. "There has been a lull in attacks—that's the good news. But we've seen in the past how a downtick in violence can mean the LRA is just gearing up for a large-scale assault. Inactivity doesn't necessarily mean peace."

"Then why the official claims that the danger is over?"

She explained that it was politically useful to exaggerate the promise of peace. The same had been true when the LRA was still active in northern Uganda. Despite the constant violence and abductions, the Ugandan government had minimized the threat. Even with tens of thousands of kids taken by the LRA, no one had kept an official record of how many children were missing. It had been more politically expedient to deny or ignore what was happening. In Congo, with Kinshasa, the capital, so far away from the affected areas, it was even easier for the official word to bear little resemblance to the truth. And then there was the complexity that followed from allowing Ugandan troops into Congo for counter-LRA missions. The Congolese didn't want a Ugandan military presence there at all, much less indefinitely.

Ida explained that obtaining accurate information in such a vast and isolated region was proving to be one of the biggest hurdles in countering the LRA. No one knew where Kony and the splinter groups were hiding. Before Operation Lightning Thunder, the LRA had used satellite phones to communicate, but they were evidently communicating now mainly through runners or predetermined face-to-face meetings. There was little way of knowing if or where they would attack next.

The only evidence of the LRA's plans or location was from the information that trickled in from communities after an LRA attack, or from abductees who managed to escape. Given the weak infrastructure in LRA-affected areas, these firsthand reports had to travel by word of mouth, often over huge distances connected only by narrow trails or unpaved roads. The reports of attacks came too late to save lives—if they came at all.

"These communities need to have a way to talk to each other," Ida said. "Not hours or days or weeks after there's new information or an attack. Immediately. In real time."

What she said made complete sense. Especially since there was concern that there might be another Christmas massacre.

On my way home, I attended a meeting in New York with Luis
Moreno Ocampo, the inaugural prosecutor of the International Criminal Court. Established in 2002, the ICC is an intergovernmental organization and international tribunal that has the jurisdiction to
prosecute individuals for international crimes of genocide, crimes
against humanity, and war crimes. Ocampo was in New York for a
United Nations conference on improving the coordination of different
institutions that work on international justice. He had reached out to
hear my updates from the region, and I wanted to know what more we
could do, right then, to help bring Kony to justice, especially now that
the prospect of more mass reprisal killings loomed. Laren Poole, then
of Invisible Children, was also in town for meetings, and I suggested
he join us at the Mercer Hotel after dinner.

I had met Laren in 2005 when he and two other young filmmakers
had shown up to pitch a grant, wearing oversized suits they appeared
to have borrowed from their fathers. Unseasoned in traditional philanthropy, full of youthful swagger, they weren't the typical grant partners.
But the atrocities they'd witnessed in northern Uganda had transformed them into activists. They were seeking funding to make a film
that would raise awareness and help repair the damage of Kony's war.

They had shown me footage that illustrated the precarious situation of the "night commuters"—the more than forty thousand children in Uganda who slept outside in groups each night, seeking
protection in numbers against abduction and murder by the LRA. The
crisis was urgent, and Laren and his friends were the ones making it
known to the world. Something told me that if what they had witnessed in northern Uganda had prompted them to give their lives to
the cause, then they could call forth in others that same passion for
change.

In the four years since that meeting, they had expanded their organization, Invisible Children, into a highly effective movement, provid-

ing support and resources to northern Ugandans who had been displaced, orphaned, and brutalized by the LRA.

In recent months, Invisible Children had begun more direct advocacy efforts. Along with their partners in DC, they had galvanized their force of nearly a hundred thousand global activists to try to move Congress and President Obama to take concrete and effective action to stop Kony. They hoped to introduce legislation through Congress: an LRA disarmament bill that would require President Obama to come up with a solution to the LRA problem within 180 days. Since the spring, Laren and Invisible Children had been tireless in working up support for the bill, flying in constituents from every single state to meet with senators, conducting mass trainings to help people speak more effectively to their elected officials. The mobilization of activists, the meetings with legislators—Invisible Children was demonstrating the absolute upper reaches of advocacy. If they managed to pass the bill, they'd be taking the counter-LRA campaign as high as I'd ever seen a grassroots effort go.

We sat in a red-upholstered booth facing the twinkling lights of the Manhattan street, Ocampo speaking with his musical Argentinean accent, waving his hands expressively after sips of his martini. I had met Ocampo a few years before when we were focused on work to end the human rights abuses in Darfur. Since our first encounter, he had reminded me of "The Most Interesting Man in the World," the silver-bearded character in the Dos Equis commercials who is so extravagantly cosmopolitan he "can speak French . . . in Russian." His warm and glittering presence always cheered me up. I was even more amused by the fact that Laren, usually so guarded and taciturn, had shown up wearing a gleaming white fedora.

"I didn't know this was a costume party," I said, laughing. Laren had brown curly hair, a narrow, clean-shaven face, and deep brown almond eyes. In the four years we had been engaged in counter-LRA work together, he had proven hard to know. He listened more than he spoke, and when he did speak, he was candid about facts but private about himself. This was the first time I had ever reached across the front he put up, the first time I'd ever teased him. It felt good to have crossed a border into friendship.

"As you know, the International Criminal Court has no arresting power," Ocampo was explaining. "We can bring Joseph Kony to justice. But we can't bring him to The Hague."

"No one can," Laren said. "We don't know where he is. Tracking Kony is like trying to find a needle in a haystack."

"It's like trying to find a needle in a *thousand* haystacks," Luis said.

"We can help coordinate efforts. We can leverage resources," I said. "What do we tackle first? What's going to have the biggest impact on the ground?"

Laren gave me a steady look, his eyes unblinking under the brim of his hat. "I have to tell you something," he said. "We just met with the person on Obama's National Security Council who's in charge of Africa. She called me and some of the other bill advocates into a meeting. And she asked us, point-blank, 'What should we be doing to stop the LRA? What kind of response are you looking for from the Executive Office?' I was launching into a discussion of past interventions, wanting to discuss what hasn't worked against the LRA so we can find something that does, and she cuts me off and starts talking about what's politically viable. People are dying right now, and the National Security Council is talking about what's *politically* viable. I always thought that activism plus policy equals results. But, even if this bill passes, I'm not sure it's really going to make a difference."

For the first time, counter-LRA efforts had real political capital and momentum in Washington and there was a huge opportunity for positive change. But the National Security Council didn't seem to be building a strategy that would decisively end LRA violence. Despite the Department of Defense's advisory role in last year's assault on Kony's camp, stopping the LRA didn't seem to be a national priority. And Christmas was only two months away.

5

A MOTHER'S WISH

"EVERYTHING OKAY?" MY mom asked, passing me the green bean casserole. It was Christmas. "Little Drummer Boy" played on the stereo and the house was fragrant with my mom's best attempts at recreating my grandmother's pies.

"I'm just missing Oma," I said. This was our second Christmas without my grandmother. A year and a half earlier she'd suffered several strokes and begun a rapid decline.

Oma had been like a second mother to me. My last year of high school I'd lived at my grandparents' home in the hill country outside San Antonio so I could graduate with my friends and play on my volleyball team instead of transferring to a new school in the neighborhood where my parents had moved. Oma and Opa's home became my sanctuary. I loved the wild bluebonnets that bloomed all over the hillsides in April, the backyard where the whitetail deer grazed. It was peaceful—no loud little brother, no daily fights with my mom over typical teenage stuff, no chaos of family life. Just long walks with Oma over the property, and afterward doing my homework at the kitchen table, where she'd bring me fresh tapioca pudding, where I'd hear Opa come in from working in the yard, whistling "How Much Is That Doggie in the Window?"

When Oma got sick, it was a very difficult time for all of us. I was sad and afraid to lose her. One morning I went to get Connor from his bed and he said, "Big Oma is in heaven."

"No, sweetie, she's resting at home," I explained. "We'll visit her today."

That afternoon, I was sitting on her bed, caressing the papery skin on her thin hands, when she stopped breathing. Just like that. "Put your hand on her heart," the nurse told me. "It will keep beating a little longer." For seven beats, eight, after her breath had stopped, her heart went on.

"Can't you feel her spirit around us now?" my mom asked at the Christmas table, gesturing at the bright cardinal centerpiece, a cherished gift from Oma.

I could. I smiled at Opa, who sat across from me, and rested in the sweetness of her presence.

After our Christmas feast, Opa pulled me away from the table and proudly handed me something he'd printed off his computer. A former civil engineer and tank driver in World War II, Opa had stayed active into his old age, walking for miles each day, mowing the lawn, spending hours at the jigsaw in his woodshop making toys for Connor and Brody and the other great-grandchildren. Now that his body was slowing down he'd taken on more sedentary hobbies: following his grandchildren on Facebook and paying close attention to my work. He regularly googled the regions where I traveled, scouring the Internet for pieces of news that he gathered and saved for me.

Tonight he handed me a short article from the *UK Guardian* published back in November. *The mother of Joseph Kony, one of Africa's most brutal militia leaders, has issued a dying wish to her son,* the article read. *Moments before dying she said, "Tell Joseph Kony to make peace."*

"It's hard to think of that man as someone's son," Opa said.

He was right. Kony was a destroyer of children, a destroyer of lives. I'd never thought of him as someone's child. And I had never once thought of what it would be like to be his mother. Instead of longing to protect her child from the harshness and dangers of the world, here was a mother who longed to protect the world from her son.

"Let's hope Kony's mother gets her wish," I said, squeezing Opa's hand.

The new year came. There were no reports of LRA violence, no reports of another massacre. At our first Bridgeway Foundation board meeting in January 2010, John and I exchanged hugs of cautious relief.

6

MAKOMBO

WHEN I GOT to Lac Kivu Lodge, in Goma, Congo, two months later, in early March 2010, the water glistened in the bright morning sun. I was in Goma for a few days, traveling with another humanitarian group, and had invited Ida Sawyer to meet up for breakfast while I was in town. She was already seated at a table on the balcony overlooking the lake.

"Hey, girl!" I called as I walked toward her. I was excited to catch up, and it was a beautiful setting for our meeting—lush tropical gardens stretched down the hill from our table. Below us the silver-brimmed lake lapped against a low stone wall.

Ida stood to embrace me and smiled. "Good to see you," she said.

"You, too! I'm so glad you were able to meet. What's up? How've you been?" I asked as we took our seats.

She let out a long sigh. "It's going to be hard to hear, but I'm glad I can tell you in person."

"You're not quitting, are you?" Ida was a Columbia grad, an experienced journalist. While I knew she was committed to her work at Human Rights Watch, there were lots of places where her skills would be valued and where her bravery and brilliance were needed. If she was ready for a new challenge, I wanted to be the first to wish her well, though her leaving would be an enormous loss to the cause.

"No," she said. "I'm not going anywhere."

She went silent, gazing out at the lake. It was a volcanic lake filled with methane pockets, risky to swim in, too huge to see across to the opposite shore. A blue misty strip of mountains was sometimes visible to the south of us. I could see that she was upset.

"I just got back from eight days in the field," she said slowly. "Shannon, there was another Christmas massacre. We just found out."

I couldn't believe what she was saying. For months there had been no indications of LRA violence. "How is that possible?"

"It was up in Makombo, near the Uele River." She reached into her bag and pulled out a map. I could see the river, a dark, twisting line. A series of dots extended down from the river and back to it in a circle, each dot labeled with a date as well as a name. Villages. Attack sites.

"The LRA hit more than a dozen fishing and farming communities in four days. We've documented three hundred twenty-one killed. But those are only the confirmed dead. Maybe as many as two hundred more bodies were never recovered or buried. The survivors we interviewed told us that this whole area, this sixty-five-mile circular route of attacked villages, was strewn with bodies. People described the 'stench of death' throughout the region for weeks after the attacks." She paused to let the facts sink in before she continued. "There were abductions, too. A total of two hundred fifty. Eighty children."

"How did no one know?"

Ida sighed again and began to recite the hard, familiar truths. There was no communication infrastructure that allowed the communities to warn each other of the attacks, no way to call for help. There was no electricity. No cellphones. The roads were so narrow they were barely passable on a motorcycle. And the LRA moved incredibly fast through the dense jungle, faster than word of mouth. Another large-scale attack had occurred one year after the first Christmas massacres, and once again the UN, despite its increased presence, had been unable to protect people.

News of the first attacks had circulated in the region, but not soon enough to prevent more deaths. In Tapili, Ida told me, residents had heard rumors of LRA violence at a fisherman's market in Mabanga almost thirty-seven miles away. They sent two people to investigate.

But the scouts had barely begun their journey when they were ambushed by the LRA. Their eyes were gouged out, and they and their motorcycles were set on fire. And then the rebels advanced into Tapili and launched their next attack.

In other places the LRA had sent explicit warnings to discourage people from sharing information about the rebels' whereabouts. In early December, weeks before the massacres, three people had been harvesting sweet potatoes and cassava on their farm near Bangadi when a small group of LRA combatants surrounded them and tied them up. The youngest LRA rebel, a teenage boy, was commanded to cut off the captives' lips and ears with a razor. Then the captives were sent home as a warning to their village not to talk about or listen to information about the LRA.

When the massacres began, the LRA swept quickly between villages, using similar tactics in each place. The combatants arrived disguised as Congolese army soldiers. They pretended to be on patrol, they spoke reassuringly in Lingala, the main language spoken by the army in Congo, asking locals where to find schools, markets, churches, water points—any place where people would be gathered. And then they attacked.

Many people were killed outright with axe blows to the back of the head. Others were taken captive, tied together at the waist with rope or wire, and marched out of the villages at gunpoint. The abductees were forced to march twelve or fifteen miles each day, carrying heavy loads of salt, sugar, batteries, clothes—all of the goods the LRA had pillaged along the way. At night, they had to sleep tied together. On the long marches, those who couldn't keep up were killed on the spot. The boys who lived were trained to fight. The commanders rubbed oil on them, saying it was magic and would protect them from bullets. The female captives were assigned to LRA commanders according to a hierarchy—first to Lieutenant Colonel Binansio Okumu (called Binany), then Commander Bukwara, then Commander "One-Eye" Obol.

"When we finally heard about the attacks, we traveled up there on motorbikes with a Congolese human rights activist," Ida continued.

Ida's treks to research violent incidents were rarely without danger or mishap. She once told me about a twelve-hour motorbike journey on a narrow, almost non-existent path through the forest, escorted by a Congolese army captain who kept wiping out on the rough trail. Each time he fell off his motorbike, his rifle and grenades and other supplies went flying around in every direction, a slapstick spectacle that would have been funny if it weren't so terrifying. At one point during the long journey, the captain picked up a live chicken he planned to cook for dinner that evening, and tied it on the back of his moto. The next time he wiped out, the chicken escaped, and it took the entire party of soldiers and moto drivers almost half an hour to recapture the chicken and resume their journey.

There was no comic relief in what Ida told me now. "We interviewed more than a hundred people last week. Every single person had a horrific story. There was an eighty-year-old man in Niangara, a chief. He was grieving for his son who'd been killed by the LRA, and what he said gave me chills. He said, 'We have been forgotten. It's as if we don't exist.'"

A waiter in a white-collared shirt and black pants came to take our order.

"Merci," Ida murmured.

"Merci, aussi," he replied.

In Congo, it wasn't customary to say, "You're welcome" or "It's nothing." In reply to a thank-you, a person said, "Thank you, too." In casual exchanges and formal settings, this thread of reciprocity ran through. Here we were in Eastern Congo, one of the deadliest regions in the world, and the everyday language was gratitude.

"There's more," Ida said. Her voice was low, guarded. "The Makombo massacre may not be the only unreported large-scale attack. We've also received reports of attacks in remote regions of the Central African Republic, but there's been little attention or follow-up from the CAR government or the UN."

The United Nations Organization Mission in the Democratic Republic of the Congo (MONUC), the UN presence in the region, now had one thousand peacekeeping troops in northeastern Congo and a proactive mandate to go after the LRA. But even the major peace-keeping presence in the region that was meant to protect innocent lives seemed unwilling to act against Kony's army. I remembered hearing after the first Christmas massacres in 2008, after Operation Lightning Thunder, that a boy had run from his village to the UN base twelve miles away, the base that was there to protect all the villages in the region. He had stood on the fence and said, "The LRA are killing people in all of our villages." The UN troops still hadn't left their compound. This time the massacres had happened much farther away from the MONUC bases. The UN hadn't been in a position to prevent the violence. But it was their responsibility to respond. I asked Ida what the UN was doing in the aftermath of the attacks.

She told me that on January 20, over a month after the attacks, MONUC had sent a human rights official up to Niangara to investigate. He stayed for an hour and a half. He had recommended that the UN form a special mission to investigate, but none had been approved. UN officials had later told her that without the GPS coordinates for Makombo village, they couldn't land a helicopter there to conduct investigations. Nor did they seem to have made much of an effort to find an alternative.

"They didn't send any sort of aid or support to the survivors? They didn't go after the LRA?"

She explained that they hadn't made any offensive operations against the LRA in more than four years, not since they'd lost eight Guatemalan peacekeepers in a counter-LRA operation in Congo in 2006, a serious loss that had discouraged them from further action.

"This can't keep happening!" I remembered Laren's long, steady stare the night at the Mercer when he'd told us about his meeting with the member of the National Security Council. That disillusionment and dread. The groups designated to stop the violence were doing nothing to prevent massacres from happening again and again. "Who else can we call on? Who can we pressure for a response?"

Ida told me that some of the Congolese soldiers stationed in the region had been helpful after the attacks, gathering corpses, digging graves. And a Congolese military team from Bangadi had come in late December—weeks before the UN had sent anyone—to conduct an investigation, walking for two whole days to reach the attack sites. But there had been no government response to the massacres. The officials Ida had talked to in Kinshasa just the week before were totally unaware of the attack. Congo's President Kabila and his cabinet continued to assert that the LRA was not a threat.

Even if the government had been more proactive and responsive, the Congolese army, the entity with the most obvious responsibility to protect Congolese civilians, was saddled with problems. With few helicopters and vehicles, abysmal communications systems, and salaries and rations that arrived late, if at all, the army wasn't equipped to pursue or protect against the LRA. Especially so when the president refused to acknowledge the threat.

MONUC had plenty of resources, several established bases in the region, and a mandate to stop the LRA. They even had an agreement to help the Congolese army with food and transport. But with rampant corruption within the Congolese military, it was impossible to make sure the UN's support was getting where it was supposed to go. And the tragic lack of response during both Christmas massacres showed that even a big budget and proactive humanitarian peacekeeping mission were not enough to guarantee safety in the region.

Ida said that the Ugandan military seemed better positioned for counter-LRA missions, and had actually sent a group of soldiers in pursuit of the LRA after the Makombo massacres. But they'd lost the trail at a river crossing. And although they were allowed to cross international borders to go after the LRA, they didn't have the troop power to adequately protect civilians in the hundreds of villages in the region. They also weren't in a position to coordinate well with the Congolese military or the UN. In fact, one of Ida's Ugandan military contacts had told her that they didn't even bother trying to coordinate with the UN anymore since MONUC had proven so ineffective at protecting civilians.

It didn't seem right to accept that we were at an impasse to stop the LRA's atrocities. And yet I couldn't see a way forward. A humid breeze came up off the lake and rustled the tablecloth. The tables near us on the patio had filled up and we could hear voices murmuring in English and French. A man laughed. The waiter returned with our coffee and tea. He smiled brightly at us before he moved away across the flagstones.

"What now?" I said. "What are we going to do?"

"We'll publish our report," said Ida. "*The New York Times* has already agreed to run a story. I have to believe that we can do something positive if we keep the world informed. If we keep the pressure on."

I wanted to believe that, too. It was what the humanitarian and world leaders I'd been honored to work with always said: that we have to work hard, we have to do our very best—and we also have to trust. Trust ourselves, each other, God. One of my favorite passages of scripture, 2 Corinthians 5:7, says: *For we walk by faith not by sight.* I had to trust that there was a solution to the LRA crisis, even if I couldn't see it yet.

I looked across the lake, trying to make out the shape of the mountains against the sky.

YOU COULD BE NEXT

David Ocitti

IN A CLEARING an hour outside Pabbo, the commanders split the children into smaller groups. David was sent one way, his brothers another. They continued to march.

Before dawn they came to a small camp. In the dark, David could see rebels standing guard around a group of women and children asleep in the grass. David and the new arrivals were ordered to find a place on the ground to sleep. When David collapsed, his whole body began shaking. He felt that the heaviness in his body would break him. He tried to slow his breathing, to search the sky for familiar stars. He stretched his body out on the rough grass. His eyes had just fluttered closed when the commander yelled and David bolted upright. The commander pulled a young boy up from the grass. In the moonlight David could see that the boy's face was streaked with tears. The commander grabbed him by the shirt and promptly shot him in the face.

"Don't cry," the commander warned the survivors. "Don't talk. Don't even look at each other—or you'll be the next to die."

————

At sixteen, David believed he was the oldest boy in his group. Most seemed to be between the ages of five and fourteen. Boys were targeted at this age, David would learn, because they were big enough to carry guns and young enough to be brainwashed. The boys were trained to kill. The girls were each assigned to a soldier. David could hear them crying out at night. Sometimes the soldiers didn't wait until night to beat or rape them.

By the end of the first week David finally wept. Even though crying meant death, he couldn't stop himself.

Each day the commander kept them moving until the sun set, when they stopped to rest. Too many nights, another child would be killed, murdered within a circle of his peers. Sometimes the victim was singled out for having disobeyed, or as an example of what happened to those who tried to run, or for talking to a friend. Sometimes the victim was chosen arbitrarily, and this was worse, because it signaled that no matter what you did, you could always be next. You could follow the rules, but you were never safe. You had no control. You could be killed for any reason, or for no reason at all.

The days of marching were exhausting, but as long as they were moving there was a respite from death. Then, a few days after his abduction, David noticed a change in the rebels who had captured them. They were edgy and even more aggressive than usual, kicking and pushing the children as they tried to march, yelling loudly. Soon David understood why. They reached a clearing where a stocky, middle-aged man was waiting. He had a mustache, and his chin and cheeks were covered in stubble. He smiled as the group approached, but even from a distance David could see his narrow brown eyes, piercing and stern. He was an upper-level commander, the one David's group commander reported to. His name, David would learn, was Okot Odhiambo. He had ordered the attack on Pabbo and neighboring camps.

Odhiambo wasn't especially tall, muscular, or physically overbearing. But he was terrifying. He spoke in a friendly way one moment, and then turned to rage. David saw him beat one of the men, an established LRA combatant, and then, as he lay on the ground, cut his shoulder open with a machete. "Move!" he yelled, kicking the bleeding man.

They didn't stay long with Odhiambo. The LRA constantly split and regrouped as they brought in new abductees. Along with the terrible violence and fear, it was a way to control the new recruits, to always keep them guessing. Just as they came to understand a commander's methods or feel a bond with a fellow captive, they were forced to adapt to new people, new behaviors. The only constant was terror, and the direction of their march. They were steadily moving east, in the direction of the rising sun, leaving home farther and farther behind them.

Soon David and the other new captives weren't just witnesses to violence. They were forced to participate. The commander shoved them into a circle. He gave them a heavy stick. He chose a boy at random to send into the middle and ordered the others to take turns hitting him with the stick.

"Keep passing the stick," he shouted. "Hit! Hit! If you refuse, you will die."

The stick was in the hands of a boy across the circle from David. The boy hesitated. The commander raised his gun. The boy closed his eyes and waved the stick.

"Harder!" the commander yelled. "Make me hear the blow, or you will be next."

David tried not to think about the boy in the middle or the awful sound, or the stick making its way around the circle toward him. He tried to remember the faces of his family. He tried to hear his uncle playing the lukeme, the trance-like, heartbeat sounds. At last, the commander said they could stop. The victim lay slumped and bloody in the middle of the circle. He was dead.

"You are alone," the commander told them. "Home is gone. Everyone you love is dead. We are your family now."

David felt more and more vulnerable and afraid each day. But he had lost the ability to cry. The worse the brutality became, the more his sensitivity to horror seemed to lessen, a knife gone blunt with use. It was how the mind survived: ceaseless distancing and endless vigilance. Don't let it in, and always stay alert. You could be next.

If he allowed his mind to wander, the terrible memories consumed him: his father falling, the question he'd been forced to answer. The guilt made him sick; he couldn't swallow. A bitter taste always filled his mouth. This was how the LRA broke their abductees' bonds with home. And David was luckier than some. He had killed his father only with his words. He would see kids forced to kill their parents with their own hands. To raise a machete over a father's head and let it fall.

Questions tugged at him under the constant stream of horrific images like a current. Where was his mother now? His brothers? Did anyone know where he was, that he lived? Was anyone he loved still alive?

God created me, he tried to remember. *God has plans for everyone.* In his pocket was a little Bible he'd been given at school. In his loneliness, to stop the haunting images, David invented a game. He'd take out his Bible and close his eyes, praying, *God, show me what to read.* Then he'd open the Bible at random. And he'd trust that whatever passage he opened to held a message from God, something to help him understand what God intended for him.

TRAINING AND
COMMUNICATIONS

"BREAK IT DOWN for me, Greg. Why can't a private foundation do this?"

US Army Lieutenant Colonel Greg Joachim sat across from me at a little table in a quiet bakery near the State Department, the comforting smell of coffee and fresh scones wafting around us. During his near twenty-year career in the army, Greg had implemented US security, stabilization, and assistance operations across Africa, even serving as a military adviser to the assistant secretary of state for African affairs. Now his role at State was comprised mostly of counter-LRA work and work in Somalia. He didn't have the stereotypically stoic look of a career military man. He was friendly and broad-shouldered, with a little star at the bridge of his nose that crinkled every time he smiled. And he smiled refreshingly often.

On the surface, there'd been progress on the counter-LRA front in the two months since I'd met with Ida and learned of the Makombo massacres. The LRA Disarmament and Northern Ugandan Recovery Act that Laren and Invisible Children had been working so hard on had unanimously passed the Senate in early March, and then in May passed the House with the support of 202 representatives—making it the most widely supported Africa-specific piece of legislation in US history. Laren had just told me that he'd been invited to be in the Oval Office when Obama signed the bill.

Despite the positive updates, I'd been sobered by the fact that policy alone wasn't going to stop the LRA. I'd initiated conversations with the US State Department, which was already supporting the Ugandan military by providing helicopters and fuel to the tune of approximately one million dollars a month. Despite the commitment and creativity Greg and his colleagues were showing in getting resources to the field, it hadn't been enough to stop the conflict or prevent the recent massacre. "What do you see as the gaps?" I'd asked Greg and other State officials. "What's needed to stop the LRA?"

In meeting after meeting, the answer was the same, and it was what I'd heard from Ida and other advocacy organizations close to the issue. There were two major counter-LRA priorities: training for the Ugandan military to be more effective at tracking and hostage release, and improving communications among villages vulnerable to attack—military training and communications.

"If we know what to do, why aren't we doing it?" I'd asked.

Funding, they told me. Despite Greg's many efforts to steer resources toward counter-LRA operations, and the then imminent passage of the LRA bill, allocating more money to fund training and communications in a region that was not a direct national security threat to the United States wasn't a government priority.

I'd suggested beforehand that maybe financial support from Bridgeway could supplement Greg's work. He'd been intrigued by the idea and had agreed to check if it was possible for Bridgeway to make a direct monetary contribution to the State Department's counter-LRA operations.

But this morning he delivered the news. He'd pushed my offer for financial assistance higher and higher up the chain, but the answer hadn't changed: while the State Department supported the cause, they were not willing to accept Bridgeway's money and use it to pay for training and communications operations in the field.

"So you're saying that training and communications could stop the LRA, and State's telling us their resources are already stretched and they can't commit to more funding. But State can't accept outside support to do the work they know needs to be done?"

"I'm sorry."

The bell on the door jingled and several men and women wearing suits came in, briefcases and stacks of binders under their arms, cellphones pressed to their ears. Greg smiled. "If you find a way to pursue funding a communications network or military training, I'll be right here in the wings, supporting you every step of the way. We just can't accept a check."

THE ONES WE WERE
WAITING FOR

"WHERE'S YOUR WHITE fedora?" I asked Laren over lunch in Los Angeles in May. He'd driven up from San Diego, where he and his wife, Courtney, lived, to see me before my afternoon meetings.

"How many times do I have to tell you?" he protested. "It's a Panama hat."

He was still glowing from his moment with the president, his happiness infectious.

"I'm in the Roosevelt Room, looking at everything. The door kicks open, and Obama comes in, like, 'What's up?' I shake the hell out of his hand. We go into the Oval Office and I'm in the front row, throwing elbows. I'm right there next to him when he signs the bill. They've told us that no one gets to talk, that the president will say some words and that's it, but I totally cut him off. I say, 'Mr. President, I'm here on behalf of hundreds of thousands of young people in America and Central Africa. I made a promise to a kid named Jacob in northern Uganda who was abducted and his family killed by the LRA. I promised him we wouldn't stop until the LRA is a thing of the past. Today is a huge opportunity to fulfill that oath.' And Obama says, 'You tell that boy Jacob that the president of the United States knows about this, and we're gonna get this done.' I'm like, 'Yes, sir.' And he picked up one of his gold pens."

"That's awesome," I said. It was a validation of what he'd always told me: change doesn't happen if you just take your seat. "You stood up," I told him.

"Me and a hell of a lot of other people. But—" His big brown eyes narrowed and his voice flattened. "It was a cool moment, I'm not gonna lie. But I don't think it's going to work. Until there's clear strategy, the bill is just a piece of paper. It's not going to change things for the people trying to survive."

I hadn't told him yet about my conversation with Greg Joachim at the State Department. About my growing certainty that if the world was going to stop the LRA, it would require taking a step beyond traditional advocacy. I had no idea yet how far beyond traditional advocacy we would go. I just knew that more direct action was necessary.

I had been trained in the power of direct intervention early in my humanitarian career. After law school I'd accepted a job as a defense attorney at a downtown Dallas firm, planning to work just long enough to pay off my school loans, and then make the switch to the work I really felt called to do. But when a friend who understood my desire to work in international human rights gave me a copy of *The Good News About Injustice,* by Gary Haugen, the founder of International Justice Mission, I realized I couldn't delay aligning my life with my deeper purpose. I put my hundred thousand dollars in law school loans on deferment and moved to Washington, DC, to work for Haugen's small nonprofit. International Justice Mission's efforts were focused in part on ending child slavery around the world. IJM was founded on the principle that we don't have to stand by and watch our fellow humans suffer. Its work showed me that we can, and must, act.

While I was working with IJM in 2003, we collaborated with local authorities in Cambodia to free young girls from brothels where they were raped for profit. Despite intense international pressure against the Cambodian government for the documented abuses—including the threat of losing aid from the United States—the status quo had continued undisturbed. The entrenched economy of sex slavery, and the corruption that enabled it, seemed impossible to overthrow. After years of research and outreach, our team of eleven went to Svay Pak, a dusty village on the outskirts of Phnom Penh, a place infamous for entrapping children in sexual slavery, and worked with local authorities to conduct brothel raids, bringing thirteen perpetrators to justice and helping thirty-seven victims start new lives. This work would be documented in an Emmy Award–winning *Dateline* piece, *Children for Sale*.

After one of the operations with the police, I'd held a little girl in my arms. She wore flowered cotton pajamas. I remember her long dark hair pulled back into a ponytail, her tiny gold earrings, her small hands holding on to my neck. At the safe house, she was quiet and withdrawn, afraid to trust anyone. I did my best to comfort and reassure her and the other girls, to let them be children again—we sang songs and blew bubbles. Before we left them to sleep in peace through their first night of freedom, I noticed that one of the girls had a number of small, pale crescents that ran up and down the length of each arm. I realized they were the scars of her old life—the places where the perpetrators had extinguished cigarettes on her bare skin.

In one night, several dozen young girls had seized their freedom, and the power of tangible, direct action was life-changing. But there was also a lot to wrestle with. A single brothel raid didn't upend an entire system of exploitation and injustice. Without justice for the perpetrators, girls leaving brothels just created space for new girls to be forced in. Lasting change needs to tackle the system itself. IJM taught me that if we also focus on bringing perpetrators to justice and building a justice system that citizens can rely on, then the change can be wide, deep, and sustainable. This movement to enforce laws and make people safe must be owned and led by national government and citizen leaders working together to protect their people from violence.

The night of the brothel raid in Svay Pak, some brothel owners had been tipped off, and had hidden their captives away where they couldn't be brought to safety. And even for the young girls who were able to leave a life of sex slavery, the danger didn't end when they were transported to a safe house. There was the constant threat of recapture. A number of the girls were Vietnamese and had been smuggled across the border. Even though they had crossed into Cambodia unwillingly and had been held hostage, they could now face prosecution for immigration violations. On top of the physical and legal threats, they had experienced significant trauma and needed careful attention and support for years to come as they healed and built new lives. An effective intervention required careful partnerships in government, law enforcement, and the courts, and close work with local medical and mental health providers, social workers, and educators to ensure top quality, long-term care and opportunities for the girls coming out of the brothels. It takes years for this kind of effective intervention to build lasting change.

Direct intervention is often difficult and dangerous, but with patience and perseverance it bears fruit. When I first went to Cambodia with International Justice Mission, the Cambodian government estimated that the prevalence of minors being exploited in Phnom Penh's sex industry was between fifteen and thirty percent. The children being exploited were as young as six years old. Now, fifteen years since that initial operation, studies show the exploitation of children in the sex industry has dropped to two percent, with hardly any minors under fifteen years old being sold for sex. This is the result of more than a decade of collaboration between the government, police, courts, social services, NGOs, and the public.

In contemplating what role Bridgeway could or would play in trying to stop the LRA conflict, I was thinking deeply about what we could accomplish, and how. And I was assessing the risks, the ways in which our involvement could endanger the very people we hoped to help protect. I wanted to make sure, if we took a step beyond traditional philanthropy, that other committed people I trusted would go there with me.

"Maybe we're thinking about this backward," I said to Laren now. "All this time we've been trying to figure out how to convince people to take action, or how to get resources to the people who are taking action. But what if it's not about waiting for the right people to show up? What if we're the ones we've been waiting for?"

I had his attention. "What are you saying?"

"I'm saying come with me to Congo in June. We'll talk to the UN presence in northeastern Congo. We'll talk to survivors of recent LRA attacks. And we'll find out if there's anything we can do to help make the violence stop."

PANGA

David Ocitti

DAVID'S GROUP REJOINED Odhiambo for a few days. One afternoon they stopped their endless march for a short rest. David sat shoulder to shoulder with Maxwell, a boy near his age with whom he sometimes exchanged glances, even a few quiet words when the commander's back was turned.

"Hey," Maxwell said.

Odhiambo, who was sitting near them, turned their way. "You!" he yelled, pointing at Maxwell. "No talking allowed." Odhiambo stood and walked toward David, shoving a panga—a machete—into his hand. "Those who talk must die. Your friend talked. You must kill him."

Maxwell stiffened beside him. The handle of the panga was still warm from Odhiambo's hand. David stared at the rust and silver of the blade.

"No," he heard himself say.

"What did you say?" Odhiambo loomed over him.

"No. I'm not going to do that."

"What gives you the right to refuse?"

"I won't do it."

"It's not a choice. You have to do it."

"Then take my life. I'm not taking his."

Odhiambo grabbed the machete from David's hands, raised it over his head. David closed his eyes. Blood pounded in his head, a river of sound. He imagined his father in his mind. *You're here for a purpose,* his father used to say. *You're not here just by chance.* When the blow came it was with the blunt edge of the handle, not with the blade. He felt the pain grow big around his skull like ripples forming in the water where a rock lands. Then the pain narrowed and sharpened, a fierce prick of light. He waited for the next blow. When it didn't come he opened his eyes.

"I'm not going to kill you," Odhiambo said. "Not yet. I'm going to make you pay first." He gave the machete to David's friend. "Beat him, don't kill him," he said.

When the beating was over it was time to march again. Odhiambo commanded David to carry a heavy pack filled with salt. It weighed forty pounds at least, a significant weight for David's rail-thin frame. He staggered on the steep trails grown muddy from rain.

"If you drop the load, you will have dropped your last breath," Odhiambo told him.

David had to carry the pack of salt for three days. His head still ached, his back ached, his whole body ached. Again and again he stumbled. If he were already dead he'd be beyond pain and fear. It was what Odhiambo and the other commanders wanted him to think: *Next time, just kill me.* They were more useful, more lethal, when they had nothing left to lose.

A few nights later, David's group arrived in a village where everyone was asleep in their huts. Odhiambo was still traveling with them. He ordered them to go into every home, to kill all the adults—no exceptions—to leave only the children age twelve and under alive, then burn the huts. It was an attack similar to the one they had survived in Pabbo. But now they were forced to be the perpetrators.

Odhiambo led the attack. He wielded a panga. "You better call out, 'Save me!'" he taunted his victim as he raised his weapon above an innocent's head. "I'm your god now. You better cry to me." He didn't wait for a reply before smashing the panga down.

When they marched away afterward with the new abductees, David felt numb. He was glad for the dark. He couldn't see the fear in the new captives' eyes. He was afraid to see himself as they saw him. He was just like them. Terrified. Scarred by loss. Left with nothing, with no one.

9

ZEBRAS

A FEW WEEKS later, the blinds in my room were still drawn tight against the morning light when the door sprang open. Connor pitter-pattered over the wood floor and pounced onto the bed.

"Is it today?" he asked. "Today you go to Africa?"

"Today, baby." Sweet boy with his hair all a mess.

He sat with his knees tucked into his chest and rubbed his bare feet back and forth across the blue flowered bedspread. "But I want you to stay."

"I wish I could stay right here with you," I said, lifting back the covers so he could squirm under. "I wish I could stay right here." I pulled him close for a snuggle. He wrapped his lanky arms around me but was too wiggly to rest in our perfect hug. He scooted away from me and moved his arms and legs up and down, out and in, like he was making a snow angel under the blankets.

"Bare toes are for tickling," I warned. He shrieked and flailed as I reached under the covers and grabbed for his feet.

His screams of laughter brought Brody toddling to the bedroom door, bib still on over his pajamas, Sam chasing after him. "Hold you, hold you!" he cried, and I lifted him onto the bed, where both boys wriggled and yelled as I tickled them. "More, more!" they begged. I tickled Brody's perfect chubby tummy. I nuzzled Connor's rosy cheeks. I caught Sam's eye in the doorway, and he smiled at me. But under the smile I could see tightness at the corners of his eyes. He looked tired.

"We wanted to let you sleep," he said.

Sam had finished his law degree and now did some legal charity work a few hours a week, but he was primarily home with the boys. It was a choice we'd made together—but one that had surprised me at the time. We'd been taking a walk in our neighborhood one afternoon when Connor was a baby, following the trails that wound through the greenbelt behind our house. We were trying to figure out how to manage our lives, how we could be the parents we wanted to be and also do the work we felt called to do in the world. At that time, Sam was a college admissions director, and I was vice president at Geneva Global, a philanthropic consulting company based in Philadelphia. I didn't know how to reconcile the extensive travel my job required with our desire that one of us always be present to hold down the fort. Sam had listened as I sketched out different scenarios, and then said, "There's no conflict, babe. It's simple. I'll step away from my job for a while and stay home."

"You would?"

"Why wouldn't I?"

Both of our mothers had worked when we were young—his mother, Joan, as a pianist and organist, and my mom as a youth pastor—but our fathers had been the primary breadwinners, our mothers the primary caregivers to the kids. That was still the division of labor in most of our peers' families, too. Knowing Sam's generous nature and his commitment to our family, I should have anticipated his willingness to break the familiar mold. But I was so accustomed to what the world, and especially Texas culture, had to say about gender and work and home that I had presupposed my own husband's reaction. I'd anticipated a struggle to find a balance that worked for us. Sam had made it so easy and clear.

I knew how lucky we were to have been able to make that choice. Lucky, too, that my parents—my mom especially—would be there while I was away, helping Sam care for the kids. My work was really a family effort. While grateful for the solidarity, I was aware of the unevenness, too, the things Sam and I each took on alone, the way life often required us to partner at a distance instead of side by side.

Connor stopped his flailing and watched us carefully, his blue eyes studying our faces the way he often did when he was about to ask a big question. *Will you die, too, like Big Oma? Will I?* His big questions always made me catch my breath. They came out of nowhere, it seemed. There was never a chance to think out a response in advance. And I had made a promise to myself that I would always try to be completely honest with my children. I wouldn't tell them the little white lies meant to soothe. If the shot was going to hurt, I said so. If they asked for ice cream and the answer was no, I wouldn't pretend there was none left in the freezer to avoid an argument or tantrum. But to answer Connor's questions honestly sometimes seemed cruel. He was only four.

"Bro Bro," he said solemnly, tugging on Brody's pajama sleeve. "Mommy's leaving today. She's going up in the sky in an airplane. She's going to Africa to see the zebras."

I looked at Sam. So much of parenting is choosing which version of the world you invite your children to see. Part of me wanted to just enjoy the innocence of Connor's idea of why I was always going to Africa, to let him picture me traveling a vast savanna, marveling at the wild animals he had only seen in zoos. But I couldn't stand for him to think that zebras were what took me away from him. And I couldn't shirk this opportunity—and our responsibility—to guide his sensitive heart. Since early toddlerhood he had shown a mature compassion. At the park, at preschool, gathered with family and friends, he had a special knack for noticing people who were in pain. I recognized his awareness of suffering as a gift that would guide him to help others— and as a vulnerability. He had the potential to get hurt. A lot. As much as I wanted to protect him from heartache, I understood that it would help him more in the long run if Sam and I, instead of shielding him from suffering, could show him ways to face it. Ways to move forward even when his heart was broken.

Sam tousled Connor's hair and said, "Mommy's going to be in a lot of meetings, not out on safari." He turned to me, giving me the space to decide how much more I wanted to say.

"My love," I told Connor, "wild animals couldn't take me away from you. Mommy's going to Africa because there are some families there in danger. There are mommies and daddies and children who are getting hurt. I want to see if there's anything we can do to help the mommies and daddies make their home safer."

Brody threw himself back onto my lap and begged for more tickles. Even though he had hardly left babyhood, he was already so different from his brother, life a simpler exercise for him. They were both affectionate boys who exuded love. Connor's love rippled out in careful, thoughtful waves. Brody's expressions of love were boisterous and daring.

Connor squinted at me. "Why are they in danger?" he asked.

"There is a man who is hurting people there."

"He should stop hurting people."

"Yes," I said, "he should."

Brody was bouncing on the bed, dangerously close to the edge. I reached my arm out to keep him hedged on the bed.

"Are you going to make him stop, Mommy?"

"There are some really special people in Africa who are trying to make him stop, and Mommy is going to try to help those people."

He nodded his head. "Okay," he said. He climbed into my lap for another hug. Sam opened the blinds and the sunlight poured in.

RED TAPE AND RIVER RAFTS

A FEW HOURS later I was on a plane to Chicago, where I'd connect to an overseas flight to Brussels. From Brussels I'd fly to Kigali, Rwanda, where I'd meet up with Laren and his Invisible Children colleagues, Jason Russell and Ben Keesey. We'd spend the night in Kigali before driving first thing in the morning to Gisenyi, where we'd cross the border into Congo on foot and catch a short flight on a UN plane up to the UN's headquarters in Bunia for our first meeting.

During my short layover at Chicago O'Hare I wandered around the airport, too restless to sit at the gate waiting for the plane to board, needing to stretch my legs. I found myself standing in front of a spinning rack of fuzzy neck pillows. In my twenties, when I'd left my job as a lawyer to work for International Justice Mission, I'd been able to travel all over the world without experiencing any jet lag, but after years of cramped and constant international travel my body was starting to complain. My mom had made me promise to do something this trip to protect my back. I flipped through the pillows, trying to find one that wasn't pink.

My mom was the first person to teach me about generosity and presence. She had served as a youth pastor since before I was born, retiring after thirty years to run a large, inner-city ministry, working to rebuild homes in San Antonio, one of the worst cities in the US for substandard housing. I understood what a model she has always been of intuitive caring, of a desire to make a difference in the world. I chose a career in law, not the church, but I think my thirst for justice comes from the same place: from what my mom and my faith community have taught me about aspiring to a life of service and sacrifice.

Now I could see that my work was both an extension of what she had modeled for me in the world and the expression of her unfulfilled longings. She had graduated high school with the burning desire to be a part of lasting peace in the world, and she had decided to apply to the Peace Corps. But her parents—my wonderful Oma and Opa, warm and loving as parents could be—weren't willing to let my mother go so far from home. She chose to honor them and not go. Maybe that was why my mother had raised me the way she had—never throwing up a roadblock in the path of my ambitions and passions, supporting me 100 percent in my work and my calling.

"I don't know if you ever knew this," she'd told me recently, "but when I was spending time with Oma during her last months, I'd tell her about all the work you were doing. She was so proud of you and so amazed. Then one night she said to me, 'We should have let you go to the Peace Corps.' I told her it was for me to stay and get to have a daughter who would change the world."

The neck pillows only came in the one obnoxious shade of hot pink, but in honor of my mom and in deference to her advice, I bought one anyway.

I closed my eyes as soon as I reached my seat and held my boys' sweet faces in my mind like prayers.

When we arrived at the stark and sparsely furnished UN headquarters in Bunia, Brigadier General Ziaul Hasan, whom colleagues called General Zia, sat at one end of what seemed like a mile-long table, and offered me a seat at the opposite end. Laren, Jason, and Ben sat along one side of the vast table while dozens of UN representatives, all wearing official badges, lined the full length of the other side. General Zia decorously introduced each of the numerous staff by name and function. When it was my turn to introduce Laren and the others—my "delegation," as General Zia called them—I felt as though I had to shout at him to be heard, he was so far away.

A long line of well-groomed faces looked at me expectantly, the fluorescent lights glinting off of many pairs of glasses. In times of crisis, countries from around the world volunteer their troops to join UN peacekeeping missions. If Bridgeway could invest in direct action to stop the LRA, it made sense to try to work with the peacekeepers already in the region.

"General Zia," I called across the enormous table. "The UN has about twenty thousand troops in the Democratic Republic of Congo right now, is that correct?"

He nodded. "Eighteen thousand, six hundred and fifty-three, to be precise," he said, pronouncing each syllable carefully. "But keep in mind that only a fraction of the UN's peacekeepers are forward-stationed for the LRA. We are also here to address violence in the Kivus, and Ituri, and elsewhere. The LRA is unfortunately just one of the many armed groups operating in Congo."

"And how many LRA combatants are operating now?"

"That is difficult to say for certain, but we estimate there are approximately six hundred LRA combatants in the bush at this time."

"And the LRA is attacking communities not far from UN bases."

"Occasionally, unfortunately, that is correct."

"And all those troops couldn't defend those communities?"

I had to stop because the entire UN side of the table started to laugh. What was the joke? I looked at Laren, Jason, and Ben for an explanation. Laren sat stone-faced. Jason's eyebrows were raised. Ben was staring at me.

Twenty badged international officials giggling because I had failed to understand what was obvious to them: despite their proactive mandate to solve the LRA crisis, the UN didn't do that. My questions about their lack of success hadn't made them embarrassed or uncomfortable. I had only exposed how little I understood about the system in which their peacekeeping work was entrenched. I was the naïve fool.

"Sir," I shouted down the table. "We're here because we want to help you stop the LRA. Please tell me, what are the gaps? What can we do to help?"

General Zia gave me a tolerant smile. "The LRA operates near the rivers," he said. "If we had river barges at our disposal, we could patrol the rivers."

"How many barges do you need?"

"I believe two would suffice."

"Great. If these barges are truly critical to the cause, I would like to supply the money. Can you walk me through the logistics?"

He blinked at me.

"Do we write a check to the UN?"

He gave a wry smile. "No, I would not recommend that, no. Our base, you realize, is not centrally located. If you submit money through the United Nations, it will never get to us here in Bunia."

"So, can I write you a check, or wire you cash?"

"Oh no, that is against regulations."

"Sir," I called. "If the river barges are needed and the lack of them is preventing you from tracking and stopping the LRA, and my foundation is willing to purchase them, then what is the procedure for getting the assets to you?"

General Zia seemed mystified that he had to explain the protocol. "You can simply requisition the boats," he said, "and have them delivered."

"What kind of boats do you need?"

He went on to describe inflatable pontoon boats with motors at the back.

"And what is the cost estimate for these?"

"I am certain they can be sourced for around five thousand dollars each."

Was he really telling me that the UN peacekeepers in Congo, with a $1.4 billion annual budget, couldn't stop the LRA because of a lack of two inflatable boats costing a total of ten thousand dollars? As we ironed out the logistics I couldn't shake the feeling that as much as

General Zia wanted the new resources to make a difference, he also knew that nothing was really going to change.

We were about to wrap up our meeting when General Zia cleared his throat. "Ms. Davis," he said. "Before we adjourn, I must tell you that there has been an adjustment in the next part of your itinerary. Security risks prevent us from transporting you to the MONUC base in Niangara, closest to the Makombo attacks. We will fly you to Bangadi instead. It is near a recent attack site. And I am going to send my chief of staff along with you as an escort." He gestured toward the trim Bangladeshi man sitting beside him who gave me a half smile.

11

A CLOSE CALL

WE FLEW IN a UN plane to Dungu, one of the largest towns in northeastern Congo, and spent the night in refurbished, air-conditioned shipping containers set up by UNHCR, the UN refugee agency. IKEA Foundation had furnished the units, and walking into the shipping container was like touring a showroom staged to look like a college dorm room.

We woke early to board the aged Russian Mi-17 helicopter that would take us to Bangadi, where there had been a recent LRA attack. It always seemed a bit like a roll of the dice when we got into these ancient helicopters—Congo was known as the world's helicopter graveyard, where all helicopters eventually go to die. Laren, Ben, and the anxious chief of staff squeezed in across from Jason and me. There were no seats, only two long benches that lined either side of the helo. We had barely clicked our seatbelts before the propellers swung and the engine roared. I settled against my little pink neck pillow as the helo lurched into motion. In the back cargo area, a stack of big tin roofing sheets rattled noisily. We lifted off the dirt runway.

A strong breeze blew in through the windows, refreshing against the heat. We straightened out above the dense canopy, a thick green tangle that stretched in all directions like a sea. Cutting through the green were two fast muddy rivers—the Dungu and Kibali—that merged to form the Uele, the river the LRA had crossed the morning they began the massacres. I looked back toward Dungu and saw a one-lane stone bridge and a giant, medieval-looking building beside it on the shore.

"Dungu Castle," Laren yelled over the engine's thrum. "One of the Belgian colonialists built it. That's why the bridge is so narrow. He stole half the bricks meant for the bridge to build his castle."

"Do you remember everything you read?" I asked.

"Pretty much." He grinned.

It was too difficult to carry on a conversation over the engine's ferocious noise, so we put our earbuds in, switched on our music, and gazed at the scenery. Soon no human-made structures were visible, just the vast and abundant jungle, veined with brown rivers. This was the same terrain that Joseph Conrad's *Heart of Darkness* had described as an impenetrable darkness, an environment of madness and moral decay. His description of Congo didn't mesh with the landscape below. The whole Great Lakes region—soil rich with iron, waters teeming with fish, the jungle a deep breathing green—looked like Eden to me. It seemed a place where life was born to thrive. It was a disgrace that a place so lush and beautiful had become a killing field.

Suddenly there was a loud bang at the back of the helicopter, a sound like a gunshot. We pitched violently. The co-pilot shouted at us to put our heads in our laps with our arms around our heads.

The helo shook violently and the hum of the engine had a drag to it. We swayed on a funny axis. It felt as if we were falling. Ben started recording a message on his phone, a goodbye video for his wife. I closed my eyes and clutched my head against my knees. As we fell I heard the words form in my mind: *I'm going to die.* Jason reached for my hand. I squeezed his fingers. He had young children, too, a son and a daughter. I tried not to panic. *I love you, I love you, I love you,* I said to Sam and my boys over and over in my mind.

Then, just as suddenly as the helo had pitched and started to fall, the engine roared and we started flying again, but at a tilt.

"What the hell was that?" Ben yelled up to the co-pilot. "Were we shot?"

"Mechanical issue," he called back.

"The tin sheets," Laren said. "They slammed against the interior of the helicopter. I think that's what made the sound."

I laughed with relief. Not an explosion, no bullet or bomb—just someone's future roof banging around in the cargo area. "So, we're good to go?"

"Negative. There's a mechanical issue," the engineer assisting the pilot called back. His face was set in a grimace and I could see from the pilot's rigid shoulders how hard he was working to keep the helicopter steady.

"Are we going to try to land?" Laren asked. He gestured out over the canopy. "Is that even possible out here?"

"No, we can't land here," the engineer said. "We're turning around."

It was a silent, somber hour back to Dungu, retracing all the ground we had just covered. Finally we landed on the dirt airstrip. My legs were so shaky I could barely stand. The UN official who had helped us when we boarded the flight ran toward us as we stumbled out of the helo.

"I heard the distress call on the radio," he said. "I prayed for you." He held my arm tightly. "I thought we wouldn't see you again."

A lump rose in my throat. "How long, do you think, until the helo is fixed?" I asked.

"We won't know until the problem has been diagnosed. We'll try to get a mechanic on the job as soon as possible." He looked at me thoughtfully. He wasn't much older than me, but something in his eyes, the intelligence and concern, reminded me of Opa. "You still want to go to Bangadi?"

I nodded.

"I'll find you another helo. You can try again first thing tomorrow."

The propellers whirred and the seats shook as we boarded the Mi-17 the next morning.

"You think it's really a new helo, or did they just scotch tape the old one?" Laren asked.

I flashed him a wry smile and willed myself not to get rattled, especially when Ben started reeling off helicopter crash statistics, which he must have memorized long ago, because we hadn't had Internet access since the hotel in Rwanda. Despite our collective anxiety, we lifted off without incident and banked, heading out again over the green-canopy sea. The jungle did seem as vast as an ocean, and as isolating. I tried not to imagine how difficult it would be to find us if the helo actually crashed this time. I tried to dispel my unease. But my body clenched every time we hit slight turbulence, and when Jason's water bottle slid off his seat the sudden thud made my heart pound.

Eventually, the green canopy opened below us, the red dirt dotted with small white cement buildings strung through the clearing like teeth. We had made it to Bangadi. I felt my shoulders loosen. The pilot announced our descent and explained that because we were entering a red zone he wasn't allowed to power down. He would land the helo near the UN base, and we'd jump out. He'd return in three hours, after dropping off the tin roofing sheets someplace else.

When the helo had landed, one of the airmen opened the door. The noise of the propellers pummeled us. My whole body shook with nerves and vibrations from the aircraft's noise. We jumped out. As soon as our feet touched ground the helo began to rise, the chest-rattling noise of the propellers diminishing to a hum as it flew away.

We stood in the hot sun and sudden silence, gathering our breath. Laren pointed to a nearby building emblazoned with the blue UN logo. Just then a horn honked and we saw a white UN truck driving slowly toward us.

"Please get in," the driver called out his open window, motioning toward the bed of the truck. "Have a seat back there and I'll drive you to the base."

"Isn't that it just ahead?" I asked, pointing at the building just a few yards away.

The driver nodded. "Yes, we will drive you there."

There was no time to argue about our ability to walk to the building. We climbed into the bed of the truck where a few armed soldiers already sat. Armed escorts, for a drive of no more than five hundred feet. The driver began a slow, wide turn toward the UN base. Suddenly, a noise pounded over us. A helicopter came into view.

A lump of panic rose in my throat. As the helo descended and hovered over the ground I realized it was our helo, the one we had just jumped out of. Were we being called back? Had General Zia changed his mind? Had our pilot just been radioed a warning? Was Bangadi under attack? The door opened and the crew chief who had helped us with the door jumped out and ran toward us, wildly waving his arm overhead.

"Stop, stop!" he shouted. "Madam! Wait! Madam!" the crew chief called again as he reached the truck. "You forgot something!"

I had my passport, I was wearing my glasses. What was the emergency? The crew chief leaned into the back of the truck. Clutched in one hand was my bright pink neck pillow. I had intentionally left it behind on the helicopter for our return flight. I would have felt awkward carrying it along. Now my face flushed and my ears tingled with embarrassment. I took the pillow. "Thank you," I stammered. I could feel Laren and the others choking back laughter. The soldiers sat rigidly on alert, their guns at the ready. I looked at my lap, afraid to meet anyone's eyes. The airman ran back to the helo and hoisted himself inside. Only when it had risen into the sky did the truck begin to crawl again.

Laren, Jason, and Ben couldn't contain their laughter. They doubled over, unable to stop.

"A visit to a red zone," Laren finally said, "should never be attempted without the following crucial items. Number one, an armed escort. Number two—" He fell apart again, collapsing into more laughter. "Number two, a fuzzy pink neck pillow."

I began to laugh, too. A full-body laugh. A laugh that wouldn't stop. The pure-joy laugh of my sons when I tickled them. A laugh that didn't let up until my body felt emptied out and my eyes were misty with tears. I couldn't remember the last time I had laughed like that.

12

RED ZONE

IN THE DIM foyer of the base, we were greeted by the head of the UN military contingent in Bangadi, a cheery Moroccan man. He led us down a tight hallway and into a sunny room where he pointed to a low table surrounded by intricately embroidered Moroccan pillows to sit on. Ornate dishes covered the table, steaming platters heaped with couscous, vegetables, fruit, and fish laid out whole, looking up at us with dead glassy eyes.

"Please sit down, take some tea," he said.

Breaking bread is often a component of my work. A meeting begins with a meal, a ceremony of welcome and cultural exchange. Food is such a universal part of being human. When we eat together, we acknowledge what unites us. To offer sustenance is a fundamental way of showing respect for a visitor. And to accept it is in turn a sign of respect to the host. It's like saying, *I feel at home in your home, I'm comfortable on your turf.*

The Moroccan battalion was known for serving the most delicious and lavish meals among the peacekeeping contingents in Congo. On any other day, I would have been honored to partake of the elaborate meal prepared for us. But today we had less than three hours to accomplish the one thing we'd crossed the world to do. I couldn't bear to spend precious time lounging on an embroidered pillow and stuffing my face with a multicourse meal.

And yet, there was no way around it. We couldn't be rude. I sat at the table. I diligently spooned something from every single platter onto my plate. And I began eating as quickly as basic etiquette would allow. If I could have shoveled the food directly into my mouth with my hands I would have done it, so urgent was my desire to get to the communities and have the conversations we'd come to have.

But the meal was like a feast in a fairy tale that constantly replenishes itself. As quickly as I could empty my plate, more trays of steaming platters were laid on the table. An hour passed and my heart sank. This meal would never end unless I made a move.

"Sir," I said to our host. "I am so honored by your hospitality and grateful for this delicious meal. But we have only two hours until our transport returns. I want to make sure we are able to do what we have come all this way to do."

He squinted at me. "What do you mean?"

"The interviews we have come to conduct. In the nearby communities."

"I don't understand."

"We are here to speak with survivors from recent massacres."

He grinned in bafflement and began to shake his head. "Oh, no, no, no," he said. "Madam, I am very sorry, but there has been a misunderstanding. This is a red zone. We can't take you out there."

Out there? On a Human Rights Watch map I'd seen of LRA attacks in the Haut-Uele region since August 2009, the attack sites were marked with stars, the UN bases at Bangadi and Niangara marked with triangles. Sometimes the space between a triangle and star was less than a pinky's width. When he said "out there," he was talking about villages mere miles away.

"Sir, I'm sorry, but I must insist. This is the reason for our trip, to speak to people directly and understand exactly what they need."

He looked for General Zia's chief of staff, who left, presumably to make a call to General Zia.

"We can just walk to the villages," I said. "And we really must leave now."

His face flushed. "The risk is too great! I cannot allow you to leave the safety of our compound."

Just then General Zia's chief of staff came back and told the Moroccan head of the UN delegation that General Zia had confirmed that he had already approved our trip to the villages. Our host bowed his head in concession.

We loaded in the back of the UN trucks and drove along a narrow dirt road, the jungle crowding in on both sides. The only other travelers on the road were men carrying farm tools and women in long floral wrap dresses with goods from market on their heads. They pressed back against the green so we could pass.

In the village, people rushed up to us, brimming with urgency. A community leader stepped forward to greet us.

"Thank you for coming and for caring about what is happening to us," he told us through our interpreter. He handed me a notebook with a handwritten log of the people killed and abducted in recent attacks. He had recorded the names and ages of those missing and dead, and details from witnesses and escaped abductees. I scanned the accounts from the survivors, the roster of brutality.

As I paged through the dust-streaked notebook, what struck me most was the incredible resilience of the survivors—and the fact that the trauma and threat of violence were far from over. All day, every day, these people who had already experienced unthinkable horrors were living in danger of more violence.

To have survived the brutality once wasn't enough. Those who had witnessed their neighbors and friends and families being hacked to death mere months ago were at risk of being the next to die. Those who had been captured by the LRA and had managed to escape and return home were the most vulnerable of all. The consequences would be especially horrific if the LRA returned. Meanwhile, the regional and UN forces close enough—and with the weapons and mandate to protect the many communities like this one—weren't showing up.

The most painful part of the trip for me was when we headed to an area with thatch-roofed homes where a nine-year-old girl came to speak to us, accompanied by her father. She had closely cropped hair and wore a brightly colored T-shirt and a long skirt. She approached us with her head lowered. Through a translator she haltingly began to tell us her story. She didn't lift her face as she spoke.

I always struggle with this part of our work. When people in affected areas share their experiences, I worry that they feel they must tell their stories to the white person who came to hear. To share something so deeply personal and vulnerable—to relive the trauma—must lead to change. The listener has no right to hear without accepting responsibility for participating in the work of change.

The girl sat carefully in a hand-carved wooden chair. I knelt near her feet. Staring at her small hands, speaking to the translator in spare sentences, she told us she had been captured by the LRA and held captive for three days. They had raped her. On the fourth day, she and her friend were left alone in a hut while their captors went to pick food from the fields. She knew it was their chance to run. But her friend was too terrified to go. She hugged her friend and ran. She didn't look back, she didn't stop until night fell and she couldn't see where she was going. She slept alone in the bush, she woke with the dawn and kept running, she ate nothing but the occasional wild yam she could dig up in her flight.

She wore a strand of green beads around her neck and a gold Saint Christopher medal on a pale string—a pendant worn to show devotion and ask for blessing, a gift from the NGO worker who had helped her after her return. She sat folded inward when she was done speaking. I felt awed by her resilience—she was closer to Connor's age than to mine, and she had experienced something most adults would never have to: she had saved her own life. But her incredible bravery couldn't bring back the life she'd been robbed of.

Her father hovered behind her, a hand on her shoulder. "I'm frightened," he said. "The LRA returns for those who escape. This time they will kill her."

I could hear the fear in his voice, and the thing that as a parent I know must hurt worse than almost any other pain: the feeling that you are helpless to protect your children. Beneath the fear I saw his hope, too, that in sharing her story, his daughter could help make a safer world.

I couldn't stop thinking of her or of her father's face.

After we left Congo, we stopped over in Rwanda. In Kigali, before we flew home, I took Laren, Jason, and Ben to pay our respects at the Kigali Genocide Memorial, a place they had never been, that honors the victims of the Rwandan genocide. The memorial garden and museum house the final resting place of more than 250,000 victims. A long granite wall lists the many, many names of the dead. In darkened chambers hung with black velvet curtains, photographs of the dead are displayed. Mothers holding babies, couples embracing in wedding clothes, cutting into flowered cake, children holding schoolbooks, families gathered around picnic tables, young people in graduation gowns. In glass cases, artifacts from the dead: children's shoes, rosaries, skulls shattered by a machete's blade. A plaque at the entrance to the Children's Room reads: *In Memory of Our Beautiful and Beloved Children Who Should Have Been Our Future.* This was always the hardest room for me—life-size photos of children killed, engraved plaques with their names, ages, their last words, their favorite things, where and how they died: *Hacked to Death; Tortured to Death; Shot to Death; Grenade in Shower; Hit Against Wall; Eyes Stabbed Out.*

After a somber tour of the museum, we made our way to a bench in the memorial garden, overlooking the green hills of Kigali. Around us, visitors rested and walked in silence. Some offered flowers. Some cried. It was a place to grieve, to face an evil that flourished in a world that did nothing to stop it. And a place to heal. To say we are better than the worst in us. To say never again.

13

LEATHER SHOES AND RADIOS

ONE OF THE most depressing aspects of the current LRA situation was the lie at the heart of the UN presence in Congo: the protection they offered often was only an illusion. And the illusion itself was dangerous. Thinking that a group was there to protect them gave communities a false sense of security. I knew we were going to have to try something different. That until we did, we were part of the broken system.

There was no road map for how a private humanitarian foundation could truly engage in the operational aspects of trying to stop a conflict. *Training and communications. Training and communications.* These were the needs our friends at Human Rights Watch, the US State Department, and, most important, community organizations in Central Africa had identified. Better communications between communities, and better-trained troops to stop the perpetrators.

Everyone was telling us that military training was necessary because the tactics the Ugandan military had employed against the LRA in northern Uganda weren't working in the current environment. After Operation Lightning Thunder, the failed assault on Kony's camp in 2008, the LRA had broken into small, agile groups, while the Ugandan army continued to operate in large, slow units. While the LRA had adapted to the jungle environment, crossing rivers and employing countertracking strategies, the Ugandan army hadn't altered its standard operating procedures. Yet, the Ugandan military was the only group on the planet that knew the LRA's devastation firsthand and had a proven track record of combating the LRA.

"Let's stop in Kampala on our way home," Laren said that night over dinner in Kigali. "We can see if the Ugandans are open to collaborating on an intervention."

In Los Angeles, just a few weeks before, we had talked about the need for an out-of-the-box, creative solution to the crisis. But this was the first time either of us had put words to a specific strategy, especially something that was potentially so far beyond the bounds of traditional philanthropy.

Laren could sense my hesitation. "We can't go home without at least asking the question," he said.

The next afternoon we sat in the office of Henry Okello, Uganda's Minister of State for Foreign Affairs. A thickset, amiable man with gray hair and eyebrows that arched in a way that made him look perpetually surprised, Henry Okello was the son of General Tito Okello, the Acholi leader who had been president of Uganda for six months before being overthrown. The minister now served in the government of President Yoweri Museveni, the man who had ousted his father.

Laren had built effective relationships with most of the Ugandan government ministers and knew Henry Okello well enough to get straight to the point.

"Would the Ugandan government be open to receiving support from a private foundation in filling the identified military training gaps in the counter-LRA mission?" he asked.

At the word *military*, my body tensed. Despite the unanimously expressed need for counter-LRA military training in the region, I was deeply uncomfortable with the idea of collaborating with a military entity. I had been willing and eager to support the State Department's contributions to a counter-LRA intervention, but to do it directly ourselves still seemed impossible, even ludicrous, to me. A private hu-

manitarian foundation didn't support military operations, and it was
beyond unsettling to hear Laren utter those words in a government
official's office. We all wanted the LRA to stop abducting children and
committing violence. But I didn't know the Ugandan government's
intentions regarding getting top LRA leadership to the International
Criminal Court.

"We're getting ahead of ourselves," I said. "I must know: Is your
plan to capture Kony?"

A silence followed. Laren seemed embarrassed by my blunt question, and Okello looked confused. He nodded his head.

"Let me be clear," he said. "Our plan is to capture Joseph Kony and
take him to The Hague."

I trusted Laren's trust in him, and I believed him, though a part of
me wondered if he was only telling us what we wanted to hear.

On the flight home, Laren and I continued to strategize. Collaborating with the Ugandan government on military training still seemed
out-of-bounds. But the communications need we could try to fill right
away. There were already numerous local leaders working to establish
communication systems that would allow villages to share information about LRA attacks in Congo. We hoped to find a way to support
and supplement the communications efforts already in place and figure out how to build an Early Warning Network that would help villages communicate with each other about threats in order to prevent
attacks. The network could also help communities collectively gather
evidence and details about the attacks—the same work that individual
communities had been doing in the notebooks we had seen filled with
careful handwriting, but that sat on dusty shelves, the information
never seeing the light of day. The incidents could be documented in
real time, offering proof of the LRA's atrocities that international bodies would find more credible and harder to dismiss.

In response to discussions with Invisible Children about setting up an early warning communications network, Bridgeway soon received a proposal Invisible Children had sourced from Father Abbé Benoît Kinalegu, a courageous Catholic priest and the president of the Dungu-Doruma Diocesan Commission for Justice and Peace (CDJP) in Congo. He was asking for a small amount of money to add a dozen radios to the existing network of high-frequency, two-way, long-range radios in communities in Congo.

High-frequency (HF) radios—similar in size and technology to ham radios—could transmit and receive signals across a distance of more than five hundred miles and cost only a tiny fraction of a cell tower. They could also be housed completely inside an existing structure, like a church, with only a small antenna running out, often from the top of a bamboo pole. One of our concerns in creating a communications network was in building something visible that would become a new target for the LRA. We wanted to be sure we didn't make the communities that housed pieces of the warning network even more vulnerable to retribution and violence. But the HF radios kept a low profile. The whole unit, including the solar panels, could be easily concealed. And the operators could be trained to use a brevity code that would mask the contents of the message. Even if the communications were heard by the LRA, the contents and location of the signal would be obscured. Plus, the network was scalable—it could be expanded over time. We could easily add HF radios to the network and eventually put a radio in a significant number, if not most, of the affected villages. From a financial and logistical perspective, Abbé Benoît's plan seemed like a no-brainer. And the proposal came from within the vulnerable communities that would operate the network, from the people most affected by the violence and most empowered to find solutions.

In collaboration with Invisible Children and the dozens of community partners already working on an early warning system, Laren and his colleagues went in search of the first five HF units needed to expand Abbé Benoît's network. The HF radios were the technology used in World War II and Vietnam, and though they could be found among enthusiasts and hobbyists in the United States, they were no longer used in commercial or military fields there. But in many parts of the world people still used HF radios on their vehicles to communicate with colleagues spread out across long distances in areas without cellphone service.

Assuming we could find the five complete HF units, the bigger problem came in transporting them. The equipment was bulky and heavy. Each unit included a long antenna connected to a twenty-pound radio pack and a receiver and a microphone, powered by a seventy-pound battery connected to solar panels. You couldn't just drive a truck across the vast distances and into the remote locations where the units were most needed. The units had to be flown in, which meant chartering a plane or negotiating passage on a UN aircraft.

In late summer, Laren wove through a crowded, dusty market in Goma, Democratic Republic of Congo. Music blared among the hundreds of wooden stands where vendors displayed their wares: plastic buckets, bolts of brightly colored fabric, whole goats hung upside down by their feet, warm sodas and beers, skewers of meat, and reused plastic bottles filled with homemade fruit juice. A flock of kids chased after him, calling, *"Mzungu, mzungu!"*—Swahili for white person— and flashing him a thumbs-up. He found the wooden stand where a vendor who sold Italian leather shoes and other luxury goods imported from Europe was rumored to have a supply of European-made HF radio units. The merchant smiled at Laren and said he did have five units in back. He would sell them for seven thousand dollars apiece. He accepted only cash. There wasn't time for Laren to call and have the cash wired. He was able to borrow the money from a UN contact, who also helped arrange for the equipment transport. He went back to the small wooden stand with the crocodile and Italian leather shoes, and gave the vendor thirty-five thousand dollars in cash for five HF radio units. As he loaded them onto a truck, he asked the vendor why he sold the unlikely combination of leather shoes and radios. The vendor said that the radios had to be shipped all the way from Italy, and in order to make the most of each shipment he filled each radio container full of Italian leather shoes and belts.

Laren drove straight to the airport and waited with the HF units until they could be loaded onto a UN aircraft, then he flew with them to Dungu. A few days later when he arrived in Limai, the first community to receive a new HF unit installation, a man was lying on the ground with a gunshot wound to the leg. There had been no way for them to call for help or flag transport, and the wounded man had to wait for more than twelve hours before a motorcycle could be summoned to ferry him to a clinic.

In October 2010, Laren would email me a picture of the first HF unit installation. A small group of men stand in a circle holding a long bamboo rod they gathered from the bush. Attached to the top of the bamboo rod is the radio antenna that can be raised up during use and pulled back to the ground to prevent its being detected by the LRA. The men hoist the bamboo pole above them. A woman and small child watch from the doorway of a square brick building with a thatched roof. Behind them, the immense green wall of the forest. The men gaze up at the top of the pole as it breaches the tree line.

The note Laren sent with the picture was brief. *We're in business,* he wrote.

THERE IS A TIME
David Ocitti

APRIL CAME, FOUR months since his abduction, and almost everyone in David's original group was already dead. "How long is this going to go on?" he muttered to his friend Maxwell. "Why don't we just get out?"

This was the first time he put the possibility of escape into words. After this, they would try to have quick, furtive exchanges in the dark each night. But there was never enough time to settle on a plan. Still, David felt his conviction gathering. "There's a time for everything," he whispered to Maxwell one night. "If it's our time to die, we'll die. If it's not, we'll live." Surviving or dying—either way, it was a way out of living like this.

They marched one afternoon in mid-June. It was the hottest day yet. Behind him in line David could hear a baby crying. The baby had been born in captivity. David could hear the baby's mother trying to comfort him. *Hush, baby, hush, baby.* They'd been marching all day in the heat without a break. The baby was hungry. He cried louder and louder.

"Please," his mother finally called up to the commander. "Can I stop to nurse my baby? He hasn't eaten all day."

"I'll make him stop crying," the commander said. He went to the mother and grabbed the baby from her arms. The baby wailed harder. The commander gave the mother a disgusted look. He carried the baby to a nearby tree and began to hit the baby against the trunk. *Thud. Thud.* When it was over he threw the body into the bushes. He shouted at everyone to keep marching.

David heard the mother crying behind him on the trail. If even a baby can get killed, he thought, we are all going to be killed. This time running away wasn't a possibility. It was a necessity. He was certain. Better to die running than to go on each moment fearing and witnessing death. It was time.

He couldn't picture when or how he'd make his escape. But he knew he had to try. When they stopped for the night he pulled out his Bible. *God, show me what to read,* he prayed. He thumbed the pages, feeling for the right spot. He opened the Bible to Ecclesiastes 3:1–8. *To everything there is a season, and a time to every purpose under heaven. A time to be born, and a time to die . . .* A shiver ran up his spine. The time to leave was now.

Early the next morning, a little before sunrise, he whispered to Maxwell, "If it's our time to die, let us die. But if it's our time to continue living, let us go now. We can't stay here." Then he took off running. He didn't bother trying to hide as he fled. He just moved as fast as he could. He could hear Maxwell running behind him, and saw a third boy join them, another of the remaining older captives. With every footfall, the mantra drummed in his head: *If it's my time, it's my time.* Gunshots erupted behind them. They raced for the forest at the edge of the clearing. Before David reached the trees, the boy who had joined them fell. He'd been shot at close range. He lay in a heap, motionless. David forced his legs to pump harder. *If it's my time, it's my time.* David reached the trees and looked back. Maxwell was on the ground at the edge of the clearing. He was bleeding from his thigh.

"Go!" Maxwell yelled. "At least one of us can go."

David ran into the trees.

He fled for two days, using the direction of the setting sun to guide him west, toward home. When he dared to stop for a brief rest or to check the position of the sun, he could hear what he thought to be his pursuers. When he climbed a tree to look around, to see if a river or landmark could give him his bearings, he could see the flicker of their movement in the bush. Once, when he was in a valley, following a stream, he was sure he saw the green of their uniforms winding down from a ridge.

On the second day, as he threaded his way down a steep hill, he heard voices suddenly right behind him. He could hear them talking, the tall grass breaking. *If it's my time, it's my time,* he thought, pushing himself to run.

He could hear people running behind him. It was rocky terrain this high up, craggy cliffs jutting through the green. Just in front of him the ground seemed to drop off. He was afraid to slow down. He wasn't aware that he had tripped until he was crashing to the ground, his head knocking against a rock. He got up in a haze, not sure if he had blacked out for a moment or a day. A stick had impaled his left leg when he fell. A fragment of it was still jammed in his calf, just below his knee. He was afraid the wound would bleed more if he pulled the stick out, so he left part of it in his leg and kept running, uncertain if anyone was following him. His whole body hurt. Except for the rasp of his breath as he ran, all was quiet.

When he heard no sign of anyone on his trail, David permitted himself to stop and rest. He dozed off, then startled awake, voices in the distance. He didn't know if it was the LRA, but he couldn't risk letting down his guard. He forced himself to keep running and limping, his nerves jumpy with paranoia and the desperate need to sleep. He came upon a number of paths through the dense forest, but he didn't dare follow them. Although it was slow going to cut his own trail, it was safer to create a path than to follow an established one. That way, if he heard someone behind him, he would know he was being pursued.

As darkness gathered his third night on the run, David felt fatigue and despair grip him. He couldn't tell direction in the dark. He sat on the damp earth, his back against a tree at the edge of a small clearing. When he stopped moving, he could feel nothing but the throbbing of his injured leg. *If you want to give up, it's fine,* a voice in his head murmured. *You can stop running.* He let his eyes close. He wondered how long it would take for death to come, for the pain to disappear. He merged into a state that was not awake or asleep, his mind floating. Then his grandmother's voice came to him: *Don't be a foolish hunter,* she said. His eyes snapped open. Right above him were the stars. *The brightest star will guide you home,* she had taught him. He looked for latwok, for the many colors it showed when he gazed only at it. He found it. *Are you sure?* a voice asked. What if fear made his eyes play tricks on him? What if he followed the wrong star? He found the brightest star again and rose to his feet, making his path through the dark in the direction he thought to be home.

In the morning, the sun came up right behind him. He was still moving west, on his way home.

Later that morning, the fourth since his escape, David came upon a larger road. A signpost pointed north. *Atiak*, it read. Atiak was the town north of Pabbo where three major roads met. This was the road that led south, toward home. He was close now, less than twenty miles away. But he couldn't follow the main road. The LRA traveled the main roads to abduct captives and pillage for supplies. He could be recaptured. Or the Ugandan soldiers who patrolled the roads might mistake him for an LRA member. It was a known tactic the LRA used to ambush the Ugandan military—they'd send a rebel out on the road, pretending to be bad off and seeking help, and then a group of combatants would descend on anyone who stopped to help. Even this close to home, he would have to make his own path.

Late in the afternoon, he reached Pabbo. The wound in his left leg looked infected, part of the stick still jammed into his upper calf. He could feel blood crusted over the side of his face, and the wound on his head was hot to the touch. Children scurried away from him as he limped his way through the village toward his mother's hut. He could smell the cooking fires, the evening meals. He had eaten only the fruit he could pick on the run. But now that he was within reach of a meal, he didn't feel relieved. Life went on in the camp. No one welcomed him. No one seemed to recognize him. He couldn't read people anymore, couldn't tell what they were thinking. He had grown so used to fear and distrust, to being alone in the world. Even if someone had spoken to him, he would not have known how to reply. It was Pabbo, the same town he had left behind six months ago. But it wasn't home anymore. It was the place where his life had ended.

He came to his uncle's hut first. It was still charred and crumbling from the fires the LRA had set the night of the attack. No one had restored it. The big tree that stood beside it had also been badly burned and was not yet recovered, the bark still black, the limbs without leaves.

Then he stood outside his mother's hut. He watched his hand close into a fist and knock. He heard footsteps within. His heart pounded. The door opened. A little girl stood there. An unfamiliar woman's voice called from the dim interior. "Who is it?"

"He's dirty," the girl said. "He's got blood all over his head."

"Wait," the girl's mother said. "Don't let him in." She hurried to the door.

David's mouth was as dry as dust. He tried to speak his mother's name, to ask if the strangers knew where she was now. But he was afraid to hear their answer. His voice came out in a stutter. He tried again. Finally he managed to say her name: Pyerina Alum.

The woman shrugged her shoulders. "Never heard of her," she said. She pulled her daughter back inside and closed the door quickly.

14

IRON LADY FROM TEXAS

WE SAT UNDER a white, open-walled tent on damp, sagging couches at the Hotel Africana in Kampala, where the whirring electric fans were doing little to cut the heat. Across from Laren and me sat Colonel Walter Ochora, the former Gulu District Chairman (a position similar to governor), now President Museveni's representative in northern Uganda. He was the largest man I had ever met, easily 350 pounds, and wore a traditional loose, colorful African shirt. His faint black mustache and lamb-chop sideburns only exaggerated the expanse of his enormous cheeks, spread even wider by a jolly smile. Laren, who knew Colonel Ochora from his Invisible Children work in Gulu establishing programs to help LRA victims, had already briefed the colonel on our possible collaboration with the Ugandan military.

I'd thought that in beginning to fill the communication void, in helping villages establish an Early Warning Network and achieve a modicum of safety and protection, we were reaching the peak of our direct action. But the more aware you are, the more deeply you dive, the greater your knowledge—the more responsible you become.

When we'd met with Uganda's Minister of State for Foreign Affairs in June I'd thought it impossible that we would actually pursue supporting tactical operations against Kony. But in the months that we'd been working on the Early Warning Network, new data was coming in all the time—from the UN and the existing six radios in the network. In June alone there were thirty-one separate reports of violence, resulting in sixty-five civilian abductions and twenty-three civilian deaths. Helping communities communicate with each other about attacks was only a piece of what was needed. The attacks needed to be halted. We'd stopped asking if we should investigate supporting a military intervention. Now we were asking how. What tactical action could private citizens take to stop an atrocity like this? What was legal, what was just, what was right? The legal and ethical implications made my head spin. I'd begun consulting with lawyers to determine whether funding military training for a foreign army was compliant with US laws. If all went well in our meeting today, Ochora would broker a meeting with General Aronda Nyakairima, commander of the defense forces, the head of the Ugandan military.

Ochora was notorious for being a heavy drinker and carrying multiple phones that rang incessantly during meetings. True to form, he opened our conversation by setting a satellite phone and at least three cellphones on the table before ordering his very unusual usual—a drink he called "seven of seven": seven shots of Bond 7 whisky served in one tall glass, no ice. He bobbed his large head agreeably as I described our current work on the Early Warning Network.

"Good," he murmured, his voice thick and deep. "Well done."

Colonel Ochora wasn't just physically large, he was larger than life. After seeing his father murdered in the early days of Idi Amin's regime and training at one of Africa's most celebrated military academies, he had become a rebel leader, staging a successful takeover of the State House in Kampala and serving as de facto president of Uganda for three days before withdrawing. He had waged war against President Museveni in the 1980s. Now he was Museveni's most trusted official in the north. And he had a long and complicated history with the LRA: on at least one occasion Kony had reportedly sent a hit squad to his home in Gulu; the LRA had also invited him into the bush multiple times to try to broker peace with Kony.

As I watched Ochora contentedly empty his glass, I wondered what was going on in his mind. Did our offer to help the Ugandan military to defeat the LRA seem outlandish to him? Was he suspicious of our motives? Or did he even take us seriously? I'd been so eager to meet him and put our plan in motion. Now I was nervous. This was my one shot to make the pitch. And I was all too aware how easy it would be to misunderstand each other, or for something simple to trip us up.

"Sir," I began carefully. "The communications projects are a start, but we are prepared to consider going even further to put an end to the LRA. The community leaders we partner with throughout Central Africa have been demanding for years that the international community finally arrest Joseph Kony, or that local armies receive the training they need to get the job done. The UPDF seems to be the regional force most dedicated to this end. We are considering the possibility of hiring a private, professional military trainer to train the Ugandan army in counter-LRA tactics."

I almost hoped for Ochora to laugh. To pull us out of this crazy scheme. To thank us for the help with communications, and wish us a good journey home. But he didn't laugh.

"Come to the Emin Pasha Hotel this evening at six p.m. You will take tea with General Aronda," he said. He shone his wide smile like a flashlight beam on me. He shook my hand warmly. "When you get back to Texas, tell President Bush, Jr., hi for me."

I laughed and jokingly agreed.

In the dark-toned library sitting room of the Emin Pasha Hotel, I sat with my cup of milky African ginger tea—my fourth in as many hours—trying not to lose hope. The general was late, very late.

He had every reason to be. He had every reason not to show up at all. On any given day, he was incredibly busy, his schedule often booked late into the night and even into the wee hours of the morning. Today he was navigating a national crisis. Just a few days prior, al-Shabaab, an Islamic Somali rebel group, had launched suicide bombings at two locations in Kampala, attacking crowds gathered to watch screenings of the final match of the World Cup, tragically killing at least seventy people, including one of Invisible Children's longtime volunteers and roadies, Nate Henn, who was watching the game with an Acholi friend he'd met while interning. As head of the entire Uganda People's Defense Force, the national military of Uganda, General Aronda was charged with maintaining security for both civilians in Uganda and his troops stationed in Somalia and elsewhere. All day I had expected to hear that he had canceled our meeting. But Ochora kept insisting that the general was on his way.

He arrived at 11:00 p.m., a tall, imposing man, his uniform weighted with decorations, his eyes heavy with exhaustion. When he called Colonel Ochora out into the hall to brief him prior to our meeting, the absurdity of the situation hit me. I didn't know what I was most afraid of—that General Aronda would consider us a waste of his time, or that he would agree to work with us.

He came somberly back into the library and took a seat in an armchair near the long couch where Laren and I had spent the last five hours worrying that he wouldn't be able to come. Ochora sat in an armchair across the room, smiling to himself, doodling on a napkin. The general nodded at me sleepily, my signal to begin.

I familiarized him with our work so far in the region. He listened with his eyes half closed, appearing not to register my words. I wondered if he was even awake.

"General, our understanding is that you're on a thin string out there fighting the LRA."

He nodded.

"We've been told there are some gaps you're contending with in the counter-LRA mission, and we'd like to help," I said. "We understand that the biggest hurdles to stopping the LRA are in training and communications. Would you agree?"

"Yes," he said. One tired, detached syllable. No elaboration. He sat completely still, his shoulders sagging down wearily, his eyes still half closed.

"General, we have some resources. And we'd like to use them to help you capture Kony and put an end to the LRA."

"I've already put in orders to cut our counter-LRA troop allocation in half," Aronda replied. He had spoken so few words that the sound of his sleepy voice took me aback. "There's an election coming up next year," he continued. "We need the security here at home."

I felt a strange mixture of disappointment and relief. It wasn't going to work. And yet he had agreed to meet with us amid a national crisis. I had to at least ask if he could accept our help.

"I know this is a busy time for you," I said. "And I know your army is stretched extremely thin. What would it take to keep your counter-LRA efforts on track? To help you finally bring an end to this conflict?"

The general didn't answer right away, and I worried that he had actually fallen asleep this time, or that we had hit another dead end. That even the head of the Ugandan military was resigned to another decade of violence. But then Aronda spoke.

"We need intelligence support," he said. "Cellphones, satellite phones, GPS tracking devices. Fixed-wing aircraft for surveillance. And we need increased mobility. Our Mi-8s are on contract and they're not cutting it. We need Mi-17s for moving troops and supplies."

"What about a private military contractor to train your troops?"

"That would help," he said. His tone was straightforward, but guarded, his eyes so droopy I almost wanted to take the toothpicks on the table and use them to prop open his eyes, to make sure that he was really seeing and hearing us at the end of his very long day. It was now well after midnight.

"If we find and fund the right partner, would you want to train a specialized group within your army to stop Kony?"

"Agreed," the general said.

It was a wary response, more circumspect and seasoned than optimistic or engaged. But it was a yes.

When we stood to leave, Colonel Ochora handed me the napkin

he had been doodling on. I saw a picture of a woman with bouncy hair in tall boots. I realized it was meant to be me. Below the picture he had written: *Iron Lady from Texas.*

He was only teasing. But I didn't feel like a person steeled for action. I felt like I'd waded in too far, too deep.

15

NON-NEGOTIABLES

IT WAS IMPOSSIBLE to sleep that night. Laren was amped with excitement. I was flooded by reservations and second-guessing. We sat up in the empty restaurant at the Lake Vic Hotel. Outside, lights glowed along the path that led through the groomed lawn to the deserted pool. The bartender slowly threaded his way among the dark tables. Laren and I went over the details of our crazy day, trying to hash out next steps, the first of which was to find someone much more experienced than we were who could help us with this project: a private military entity we could contact about training the Ugandan army.

I had never imagined that the conversation about a possible military intervention would go this far, and short of contacting Greg at State for potential contractors, I had no idea whom to call for help. The only military contractor firm I could think of off the top of my head was Blackwater—and only because of the terrible media stories I'd read about the Blackwater contractors and their horrific behavior in Iraq. How was I going to find people capable and trustworthy enough to work with us and train a specialized force in the Ugandan army to pursue the LRA?

"I've already got a short list," Laren said. "I started doing some reading on the best bush fighters in the world as soon as it looked like we might consider doing a tactical intervention."

He showed me his list of names: James Acker*, the head of a UK-based company that claimed to handle a substantial number of the US Department of Defense private military contracts; Lafras Luitingh, head of Saracen International, which had an office in Uganda; and Eeben Barlow, the chairman of Specialised Tasks, Training, Equipment and Protection (STTEP) International, in South Africa. Laren thought that Luitingh and Barlow were the most promising. Eeben Barlow was often referred to as the grandfather of private military contractors. He had founded Executive Outcomes, the world's first-ever private military group, and had waged successful—though controversial—campaigns against rebel groups in Angola and Sierra Leone. Lafras Luitingh had been Barlow's business partner at Executive Outcomes for a time before they had parted ways.

As Laren shared his months of research, I felt another wave of unease. Only months ago, I'd been the one pushing hardest for an intervention, running full speed like a horse out of the gate. Now Laren was racing and urgent, and I wanted to pull back on the reins. It had been such a leap for me to even consider doing anything militarily against the LRA, and now that a partnership with the Ugandan military seemed viable, all I could see were the potential risks.

The Ugandan Minister of State for Foreign Affairs' assurance that this would be a mission to capture, not to kill, was a start in addressing my extreme discomfort. But there were other conditions that had to be met before I could agree to move forward. These had to be crystal clear before we began the search for a potential partner. In the dark, quiet bar I listed my non-negotiables.

Traditionally, private military contractors charge a project fee on top of salary and expenses, but my first non-negotiable was that Bridgeway would pay no extra fees to a private military organization—just basic expenses and salaries for the trainers. This mission wasn't about lining pockets. It was about giving a local group the training they needed to protect civilians, free people in captivity, and pursue and apprehend LRA commanders, and I only wanted to work with someone who shared that sense of purpose. Second, we would need to establish a vetting process of all the soldiers involved to avoid putting tactical resources in the hands of people who had committed or might commit human rights abuses. Last, the Ugandan military needed to bear the operational costs of the mission. This was a collaboration—a partnership—and we needed to share in all the pieces of the project, from planning to financing to implementation. And if at all possible, I wanted to hire an African private military company, professionals who would have a closer contextual understanding of Central and East Africa, and who believed that the solution lay within.

As I named my terms, Laren shook his head in dismay. "There's no way," he said. "That's not how these guys work. These are completely unrealistic terms. There's no way we're going to get this."

"We can't erode our principles," I insisted. "These terms are not negotiable."

"Okay," Laren said. "But if this is going to work, I think you're going to have to be ready to compromise."

We agreed to split the list. Laren would contact Eeben Barlow and Lafras Luitingh, and I would reach out to James Acker. We had a short window. If we were going to partner with the Ugandan military, we had to offer a specific plan before General Aronda began the drawdown of counter-LRA troops.

16

AL DENTE

"I WANT TO own an island," James Acker said in the blue light of the rooftop Italian restaurant in Georgetown where he had agreed to meet for dinner after a full day of Pentagon meetings in the summer of 2010.

He laughed, but I had the strange feeling that he wasn't entirely joking.

He had been talking almost exclusively about money the whole evening, and I couldn't tell how seriously to take him—or how seriously he was taking me. Over aperitifs Acker had gone on a lengthy diatribe about the extreme wealth of African presidents, comparing how much various leaders spent flying on private jets, staying in penthouse hotels. He'd spoken with unfiltered disgust about what he saw as pervasive African corruption. "The Ugandans have plenty of money, don't let them fool you," he said. "And don't let them prey on you as a soft target for a few million."

Maybe he was trying to be helpful, schooling me in his worldview, but it felt more like he was trying to shock me than inform me, going for the brash and sensational angle, not the nuance or heart. But his company handled a lot of the US Department of Defense private military contracts. He was well vetted in the field—I just didn't have any personal comfort. Later I would add a fourth non-negotiable to my list: I would have to have some basic, instinctive trust in any future potential partner. I plowed on with the meeting, asking whom he'd recommend to train the Ugandan military.

He didn't ask for more details. He didn't pause to consider the job at hand. He just said, "No private military contractor in his right mind will accept this job for less than a $25 million fee in addition to costs. You better budget thirty mil, minimum."

I'm sure he could see my jaw drop. The figure he named was such a far cry from my non-negotiable number: zero. I felt a surge of discouragement. It seemed Laren was right, that my ideals were too pie-in-the-sky. I knew that private military entities were businesses, and those involved needed to make a living. But I had hoped that people in that world were also motivated by the need to protect. Now it seemed that finding someone who would meet even one of our terms was going to be impossible.

I hoped the meeting would turn around, but our disappointing dinner went even further south. First Acker berated our server because his pasta wasn't al dente. (I wasn't even sure what al dente meant.) When the check came he complained to the server again until her eyes brimmed with tears. He demanded to talk to a manager and insisted that his overcooked pasta dish be removed from the bill. Then he handed me the check.

By the time I sank into my hotel bed, a terrible taste lingered in my mouth. I was ready to cut our losses and find a different way to help stop the LRA.

17

IMPOSSIBLE TERMS

IN LATE JULY, Laren called from Johannesburg.

"I found our man," he said. "How soon can you get here?"

A few weeks later Laren and I flew to South Africa for a meeting with Eeben Barlow, the chairman of STTEP International. I trusted Laren's respect for Eeben's résumé: his impressive track record fighting a rebel group in Angola; his success in containing the "blood diamond" violence—rape, torture, severed hands, murders—in Sierra Leone. His work in Sierra Leone was especially important to us because the topography and brutality were similar to those in the regions threatened by the LRA. His company had succeeded in stopping a war where nearly eighteen thousand UN peacekeeping troops had failed to curb the violence. And the Ugandan government had called on him to do a threat assessment of the LRA back in 1996. He had knowledge and firsthand experience with the LRA context that no one else in the industry had.

But he had an undeniably checkered past. He had worked for the apartheid government. I found it difficult to believe that someone who'd been on the wrong side of those dark years of oppression and violence would feel a responsibility to stand beside the world's most vulnerable populations.

Eeben came to the airport in person to pick us up. He was not at all as I'd imagined him; he was of a medium build, with a low-key presence and graying hair. He wore wire-framed glasses and his smile was warm. On the drive to his home in Pretoria, he smoked menthol cigarettes, one after another. He seemed comfortable in silence, and I resisted the urge during our forty-five-minute drive to clutter the space with words.

We took tea on the veranda of his beautiful, art-filled home, and then met his wife and teenage son for dinner at a local restaurant. Chris, his wife, was delightful. A reporter, she had a fierce spirit for exposing wrongs, from corruption to domestic violence.

"You wouldn't be here tonight if it weren't for my son, J," Eeben said, affectionately thumping his son's back. "Laren had sent me this urgent message through the 'contact us' button on my blog. I had no idea who this guy was, and I was ignoring him. But my curiosity got the better of me. We met, he gave me an Invisible Children film, and J happened to walk by just as I was sitting down to watch it. We ended up watching it together, and at the end he said, 'Dad, you've got to help them.'"

We hadn't even talked about the project yet, and I hadn't resolved my misgivings about Eeben's past, but I felt unexpectedly at ease in his presence. I found myself nodding again and again in agreement with the things he said, and I liked how his wife and son seemed to support and even motivate his work. But we hadn't talked specifics, and I couldn't tell if my list of non-negotiables would turn out to be a bridge or a block to our partnership.

When we returned to Eeben's house after dinner, Eeben and I sat alone on the veranda. It was time to talk business. I outlined what we were considering. When I was done speaking we sat together in another long silence.

"I want to do this," he said.

"Why?" I asked. His motivation was more important to me than his willingness.

He answered carefully. "I'm African," he said. "And Africans are the solution to Africa's problems. I'm so invested in a solution to the LRA conflict that I won't accept a fee for the mission, and I will discount my trainers' salaries." He added that he would only agree to the mission if the Ugandan military agreed to do their share, and if we could have some say in regard to screening soldiers for the work ahead.

We'd thought my non-negotiable terms would be impossible to fill. But he was meeting all of them. Despite my qualms over what I knew of his former career, I was beginning to feel strongly that Eeben was our guy.

Now I was really scared.

18

DRONE

THE NEXT DAY, Laren and I flew with Eeben to Kampala to meet with General Aronda. To forge this collaboration we needed more than everyone's agreement to work together, more than a concrete and thorough plan: we had to overcome differences across three cultures and navigate multiple triangles of trust.

We convened once again at the Emin Pasha Hotel, this time in a private suite. Our first encounter had been in the middle of the night. Now we were actually laying out potential terms of our proposed support. And now Aronda's eyes were alert instead of half closed. He agreed with many of Eeben's suggestions, and seemed to respect his outside-the-box thinking.

Then Aronda reminded us that the Ugandan army was covering a distance twice the size of Uganda in pursuit of the LRA. That tracking by foot ended when the food ran out. That the specially trained soldiers would not be effective unless the Ugandan military had the ability to airlift food, fuel, equipment, troops. "If we had three Mi-17s we could transport nearly one hundred troops," he said.

I was suddenly uncomfortable. Although Eeben had also spoken to us about the advantages of air mobility, I had been very clear from the beginning that Bridgeway was offering to pay for the training of Ugandan soldiers, not buy expensive equipment for the armed forces. James Acker's warning flashed in my mind: *Don't let them prey on you as a soft target for a few million.* I knew General Aronda was already twenty layers deep in counter-LRA work, that he knew a million times more than we did about the hurdles and necessities in fighting the LRA. And I realized how strange we must have seemed to him, how alien it was for a private group to propose assistance with a military action on humanitarian grounds. He had every right to be critical of our inexperience, and even to be suspicious of us, to wonder what favors we might require in return for our resources. But the tentative trust worked both ways. I had a strong fear that something more than shared purpose could be motivating him, that he might be trying to cherry-pick expensive equipment off a gullible donor.

That fear only intensified when he said, "We need intelligence collection. We need a drone."

I didn't know then what I came to know later. That the mission would need air support for troop and supply mobility, and that aerial surveillance was needed to locate the LRA. That once the Ugandan military found them—if they found them—they would need video and infrared capabilities to keep an eye on the rebels night and day. That a manned aircraft couldn't even fly the fourteen to twenty continuous hours to the Central African Republic and back to gather and convey intelligence. That when the general asked for a drone to capture Kony, he wasn't trying to play me. He was absolutely right.

But in my world, *drone* was a loaded word. Drones were weaponized; drones had mistakenly and tragically been used to kill civilians; drones were completely beyond our budget. A drone was out of the question, much too great a risk. General Aronda's mere mention of one had put me over the edge of unease.

"I think this meeting is over," I said. I stood up and headed for the door.

"No, no," Aronda said, reaching out to tug on my suit jacket sleeve as I passed his chair. "There's no need to leave in haste. Sit down. Sit down."

THE FACE OF GOD

David Ocitti

THE FIRST NIGHT back in Pabbo, David collapsed in the market area and slept. At dawn he wandered the village again. His wounds were throbbing. He knocked on doors, stopped strangers, begged people to tell him if his mother had lived. By afternoon, he had to accept that his mother wasn't there.

"She might be at another camp," someone finally told him. "People have been moving around a lot after the recent attacks."

The next closest camp was Alero. By the time he reached it, his leg was so swollen he could hardly walk. He paused by the side of the road. A man passed him warily.

"Do you know Alero?" David asked.

The man nodded. He barely looked at David. He seemed ready to run.

"Please, I won't hurt you. I'm looking for my mother," David said.

The man paused, listened. When David said his mother's name, the man nodded slowly. "I know who she is," he said. "Follow me."

David felt dizzy. The man led him through the winding paths of the Alero camp, and finally stopped near a thatched-roof hut. A woman knelt in the yard, feeding a fire.

It was her. He could tell by the bend of her head, the red and magenta and green of her scarf, her dress. He tried to call to her, but his body had stopped working again. It was the man who yelled her name. She turned. Lips pursed. She saw David. She frowned slightly.

"I brought you your son," the man said.

His mother brushed ash from her hands and stood. She didn't smile at David. "Why are you here?" she said.

"Mom, Mom, it's me. I'm home."

"No," she said. "You're not."

"I am. I escaped."

"You've just come back to kill us."

She meant that she was afraid David had brought other LRA members along with him, as was commonplace when abductees were forced to lead the LRA back to their village to commit atrocities. The words fell on David like stones. *Who do you love the most?* echoed in his head. He started to cry. "Mom," he said. "Mom." The tears came rushing out.

She stepped toward him, uncertain. Then she was holding him. "My baby, my baby," she said. "You gave me a terrible scare."

David felt her strong arms circling him, her heart thudding against his ribs. He rested his head on top of her head. She smelled like the cooking fire.

"My baby, my baby." She swayed with him back and forth.

David closed his eyes.

Finally, his mother pulled away and gazed at him. She touched his face, his forehead. "You're bleeding," she said. She brought water and clean rags. She daubed the wet rag gently along his cheek, over his forehead, dissolving the dried blood. She bandaged the cut on his head. She performed the same ritual on his leg. It was the first kind touch David had felt in six months. It felt so good—the way she looked at him. The face of God could not have been sweeter.

BLACK AND WHITE

AFTER ONE MORE meeting with Eeben Barlow and General Aronda, we had a plan we all agreed on. Bridgeway would fund the training itself. The Ugandan military would cover every other cost and all aspects of the mission: room, board, and salaries for their personnel, all equipment needed for the training, and the weaponry and strategy for the mission to capture Kony and release his hostages. In the meantime, the lawyers I'd consulted had all confirmed that the proposed undertaking to fund specialized training for select Ugandan soldiers was in the clear, that we did not violate state and commerce department international traffic in arms regulations, or any other laws. We were ready to begin.

I created my own council of advisers, talking to a select group of colleagues and mentors in the humanitarian field whom I could trust with sensitive information and count on to offer me useful perspective. I especially sought out the people I thought would be my biggest critics. I wanted their advice on how to make the intervention as effective and safe as possible.

I was sure the pacifist, Quaker-like sensibility of John Montgomery, Bridgeway's founder, would help him see the risks and flaws of a military intervention, that he would tell me we had to turn away. But while he was surprised by the idea, he was unswervingly committed to making a world free from mass atrocities. And he trusted me. He'd been part of the whole journey so far, and he knew that nothing else had worked.

I expected Gary Haugen, my former boss at International Justice Mission—the first person to teach me that sometimes advocacy isn't enough, that sometimes direct intervention is necessary—would warn me about the ways a mission like this could backfire, that a mistake in the field could make it even harder to complete other projects, that I might tarnish my reputation and relationships in such a way that I'd be rendered ineffective in my humanitarian work. But when we met for tacos at Chuy's, a Tex-Mex restaurant in San Antonio, he simply said, "If we're going to rid the world of injustice, there must be people as committed to justice as the perpetrators are to committing wrong."

I was prepared for the biggest pushback from Ken Roth, the executive director of Human Rights Watch. I went to his New York office ready to field a litany of concerns. He agreed that this was an out-of-the-box idea, a far cry from building a school or drilling a well. But, like the others I'd consulted, he thought the intervention was worth considering. "We keep writing these reports about LRA attacks and massacres," he said. "We keep beating the drum for the arrest of Kony and the other ICC indictees. But the ICC has no arresting mechanism. You're helping to close this gap."

He raised one area of concern, asking if we'd given consideration to the Ugandan military's history of human rights abuses. "Do you have a plan to avoid providing training to people with a track record of atrocities?" he asked.

I told him we would try to train only soldiers who were thirty years old or younger, too young to have participated in the human rights abuses perpetrated by the Ugandan military in Congo during the 1990s. During the training itself, we would insist that the soldiers receive human rights training, including instruction on how to properly handle defectors, the ethics of operating in small groups and in denied areas where supplies are difficult to find, and an explanation of Geneva Convention and basic human rights standards. Ken said he was glad we were taking these steps, and encouraged us to move ahead.

No one I consulted with said as frankly as I said to myself what I knew to be true: that we were taking a terrible risk in training a foreign force with interests beyond the LRA and a history of human rights abuses with its neighbor, Congo, and led by an aging president who had clung to power for decades. That it could end badly, that it might set a dangerous precedent. In one last attempt to gain advice and perspective before we committed, I met with the most dedicated humanitarian and pacifist I had ever encountered, the final person I more than halfway hoped would turn us back.

I walked in the serene gardens of the Fairlawns resort in Johannesburg, South Africa, with Archbishop Desmond Tutu. We had met working with The Elders, an organization of global leaders Nelson Mandela had brought together in 2007 to work for peace and human rights. At its inception, I'd been invited by a cofounder and friend in philanthropy to serve on the advisory council. I was honored to support The Elders, constantly inspired by the work and commitment of these change makers, and I treasured the personal relationships I had been privileged to build with some of the world's most loving visionaries. Archibishop Tutu—Arch, as he asked me to call him—had become a dear friend, and I was fortunate to get to visit with him several times a year.

As we strolled together, his bright purple shirt and crisp white cleric's collar were vivid against the lush green, his large silver cross catching the sun. Some of us in The Elders remarked that many of those involved had a superpower. President Jimmy Carter's was hope. Virgin founder Richard Branson's was fun. Archbishop Tutu's was joy. Even as we took slow, silent steps through the garden, Arch exuded joy. He smiled up at me impishly. He didn't look like a person who had spent a lifetime confronting humanity's worst travesties. He looked like someone in possession of a happy secret. He made joy look effortless.

On an Elders trip to Darfur in 2007—where conflict had been ravaging the nation for years, where the violence had forced millions of people into refugee camps where they faced further horrors: not

enough food or water, the constant fear of being raped, of attacks by
the Janjaweed militias—my heart had been so heavy that I'd barely
been able to hold back my tears until we reached our hotel for the
night. One blisteringly hot afternoon in the camps when I was particularly struggling against despair, Arch stepped into a throng of
refugees and started to dance. His bald head, his white collar, his
beaming face flashed in the dusty crowd of people who didn't know
when they would get their next meal, who didn't know if their children
would live through the night—and they broke into laughter when
they saw him and joined him in song.

How did he do it? How did he bring joy in such deadly and devastating circumstances? How did he find happiness amid such staggering sadness? On one of our long drives I had asked him about it, and
he said, "Sister Shannon, it's not that I'm not sad. It's that I choose joy.
Even when we're crying—especially when we're crying—we have to
work to find joy in the world."

Joy wasn't his effortless condition. Joy was his discipline.

"What's troubling you?" he asked me now as we threaded our way
across the lawn in Johannesburg, toward a shady grove of palm trees.

I blurted it out. I told him that we were thinking of doing something unprecedented to stop the LRA. I felt strongly that the international community had tried every other possible avenue for an end to
Kony's violence. But as a peacemaker and human rights lawyer, I was
afraid that a decision I might make could have the potential to lead to
more chaos and death. Despite my rigorous and careful examination
of the issue and my countless conversations with human rights advocates well-versed in the conflict, there were still variables that I couldn't
account for because they were impossible to predict, or simply invisible to me. It wasn't enough to have good intentions and committed
allies, to share a conviction for peace and justice. I was wrestling with
one of the golden rules of humanitarian work: *first, do no harm.* Our
ideals and commitment didn't protect anyone from all the ways, seen
and unseen, that an intervention could go wrong. I could choose to
take risks with my organization's reputation and resources. But these

were insignificant compared with the risks on the ground, of warfare and retribution. Of course, as I was learning, not to act was the biggest risk of all. I asked Arch to help me weigh my desire and responsibility to do right with the very real possibility that others could suffer because of choices I'd made.

Arch didn't seem at all surprised. He didn't miss a beat. It was like he already knew. He took my hand. "Sister Shannon," he said, "things are rarely black and white. But this one is clear. Put your fears to rest. You already know in your heart what you are going to do."

As vigorously as I faced and tried to eliminate the risks, I had no way to know how long the mission would last, or what the costs would be. On November 7, 2010, Eeben sent the request for authorization. I signed it. Operation Viper would begin on February 3, 2011.

PART TWO

Silence in the face of evil is itself evil:

God will not hold us guiltless.

Not to speak is to speak.

Not to act is to act.

—DIETRICH BONHOEFFER

IN AT HALF

ONE MORNING SHORTLY before Christmas, my hardworking and meticulously organized assistant, Jen, asked for me to weigh in on an odd meeting request. She'd recently been contacted by the assistant to someone she had never heard of, asking to schedule a meeting with me as soon as possible. When she'd replied that my schedule was booked solid for the next three months, the stranger's assistant had persisted, so Jen had googled the name of the man who was requesting a meeting, and discovered that he—Muneer Satter—was a high-level partner at the investment banking firm Goldman Sachs. He wanted to meet me for an hour lunch. He would fly to San Antonio, I would pick him up at the private plane terminal, take him to lunch, and drop him back to meet his plane.

No one had ever gone to such extraordinary lengths to arrange a meeting with me before and I agreed, mainly out of curiosity. But I was cautious when, a few days before Christmas, I waited in the lobby of the small airport to meet Muneer Satter. Right on time, an impeccably dressed man in a collared shirt and dress shoes walked—almost bounced, he was that energetic—through the sliding doors from the tarmac. His dark eyes twinkled from behind his rimless glasses, his face lit up.

At an Italian restaurant near the airport, after some brief pleasantries, he looked across the table and explained why he wanted to meet. He said he was very interested in the work we were doing to stop Kony.

I wracked my brain trying to figure out how he knew about the work, and what exactly he knew. Our mission had been kept so quiet, yet he seemed to be aware of details my own family didn't know. I was shocked, and scared that if he knew this much, others must know, too.

Muneer told me that he had supported Ken Roth at Human Rights Watch in going after Charles Taylor, an infamous Liberian warlord. When Taylor had been captured, he'd asked Roth who they should target next. Ken had said Joseph Kony. Muneer had immediately begun funding organizations that were working to end Kony's war, including some of the same NGOs that Bridgeway funded. But he was a results-oriented man, and he had grown weary of the advocacy-only approach to change.

Muneer explained that his mom, Patricia Templeton Satter, had attended Berea College, the first integrated college in the South, and gone on to become a civil rights activist in the Deep South during the 1950s. Much of his outrage about injustices in the world came from her, and she, along with his wife and five daughters, inspired him to use his wealth and influence to build a better world. He was looking for "Jedi warriors" in his lifetime—people doing extraordinary work on behalf of humanity, people he could bet on. He'd already supported several Jedis, including the founders of Belgrade-based CANVAS, the Center for Applied Nonviolent Action and Strategies, whose original work had led to the overthrow of genocidal dictator Slobodan Milošević.

"I look at philanthropy the same way I look at my investments," he said. "I'm looking for exponential returns." He had been on the verge of pulling some of the money he'd been contributing to counter-LRA work and putting it toward a different goal when Yvette Alberdingk Thijm, the executive director of WITNESS, another organization that he and Bridgeway both funded, had given him my name. "If you want to stop Kony, this is the person you need to talk to," she had told him.

"I believe you're a Jedi warrior," Muneer said, beaming at me from across the table. "Whatever you're doing to stop Kony, I want in at half."

A DIRTY PATH

David Ocitti

AFTER ESCAPING FROM the LRA and reuniting with his mother in Alero, David Ocitti tried to pick up his life where it had left off. But he struggled to leave the horror in the bush behind him. It was difficult to concentrate. He easily grew confused. If anyone around him yelled, he would freeze, paralyzed. He would sweat and shake. Then there were his nightmares. In his dreams, the LRA returned for him, gave him a machete, forced him to hack his mother apart.

His nightmares were an effect of the trauma he'd experienced, Kony's fear tactics still embedded in his brain. But they were also founded in reality. The LRA really did return for those who escaped. Sometimes the escapees were killed, sometimes recaptured. Sometimes their families were slaughtered as punishment. It wasn't just his own life on the line anymore. Now he also needed to protect his mother.

He wanted to continue his studies and be someone who made positive contributions to the world. But he couldn't imagine a specific future for himself. If he'd gone to a government-sponsored rehabilitation center created for the thousands of abducted children in northern Uganda, he would have had access to therapy and coaching that might have helped him through the terror and despair. But Kony had warned his young captives that if they tried to go home, the Ugandan government would hold them in military detention centers, so David was suspicious of the rehabilitation centers, fearing they were a form of punishment or imprisonment. Even if he had trusted them, what difference would it make? No amount of counseling could bring his father or his brothers back. Nothing could take away what had already happened.

David stayed with his mother and did odd jobs throughout the summer so he could begin secondary school in the fall with his friends. He couldn't stand for his primary school friends to get too far ahead of him in school. He couldn't forget the memory of his community members crying and moaning the night he was abducted, the inner sense that he had to be strong, that his community needed him back.

David walked eagerly to school on the first morning, smiling as he anticipated a reunion with his former classmates. He longed to be in the company of people who knew him well, who would welcome him home. He arrived early. He sat in the front row of his classroom, ready to surprise and greet his friends as they came through the door.

But as the other students filed in with their books and new supplies, they hardly looked at him. When the teacher arrived and began the lesson, David was the only student seated in the first row. No one sat in the row behind him, either. The other students sat jammed together in the back rows, some sitting two or three to a seat—to avoid being near him, he realized. It was as though he was contaminated, infected with a fatal and contagious disease. The other students preserved a radius around him at all times. He wasn't David to them anymore. He was an outcast, forever an LRA member who walked a dirty path.

IMPOSSIBLE CAUSE

IN JANUARY 2011, the month before the training mission was to begin, John Montgomery and I traveled to southern Sudan to help monitor the historic referendum vote: an opportunity for the south to determine whether they would officially make South Sudan an independent nation. The Carter Center, which at that time had observed more than eighty elections all over the world, trained us as short-term international observers, and we were honored to help monitor the opening day of elections in a city south of Juba. It was an unbelievable experience—deeply humbling and inspiring to witness the profound excitement and optimism of people who'd been trapped by a long and bloody civil war at last able to make their voices heard.

After the election monitoring, we traveled with a translator to a large refugee camp near New Lasu, just on the southern Sudan side of the border with Congo. Our original intent was to visit the population there, as Bridgeway had supported some aid assistance to the close to ten thousand Congolese civilians living there who had been displaced by LRA violence in 2009. But when we arrived we learned the devastating news that there had been at least one LRA attack in the Aba area, a day's walk from the camp, the week of Christmas. Many new refugees had arrived in the camp the previous week, and we were told that three to four hundred more were traveling there on foot. We met a woman whose hand had been cut off by the LRA before she managed to escape, and a couple whose five children had all been abducted. Meanwhile,

LRA attacks were continuing multiple times a week in the northern regions of Congo, eluding Ugandan army and UN peacekeeping deployments. Later we would learn that the violence was intensifying because a new LRA group—including Dominic Ongwen, one of the International Criminal Court indictees and masterminds of the second Christmas massacres in 2009—was now operating in the area.

Despite the glaring evidence of more attacks, the Congolese government officials in the capital, Kinshasa, steadfastly denied the LRA's presence, prompting the Catholic Church and Civil Society groups to stage a protest to call on the government to acknowledge the threat and protect the residents of northeastern Congo. Back home, I watched the continuing reports of violence and hoped the training would make a difference.

But then Eeben wrote to say that for some unclear reason, the Ugandan troops selected for training had been delayed in their arrival at the training site and would not be able to begin on the agreed-upon date. He wrote, *We are very frustrated with the situation and are well aware of the fact that every day we sit on our bums, we are wasting your money and simultaneously, people are getting killed or kidnapped.*

As the delay continued for days and then weeks, his outlook worsened. *This smacks of a very slack attitude re the LRA by all parties concerned in supposedly stopping Kony and his thugs,* he wrote. *Indeed, were it not so tragic, it may even be funny to see how so many are claiming action yet remain dedicated to inaction.*

I didn't want to share his worry that the Ugandan military wasn't really serious about ending the LRA. They were the best—the only—option to counter the LRA in the region, and although the meetings with General Aronda had not been without wrinkles, I trusted his desire to stop the LRA was sincere. But Eeben's concerns—that we were being used in some way, that corruption and profiteering made it useful to some for the LRA crisis to continue—ate at me.

I needed a concrete reminder to keep the faith and I began wearing a charm on my wrist, a pendant picturing Saint Jude, one of Jesus's original twelve Apostles, who preached with such passion during the most difficult circumstances that he became celebrated as the patron saint of lost or impossible causes. Sam's family had introduced me to a number of Catholic traditions, including the practice of calling on specific saints for guidance and support through challenging situations. The oval-shaped pendant I chose had a tiny relief portrait of Saint Jude in a long flowing robe, one hand holding a staff, the other a picture of Jesus against his heart. It weighed less than a penny, and I grew used to the tiny jangle it made when I moved my arm, the subtle feel of it against my skin reminding me to pray and remain hopeful.

Meeting Muneer and discovering his passion and capacity to see the kind of world change I spent my days dreaming about felt like an answer to my prayers, a sign that despite my worries, I wasn't alone.

Before he dispatched funds to support the mission, he brought me to his home in Chicago to meet his wife, Kristen, and their five daughters, including a set of triplets. The girls gathered around me affectionately. Tess, the eldest, was nine years old, a kind big sister to her younger siblings. We sat in the kitchen together, nibbling on snacks. Tess told us about going ice-skating with her friends that day, and her worry when one of them had gotten hurt. She was deeply empathetic and I thought, *That little girl will be a world changer.* Kristen, who wore her beautiful long dark hair down in a no-frills style, engaged with the girls in her patient, matter-of-fact way. She struck me as stoic, an obvious anchor for the family. Muneer looked on happily, glad to see that we were enjoying each other's company. Before we parted for the evening he said, "You are one of the most baffling people I've ever met. I mean that in a nice way. Most people don't take the risks you take."

As I curled into my bed in the Satters' guest suite, I thought of all the people who were taking the real risks. I thought of Ida on her tiny motorbike, the radio operators working to protect communities throughout Congo, and of the Ugandan soldiers who would soon deploy for the training. I was taking some risks, but others were risking their lives.

I also thought of all the people I'd met so far in this mission—
Abbé Benoît, Luis Moreno Ocampo, Colonel Ochora, General
Aronda, Eeben Barlow, Muneer Satter. Whether behind the scenes or
on the front lines, each individual, fueled by a unique motivation, was
doing something remarkable. If we managed to stop Kony, it would be
because of the beautiful culmination of a lot of people's goodwill and
our ability to lock arms and work together. For a moment, I felt a
peace. It was hope, and something as important as hope: a deep and
abiding gratitude.

USE THE FORCE

ONE AFTERNOON A few weeks later, Connor watched me posting lists around the house—reminders about school functions, carpools, playdates, birthday parties—and I saw him register that I was getting ready to travel again.

"Is the bad guy still hurting people?" he asked.

I put down the calendar and sticky notes. I would be heading to South Africa in a few days to meet Eeben's trainers and accompany them to Uganda, where the Ugandan military troops were finally ready to deploy for the first training. I knew I needed to lay a foundation for my boys to understand my absence—not just the upcoming weeks away, but all of the trips the mission might require. I needed them to try to grasp the reason I'd be gone so much. Maybe if they could see the goal and track our progress it would help something endless feel more finite and contained.

"I want to show you something," I said. I found a big piece of cardboard and taped a large map of Central Africa to it, then fished around in a kitchen drawer for some stickers. The only ones I could find were puffy *Star Wars* characters. It wasn't hard to choose which sticker would represent Kony. I showed my boys the vast region in which Darth Vader—our "bad guy"—was hiding and explained that I hoped each day would bring us closer to discovering his location. I put two Jedi star stickers, one orange and one green, in northwestern Uganda

to show them where Mommy and Mr. Laren would be for the training. Connor and Brody studied the map and stickers carefully.

"Is there anything you want to ask me?" I said.

Connor shook his head. "Use the Force, Mommy," he said, and
threw his arms around my neck.

The day before I left for Africa, my parents came over for dinner. Usually our family gatherings were raucous, the boys running full speed
through the house, the adults yelling back and forth to get things on
the table, but tonight the mood felt somber. My father, so loving and
protective, was withdrawn, frowning down at his steak. Sam kept trying to draw him into conversation about the boys, about San Antonio's
NBA team. I realized that without knowing any of the details of the
mission, my dad was terrified. He had raised me with such warmth
and support, attending every volleyball game and school play, teaching
me that there was no limit to what I could accomplish. Now I could
see how scared he was to watch me go. As we were clearing the plates
away after dinner, my mother took my hand.

"I know you can't talk to me about what you're doing over there,
but I just want you to know I've started a twenty-four-hour prayer
group to pray for your safety and success," she said. I would later learn
that she always signed up for the 3:00 a.m. shift—the hardest one.

At bedtime, Connor held out the love-worn froggy blanket he
slept with every night. "Take it with you to Africa and then you won't
feel lonely," he said, placing it ceremoniously in my hands. I lay down
beside him on his little bed, trying to drink in his sleepy warmth, to
memorize the sound of his soft breath easing him into sleep. I thought
he was already fast asleep, but then he turned to me in the dark and
planted a kiss on my forehead.

"I just have to count to ten and then two more and you'll be home,"
he said.

OPERATION VIPER

"LET'S NOT BE under any illusions," Eeben lectured the large men gathered on his back patio in Pretoria. He was giving his team their pre-deployment briefing and orders. "There's no magic solution. We're going to be training these men to do something extremely difficult."

I sat sipping a Krest bitter lemon, a quinine and lemon juice soda sold all over Africa, and watched the sun dip behind the tops of the acacia and yellow-wood trees that towered over Eeben's grassy lawn. Laren's flight had been delayed. He was missing the opening meeting with the trainers and I was struggling to connect with them. I motivate and operate out of relationship, and I had from the beginning felt a connection with Eeben. But now the circle had widened to include his team, and they were such a different breed from the humanitarians and government officials I was more accustomed to partnering with.

They were very polite and respectful. But they were also cagey, sitting aloof and stiff-jawed in a way that was both physically imposing and disconcertingly reserved. Trying to gauge them—their personalities, their motivation for being here, their hopes and fears—was a challenge. Later I would understand that they had a long experience of being painted poorly in the press and that the sensitive nature of their work made them wary of outsiders. I searched their terse faces for common ground, trying not to stare at the biggest, tallest man, who had a permanent scowl on his face.

"The LRA are running around in 360,000 square kilometers of

jungle," Eeben continued. "Finding them and stopping them isn't just going to happen on its own. The Ugandan soldiers will be chopping their way through an overgrown jungle where there aren't any roads or paths. If they move even one kilometer in an hour, that's a good pace. They'll be lucky to move six or seven kilometers in an entire day. Just locating the LRA's trail will be their biggest challenge. If they manage to discover signs of the LRA, they'll already be days old. When the rains come, the work will get even harder. Everything—the terrain, the rain—favors the LRA."

All that Eeben said was painfully true. But it wasn't the pep talk I'd imagined. I wanted to talk to the men not just about the risks and impediments to the mission, but about why they were here at all. To find the heart in each man that motivated his sacrifice. Most of them were fathers, Eeben had told me. They were used to shutting that part of themselves off to do the work of war. But I wanted to make sure that for this mission they turned that part of themselves completely on. I wanted them to operate in the field not just from the framework of force, but through the lens of protection. I wanted to beckon their paternal instincts, their moral mandate.

And so when it was my turn to speak, I began to talk about the children I'd met and the atrocities they'd endured—the terror that would continue as long as the world failed to intervene.

"It's such a small number of perpetrators getting away with so much," I said. "And until now, no government entity or international body has responded in a way that stopped the conflict.

"And here you are, a concerned group of men taking risks—and for less compensation than you usually receive—when entities with greater resources and capabilities are doing so little. We spend so much time talking about how difficult situations are, how things are so complicated, instead of just looking at the essence of our humanity—that we have quite a bit more power than any of us probably realizes we do.

"Stopping mass atrocities relies on the power of the individual, not the power of institutions. Institutions don't have hearts or souls. But people do. Mothers and fathers do. You do."

The men sat still, immovable as stone, arms crossed over their large chests. But in some of their faces I could see the veil had lifted. Eeben had told me that this mission was a unique opportunity for his team—to be contracted to help stop a conflict, to work with a well-articulated goal, instead of being pulled into the machinery of a forever war. One of the head trainers, a man built like a brick, approached me after the meeting.

"I've been a soldier all my life," he said. "This is what I enjoy doing, what I'm fairly good at. It's my job. But I also like to know that I'm part of doing the right thing. When I fly to Uganda tomorrow, and every day I'm there, I will know that this is the right thing to do."

FLIGHT MANIFEST

"WEAR PLAIN CLOTHES," Eeben ordered. "Blend in. At the airport, act like you don't know each other." A former covert operative for special forces in the South African army, he was chronically suspicious. Not wanting to call any attention to the deployment, he insisted we take different vehicles to the airport the next morning.

Laren and I arrived three hours early for our flight to Entebbe. We tried to keep busy and look inconspicuous, but everywhere we went, from the coffee shop to the newsstand, we kept running into the trainers. In order not to compromise us or the mission in any way, Eeben had told us we were supposed to pretend not to know them. It was awkward to keep my face blank, to dart my eyes away.

"I'd make a terrible spy," I whispered to Laren.

With still more time to burn and an overwhelming reserve of nervous energy, we finally deposited ourselves in the chair-massage booth. I knew I wouldn't be able to relax. I just needed a safe place to sit for thirty minutes where I didn't have to worry about accidentally making forbidden eye contact with a private military contractor.

We didn't realize until too late that the massages had taken so long. By the time we reached our gate we were among the last passengers in line to board. We could see Eeben and his men interspersed ahead of us, but it was hard to pick them out because almost every person in line ahead of us seemed to be a buff man with a crew cut, wearing desert tan pants and a T-shirt, G-Shock watch cinched around his thick wrist.

"Is there a private military convention in Kampala?" Laren joked under his breath. "I've never seen this many private soldier–looking dudes in one place."

I felt as if I was the only female passenger on the entire flight.

On the tarmac, my rolling suitcase rattled, making my arm vibrate. I never check my bags when I'm flying overseas. It's not worth the risk of losing baggage and time trying to replace essentials in a remote area. Now I was headed for a training camp where we'd stay in tents without electricity or running water, much less a store where I could get a toothbrush or underwear.

Just as we reached the stairs to the airplane, the gate agent stopped me. "That bag won't fit in the overhead," he said. "It has to go under, ma'am."

"It will fit," I said. "I fly a lot, and I know how to pack for small overhead bins."

"We're low on bin space," he said. "I'll be happy to gate check it for you."

"Thanks, but I'll take it on board with me." I was imagining what instructions I'd have to give on the lost luggage form. I wasn't even sure exactly where I was going.

"Ma'am, it's too big, it won't fit."

"It will fit. It came all the way from San Antonio, Texas, in an overhead bin. I know it will fit." I looked at Laren to back me up, but he rolled his eyes at me. He was clearly thinking I should just check it. But I was too mad and frustrated to back down. "I'm bringing this bag on board with me."

"No, that is impossible," he said. "The bag must be checked."

I don't know what possessed me, but I began to empty the bag, toiletries, clothes, computer cords, journal, into Laren's arms. "Go ahead and check it," I said, handing the flight attendant the empty bag.

Eeben later joked that Laren looked like a supermarket when he boarded the plane, his arms full of my belongings. I walked on behind him, still on a tirade, looking into the open overhead bins. "There's bin space here, there's bin space here," I said, jabbing my finger at the numerous places where my bag would have fit. I was so indignant over the bag situation that I didn't notice Laren had frozen ahead of me in the aisle until I bumped into him.

"*Lar-en!*" a stranger in an aisle seat called out.

"Shannon," Laren said, turning back to me, his eyes wide. "I'd like you to meet someone. This is Lafras Luitingh. Lafras, this is Shannon Sedgwick Davis."

Lafras Luitingh was Eeben's ex–business partner in Executive Outcomes. His security company, Saracen International, was one of the candidates Laren had investigated when we were looking for someone to conduct the training mission. Since hiring Eeben, we'd learned that the two had had a major disagreement and had stopped talking to each other. Completely by chance, we were flying to Uganda with Lafras and his band of private contractors.

Lafras flashed me a genial smile, showing his large, even white teeth. "It's a pleasure, Ms. Davis. From the looks of it your little project is going well and you've hired the A-team to do it, eh?"

I managed a polite smile before proceeding down the aisle and squeezing into my center seat between Laren and a man built like a linebacker. All around us were men whose shoulders were so broad they took up a seat and a half, their necks as massive as trees. We would learn from a *New York Times* article that Lafras's group, four times the size of Eeben's, was deploying on a mission commissioned by Erik Prince—America's most notorious private military contractor—to intervene against Somali pirates. Almost immediately after landing they would be sent home.

We later learned through a contact at State that within twelve hours of our flight, the US State Department received a cable about a suspicious plane manifest: a flight from Johannesburg to Entebbe that included both Eeben Barlow's and Lafras Luitingh's private military groups, plus two American citizens, Laren Poole and Shannon Sedgwick Davis. Lucky for us the cable came across a friend's desk at the State Department. If he'd been off that day, or if the cable had been delivered to someone else, he wouldn't have been able to ease concerns within the diplomatic community. Fortunately, he reassured State that he knew what we were up to and we traveled on to the training site without incident.

IT WAS YOU
David Ocitti

AT LUNCH ONE day, a boy approached David in the schoolyard. David's heart leapt. Someone was daring to reach across the divide that kept him isolated. His face opened into a grateful smile.

But his schoolmate didn't return the smile. "I saw you," he said, his voice ragged, as though holding back the desire to cry. "You were in the group of LRA who killed my dad."

David felt a terrible pinching in his chest. He began to sweat. His mouth went dry.

"I saw you," the boy said again. "I saw your face. It was you."

In the six months of David's captivity, there had been countless raids and attacks. It was LRA protocol to push the young recruits to the forefront during an attack—to put them on the front lines of danger, but also to ensure that their faces would be seen, that the communities would identify children as perpetrators. It was part of the strategy to sever the kids' ties with home, to make them feel they could never return. On the worst days, memories of that terrible night intruded: Odhiambo with his machete raised, yelling, "You better call out, 'Save me!'"

"It was you, I saw you," the boy repeated. His face was gaunt, dark circles under fierce eyes. "You killed my father."

David wanted to run—from this boy's pain, a mirror of his own, from the bitter taste in his mouth, the images he couldn't stop in which he was the one holding the stick. He was a victim, he knew. But to his classmate, he was a perpetrator. He wasn't another child who had lost a father. He was the enemy.

"If you saw me, I must have been there," David said, the words barely escaping his tight throat. "But it wasn't my wish."

The boy lunged closer, as though he was about to hit David, or throw him to the ground. But he stopped short, pulled back. "I saw you!" he screamed again as he fled.

Some days it was David who recognized someone's face from an attack. He would remember on what day the attack had occurred, at what time, what weapons had been used against the person's family members. Many days, he broke into tears while at school, the onslaught of grief and remorse so intense that he had to ask the headmaster for permission to leave school for the rest of the day to hide in the dim quiet of his mother's home.

Doubt battered him. *What have I done?* he thought. *Do I even deserve to be here?* As much as David wanted to run from the past, he knew that the only way forward was to admit, yes, it happened; to remember, it's not happening now; and then to ask, What can I do now?

FALSE RIDGE

A LATE FEBRUARY attack on Bamangana, a village near a small Congolese military camp, made the need for the training more urgent. Every household in the community was attacked, food and goods stolen, and thirty residents kidnapped. Six Congolese soldiers were killed, their camp burned. A number of civilians were dead, including a village elder, a woman who was burned alive in front of the community, and a fourteen-year-old girl who was shot in the chest.

Despite the necessity of taking action to curb the escalating crisis, there were still risks to mitigate. There's always a danger, not just in military training, but in any kind of development work, to come into a foreign country and say, "Here, let me teach you what I learned someplace else, because it's the only thing I've seen work." But importing strategies from other situations, applying them in new contexts, isn't always effective. The Ugandan military had received training from foreign armies in the past, and the Ugandans had been responsive and disciplined about incorporating new tools and strategies. But they'd sometimes been given the wrong tools, strategies effective for European contexts that didn't work against the LRA. Eeben's men were extremely experienced; they'd operated with armies from diverse African countries, in diverse conflicts. They'd dealt in the past with LRA-type organizations. Along with the irreplaceable credibility of having done it many times themselves they had the flexibility to tailor their previous experiences to fit the current needs. This is a critical reason why we had picked them to conduct the training. And this is why the Ugandans accepted them, too. For someone in the UPDF who'd been in active combat for a decade, the training was no good if it was purely theoretical. Eeben's team was the most experienced and effective option to navigate the terrain and conflict.

As many as 1,200 Ugandan soldiers applied to participate in the training, and the 280 most promising were brought to Bondo to undergo a selection process for the four-month program that would cover all aspects of hostage release in a rural environment, including: operational design; tactics, techniques, and procedures; patrols and reconnaissance; tracking; rigorous physical training; and, most important, target discrimination to avoid at all costs harming captives and civilians.

Out of the 280 Ugandan troops brought to Bondo, fewer than half would pass the selection to complete the training. On the first day, each soldier was given a hundred-pound backpack filled with sandbags and told to run. "Be the first one back, don't be last!" the trainer yelled. The course was seven miles long and went up a mountain with a seven-hundred-foot elevation gain. When the men came to the end of the course, sweating and panting, relieved to have completed the first arduous task, they were told to run it again. They ran three rounds in all.

The selection course was physically demanding to the extreme. But the challenge was also psychological. "Out there in the bush there are lots of false ridges," Eeben explained. He meant the terrain, and also the metaphoric false ridges of hardship, hunger, thirst, exhaustion, and threat. "You keep thinking you're about to reach the top but then there's another ridge ahead of you. You have to have the physical capacity to keep going. You have to have the heart and eagerness, too."

After the selection process, a tight training schedule followed: GPS navigational system training, pseudo ops, human rights, and contact drills that ran all day long. The soldiers learned how to cross a road while covering their own tracks, move together in formation, move during live fire, track in the rain, make contact during an advance, and establish a cache of medicine and food at strategic locations. They also learned how to be comfortable and confident with their teammates, to believe in each other—and themselves. Since many of the soldiers did not have adequate basic training skills, Eeben had to stretch an already time-pressured program to incorporate basic training with the advanced training curriculum.

One of the most important lessons was in operating pseudo groups, small units that would mimic nomadic traders or the LRA themselves in their dress, grooming, habits, and language. In disguise, pseudo groups could operate discreetly in LRA-controlled areas. This tactic required a higher level of training and discipline, because pseudo groups have to operate in remote areas without Ugandan military support. If a soldier is hurt or if the group runs out of food, they can't call for help; they have to fend for themselves and maintain their cover.

Training began smoothly. Then, in early March, terrible news came in from northern Uganda. Colonel Walter Ochora was dead.

He was only fifty-four years old. It had been an election year and his doctors said that the stress of the election cycle—raising money, canvassing, his constant string of commitments—had taken a toll on his already poor health. He'd been grossly overweight, he drank more than anyone I'd ever met, he'd been suffering for years from lung disease, but I'd only seen his lively and jolly side, his abundant smiles against the backdrop of his endlessly chiming cellphones. His vibrancy and steadfast commitment to peace had launched us on our path, and it was hard to accept that he was gone. I had already allowed myself to fantasize about calling him with the news of Kony's capture. I'd imagined him saying, *We did it, Iron Lady!* and bursting into his rolling laugh. Although he had no role in the actual operations of the training mission, I had still viewed him as one of our guardians. We would never have undertaken it without his support and advocacy, and his sad death made our precarious cause feel even more vulnerable.

CAMP BONDO

TO GET TO Camp Bondo, the Ugandan military training facility in northwestern Uganda, you drive seven to ten hours, grappling with inevitable flat tires and watching elephants swagger by on the side of the road. Or you charter a flight from Entebbe to Arua and take a four-by-four to the training site, a small clearing in the dense trees.

The camp consisted of a few barracks structures with metal roofs, terrible in the intense heat, where the Ugandan army troops slept; an operations tent that also served as the camp kitchen; a cluster of ground tents where the trainers and Laren and I slept; a pit latrine; and several camp showers, where thatched grass served as a curtain around big plastic bags filled with water that would warm up during the day under the hot sun. Around the camp stood rolling hills, green and lush during Uganda's two rainy seasons, and huge trees where black mambas and at least one jungle viper lived.

I'd come into camp regularly, staying for a week or two at a time. I'd always check in with Laren first. We'd take a walk in the blazing heat and he'd give me the lay of the land, and I'd try to read between the lines for the things he left unsaid. There was no way he could bring me up to speed on every single detail of the training. He had to be selective about what he shared. And so I listened carefully to his reports, trying to hear in what he said the realities that were unspoken.

There was no road map for our intervention. We were essentially building the airplane as it flew. Laren was stationed at Bondo for the four months of training. He was my eyes and ears, taking copious notes, documenting daily life and training regimens. And he was an invaluable go-between, helping the Ugandans and South Africans communicate their needs and differences. As much as I relied on him, and as hard as I knew he was working, I could also see that he was in an impossible position. There were constant bumps and challenges to navigate: equipment shortages, and a scant supply of essentials—food, water, even toilet paper. By April several instructors had fallen ill. A number got sick from untreated water and poor food preparation hygiene—enough that Eeben put his team's medic in charge of the kitchen. One trainer contracted malaria and had to be medevaced.

Laren was the peacemaker and go-between, communicating the trainers' grievances to the Ugandan higher-ups when the camp ran short on provisions. But many of the trainers were suspicious of him, by nature wary of outsiders, and unwilling to take direction from someone they saw as a tenderfoot. I didn't know until later the extent to which some of the South Africans ostracized him. Somehow, in the tangle of relationships and cultures, Laren was able to remain singularly focused. In the many years that he'd been involved in the LRA conflict he had met so many people deeply impacted by the violence, and he was so driven to make a difference that he put up with a lot.

I'd wake in the morning to the sound of roosters crowing and someone sweeping the dirt in front of the tents. I'd walk to the pit latrine and see the morning crew checking around the perimeter of the camp for jungle vipers or other animals that might have come near in the night.

Laren, Eeben, Captain Kommando—the commander of the troops participating in the training—and I would have an early meeting over instant Nescafé or South African tea mixed with powdered creamer, our camp chairs in a circle in the dirt. Eeben and the trainers were in charge of all the training program details; Captain Kommando handled all of the scheduling and disciplinary decisions and the logistics when the camp ran short on essential supplies.

He was the youngest of our partners in the Ugandan leadership, his face round and smooth. But he had the maturity and confidence of an older man. Quiet and serious, he seemed incapable of casual eye contact. When he looked at you, he really looked, his eyes studying, examining. His experience as well as his demeanor made him a valuable leader and an asset to the mission. A former child soldier, he had spent much of his life as a fighter in the bush. The Ugandan government dissolved the West Nile Bank Front, a Ugandan rebel group, in part by pulling rebel combatants into the Ugandan military, and Captain Kommando had become an officer in the same army he had been trained as a child to fight. Given his past, he was uniquely positioned to head a group training to rescue hostages. And when he disciplined his soldiers, he didn't do so with the entitlement of someone who had grown accustomed to the comforts and authority of his office. He led from the credibility of his experience, his stern face seeming to say, *What I expect of myself I also expect of you.* Fit, strong, and athletic, he modeled not just the physical proficiency but the mental balance necessary for the work. There was no place for an action junkie in the field, but we needed aggressive leaders like Captain Kommando, men who would go all in and split hairs in order to be effective and precise.

He spoke just a little English and rarely talked at our breakfast meetings, but he listened intently, and though he didn't share stories from his past, I got the sense that he was often navigating the present through the lens of his experience. Captain Kommando exuded stability. It was inspiring to see a born leader and good man come out of a hard and violent past.

I'd spend the rest of the morning observing training drills, surprised to discover that the simplest things often made the biggest difference. I happened to be visiting Camp Bondo during one of the most crucial training lessons: river crossings. Tracking the LRA would be impossible in the river-dense jungle if the soldiers couldn't get themselves and their gear across racing water. During the rainy season the volume and speed of the water increased, the large rivers becoming precarious to cross. In every season, there was the danger of hippos and crocodiles. The men had to be comfortable and successful in the crossings. They had to know how to make a temporary raft, read the currents, and swim in tactical formation wearing their clothes, all the while carrying four or five magazines of ammunition and backpacks loaded with food and radio batteries, with a waxed canvas poncho tied over their belongings and an AK-47 secured on top.

A river often had a strong current and nearly impenetrable reeds on each side. They had to learn to choose the crossing point carefully. It was best to cross where the water was fastest and deepest, because crocs and hippos were less likely to hang out there. But the current also had to be factored in when determining how far upstream to start. Launch too early and you'd be banging up against the reeds, going nowhere; go too late and you'd end up in hippo country. On top of the many dangers was the pure and simple fact that most of the men had never swum before. Even for those who could swim, crossing the Nile was a new and difficult endeavor.

The first day of their swim class the men were visibly terrified. Dressed in their skivvies, they had shoved empty water bottles into their underwear in hopes that they would help them float. One of the trainers took the men out on an inflatable boat with a rope hanging off the back that they could grab on to if they started to go under. As the men hit the water, many would start to panic, gasping and thrashing. One man was really struggling, looking like he was starting to drown, and the rest of the guys on the bank started to laugh at him. I realized they weren't being cruel. It was how they handled the struggle, how they expressed it—not through screams or showing fear, but through a buoyant chorus of laughter. A couple of times the trainer had to dive in and fetch someone. The next day, a lot of the guys were sick from ingesting bad water. Their final test was to swim across the Nile—

a half-mile distance—with all of their equipment, ammunition, and food rations. Every single soldier passed.

We'd lunch on rice and beans and posho, a thick paste resembling grits or hot cereal made from corn flour. I'd sit at a table with Laren, the trainers, and the Ugandan military leadership, discussing the morning's highs and lows, the necessary adjustments. I asked one day about the soldiers' footwear. Some didn't seem to have adequate boots or shoes; accustomed to being barefoot or relying on ill-fitting footwear, they were completing the training in nothing but flip-flops. Eeben agreed to source two hundred pairs of field boots, two hundred pairs of gum boots, and four hundred pairs of wool socks from South Africa when he put in his next equipment order.

I knew from observing the training sessions and sharing meals and conversations with the trainers how hard everyone was working. The trainers were natural teachers, good at establishing rapport and relationships. A lot of times when foreign militaries come in they set up huge bases, they build a miniature version of home in a foreign land and they stay insulated. But Eeben's guys were living in tents in the same camp, using the same pit latrines and camp showers, eating outside even when it rained. They set a tone of shared sacrifice. Rapport and trust would have been impossible if they had kept themselves removed and left the brutally hot field each day to hang out in an air-conditioned base with hot showers and cold beers. The troops saw the trainers expecting as much from themselves as they did from their students. The more time I spent at Bondo, the more I could appreciate how effective they were. I could see evidence of the soldiers' growth and progress.

———

After lunch, there was a rest period, and Laren and I would head to the barracks to talk with the soldiers. We'd go for walks with them, sharing stories about home. I became particularly close to a few of the men, mostly because they spoke English and we could communicate easily. Their contributions ended up being particularly crucial to the mission.

Lieutenant Charles was from northern Uganda. People close to him had been killed by the LRA, and although he'd been to university to study animal husbandry, he was motivated to give up his calling to be a farmer to join the Ugandan army because of the personal losses he'd suffered at the hands of the LRA. He had deployed in Congo during Operation Lightning Thunder in 2008 and had been one of the first to volunteer for the training. Of the ten officers who started the first training course, he was one of only three who would graduate. He would prove to be one of the all-stars among the graduates, excelling in tactics and night operations, and exhibiting exceptional strength and leadership. He was not only effective, but passionate—or maybe he was effective because he was so passionate.

Lieutenant Pauson, a slim man with a neatly trimmed goatee, had also studied at university but had long desired a soldier's life. On a walk one day he told me, "My joining of the army was not, should I call it, a coincidence. It was a well-thought and sorted-out decision. I liked the army, looking at soldiers, their uniforms, the way they carry themselves, the way they march. It was within me. I liked it from my childhood. Always I wished to join."

And he couldn't forget the haunting images from his student days in Gulu:

These young girls of school-going age were being abused because of the lawlessness caused by the LRA. Particularly the night commuters. I saw these little girls going to sleep in town. Sometimes it would be in the rainy season and you'd find they stayed the whole night there, waiting, the rain on them. Some merciless men, they would offer them accommodation in return for sex. It was a great abuse. I saw so many casualties, some of them cut with pangas, a lot of disfigurements on the citizens of Uganda. I even saw an ambush on a bus, people killed. I developed that anger. I thought I should fight the LRA and maybe the war comes to an end. I always wanted to be a soldier. And I wished to join the army and give my contribution.

He showed me a picture of his kids. I asked him how he balanced his life as a soldier with his life as a father, how he dealt with the time away.

"You know, in Uganda so many people don't like you joining the army, because they have the fear that when you join, you have to die, you'll die in the battlefield. Sometimes when you share with your loved ones that you've joined, you get some discouragement. I knew I had to join, I knew it was something I needed to do, a bold decision I needed to make to be a man. So I joined and did the training and kept it a secret all to myself. I didn't even tell my wife. She was surprised one day to see a picture of me in military uniform!" He laughed.

I felt a surge of understanding. The loneliness of that life and the responsibility that gnaws at you, that won't let go. "Are you ever afraid now?" I asked him. We'd reached a small rise and stood looking out at the endless green.

"Mostly, I think it's God's will," he said. "You may try your best—but again, there is luck, and the Almighty. I don't know how my future will be in the army. Even right now I cannot predict how it will be in the next few weeks or months or years to come. I don't know. I just leave this to God. I just do my best, and whatever comes my way, I accept it."

I was struck by his remarkable resilience—his willingness to rest in uncertainty, to be up for whatever was next—and by his choice to trust in something bigger, something beyond our immediate understanding.

After the afternoon rest period and another training session, dinner was served. Sometimes the evening meal included meat, usually goat or chicken, along with rice and beans. All pieces of the animal were used, the neck of a chicken sometimes surprising me mixed in on my plate. We'd have glass bottles of soda. Even warm, they were delicious.

Everyone got extremely hot and sweaty during the day, but there was no point showering because you'd be covered in sweat again as soon as you stepped out. I'd wait to shower at night when it was cooler, trying to time it just right so I wasn't showering in the dark. The first time I used a camp shower I left the spigot on while I lathered up and the water ran out before I could rinse. I had to wipe the soap off with a wet wipe.

In the evening, we'd sit around the campfire and drink more coffee or tea—it was a dry camp, so there was no drinking—and tell stories. War stories, injury stories, funny stories about embarrassments. One of the trainers would sit quietly with his bird book, identifying wing shapes. They liked to ask me about my family and my work. And they loved to rib Laren. They teased everyone—it was how they bonded— but perhaps because he was so young, Laren was often the target of their jokes. He took it all in stride, laughing along with them.

A favorite story was about a time when Laren had been out with a group on an overnight field training—he was a tireless documentarian, hoofing it with them through the heat, sleeping out in the cold during rainy season. One particularly rainy and miserable night he'd slung his hammock up in the trees. The Ugandans were lying on the ground, mud rivers going over them, somehow able to sleep half submerged. But Laren was freezing. His hammock was full of water and he couldn't sleep. Lieutenant Pauson heard him rummaging around in his backpack. "Mr. Laren, are you okay?" he'd asked. Laren said he was fine. Lieutenant Pauson saw him pull an MRE (meal ready to eat) out of his bag. He opened the meal kit, took out the heating element you break to warm up the meal, and put it in his hammock. The men woke to a sizzling sound and saw steam rising out of Laren's hammock.

"He made his own Jacuzzi hot tub out there in the bush!" Eeben exclaimed, laughing. "Jungle steam room!"

Sometimes the talk would turn more serious. We fell into a silence one night, stars brightening out of the dark. I was struck by our being there together, the unlikeliness of it all. We were from vastly different backgrounds, we had completely different personalities, but the same thing motivated us. We had the same goal. "What do you think motivates Joseph Kony?" I asked.

"He's delusional," one of the head trainers said. "There's something wrong with the guy. He can't be normal."

"It's fear," Eeben said. "He feels fear, he feels other people's fear. He feeds off it. He's deep in the jungle; it's not an easy life. He chooses it because having the power over life and death makes him feel like he can control fear."

I thought of what Lieutenant Pauson had said on the hill—that he dealt with fear by releasing himself to God's will. It was strange to think of Kony as a person who was also confronting fear.

When the fire had burned down and the men started turning in, I'd go to my tent and lie in the dark with Connor's frog blanket. There aren't words to say how much I missed my boys those nights. I'd sing them lullabies in my mind, especially my favorite Dixie Chicks song. *Godspeed, little man. Sweet dreams, little man. Oh, my love will fly to you each night on angel's wings. Godspeed . . . Sweet dreams . . .*

DANCE FOR SAINT JUDE

ONE HUNDRED THIRTY-SIX Ugandan soldiers graduated from the training in mid-June. They became known as the Special Operations Group, called the SOG by those of us in the mission. They stood in straight lines, three deep, in full fatigues, arms pinned at their sides, ammunition vests and rifles strapped across their chests, faces serious beneath the brims of their camouflage hats. A number of guests, including local journalists, and representatives from several NGOs and community-based organizations, including Jason and Ben from Invisible Children, had been invited to witness the graduation. It was incredible to have a group of friends there, aligned in passion with a shared history, witnessing what felt like a giant step forward in the pursuit of an end to the war. Standing together in the heat, lush hills rolling on and on around us, fading out to blue in the haze, the pride and dignity of the soldiers were palpable.

I had been asked to say a few words. I'd dressed up for the occasion, putting on an outfit I'd wear to a graduation ceremony at home: black dress pants, a green silk shirt, heels. As I stood before the soldiers, I found that words failed me. All the sleepless nights I'd spent worrying over the professional risks of the intervention suddenly meant nothing. Before me stood men who had signed up to go into a hostile jungle far from home for months at a time. And they were risking their very lives to stop the LRA. A hot wind pulsed through the clearing, ruffling my blouse as I searched for the words to express how humbled I was.

"It is impossible for me to express the admiration I have for you," I began, watching their faces, resolved and somber. "As a mother of very young children myself, I am hopeful about the peace you will bring to other mothers when you deploy. You will be giving them the greatest gift anyone can: protection and freedom from fear. Every human being deserves this gift, and it is now yours to give. I am grateful to each of you for your profound sacrifices and my hopes and my prayers go with you."

Then it was General Katumba Wamala's turn to address the graduates. As commander of the land forces of the Uganda People's Defense Force, he oversaw all military deployments, including the counter-LRA units. He had commanded the UPDF in the Democratic Republic of Congo with mixed reviews from the human rights community. We found him to be a reliable and straightforward partner. We'd met a few times in his office in Kampala and he had become my most trustworthy bridge to the Ugandan military. He exuded gentleness and warmth. He wasn't the typical older man in senior leadership, hardened by turbulence. Somehow, he was free of that. He always seemed to be smiling. His whole face shone with kindness, good-natured crinkles gathered at the top of his nose and at the corners of his eyes.

It wasn't just his physical presence that put me at ease. It was his priorities and way of being in the world. In his off hours, he helped a local organization fighting child trafficking. He went above and beyond the requirements of his command to see to the well-being of his troops. A number of Ugandan soldiers deployed to Mogadishu, to help in the US-backed fight against al-Shabaab, had returned home with wounds so severe they had required amputations, and General Wamala had personally written grants to get soldiers wheelchairs and crutches. A few years later he would become the fourth African to be inducted into the prestigious Hall of Fame of the United States Army War College.

It was a big deal that he had come to Camp Bondo for the graduation. He wore a black beret, the sleeves of his uniform rolled up to his
elbows, a gold watch circling his wrist, the red decorations on his collar especially pronounced amid the mass of green fatigues and the
jungle around us. He addressed the troops first in Swahili:

First and foremost, I congratulate you. I congratulate you all for
completing your military training. You started with many, but
now only a few have successfully completed the training. That
shows how resilient you have been.

As your leaders, we are eager and anxious to see you in the
field. We have high hopes for you. High hopes that through your
hard work, the solution to the Kony problem has finally been
found. That is why we are anxious to see you commence your
work and to see this mission accomplished.

You are still young men, so jealously protect your dear lives,
and all the energy you have exhibited here during the training, all
the sweat you have lost during your training, all the knowledge
and skills you have acquired here.

I want your group to have what is called "esprit de corps."
Have strong regard for your unit, and feel proud to be a member
of your group. I want everybody to be inspired to belong to your
unit. May you serve as an example so that others may emulate
you. Are we together?

"Yes, sir," the graduates chorused.

General Wamala switched to English to thank the trainers. "The
skills that STTEP has imparted are not theoretical things," he said.
"They are practical things, because you've been at it yourselves." Then
he turned and spoke directly to me. "Shannon, please give our regards
to your family. Those small kids, tell them somebody somewhere ap-
preciates what you do. Because you care, because you feel for others—
that's why you're out here. That is why I want to thank you."

The reservations I'd had about the training mission and my role in it felt transformed by this moment of connection.

At the end of the ceremony the soldiers broke into song, voices interlocking in harmony, whistles and ululations threading through the melody. General Wamala clapped and sang along. When they raised their arms to the sky I could see the black, yellow, and red stripes of the Ugandan flags on the sleeves of their uniforms. The strength and jubilation—their sheer joy—made my heart pound.

As we filed toward the tent to share a meal, Laren and I shook the soldiers' hands. *"Apwoyo,"* they said in Acholi. Thank you. *"Apwoyo, bene,"* we replied. Thank you, too.

Before we sat down to eat, Laren pulled me aside. "I've had this pinnacle feeling before," he said. "After the years of peace talks, that day in Garamba when Kony was supposed to sign the peace agreement, the hope that it could all come to an end. It didn't. But today, seeing these troops—there hasn't been a single day for me that's contained so much hope that the war could be over soon."

I felt it, too. It had been a challenge to find hope in the journey so far. We'd hit so many roadblocks. Every roadblock meant more months of inaction—and the consequences that came from that inaction. But today was a point of hope.

After the meal the soldiers returned to their barracks. They didn't walk. They danced. I got up and danced with them. Strained by the heat and all the joyful dancing, the charm bracelet I'd worn every day of the training burst—the beads, the chain, and Saint Jude went flying. Lieutenant Charles found Saint Jude in the grass and restored the charm to me. I put it on a string around my neck.

NOT IN OUR INTERESTS

AFTER GRADUATION, THE Special Operations Group deployed to the field, working out of forward counter-LRA bases established in Nzara (South Sudan), Dungu (Democratic Republic of Congo), Djemah (Central African Republic), and Obo (Central African Republic). The South Africans stayed on in the region to prepare for the next SOG training and wait for proof of concept—for a glimmer of a sign that the training they had provided might bring the world closer to capturing Kony.

Despite the highly motivated and well-trained troops, all that was proved in the first month of deployment was the extreme difficulty of the work. On top of the geographic isolation, the SOG was operating in an intelligence vacuum. The large-scale reconnaissance patrols and former human intelligence assets the Ugandan military had used in the past were no longer sustainable given counter-LRA troop drawdowns and the LRA's expansion into more and more remote areas of operation. The Ugandan military could intercept radio calls between LRA groups, but they didn't know who was communicating or how to decode the content of the messages. The LRA communicated in a complex brevity code in which common words were coded to represent people, places, and events. The codes changed frequently. The SOG had no idea where exactly the LRA groups were operating or who was in them, no clue if they were getting any closer to ensuring freedom for Kony's hostages or justice for the perpetrators.

In fact, it would take years of institutional knowledge and creative intelligence gathering to understand where and how and why the LRA moved—to learn their sources for food and water, their river crossing points, and the routes they traveled to engage in illegal ivory trading. Eventually the Ugandan military would recruit informants— sometimes community leaders in areas suffering from LRA raids, or hunters and fishermen who would occasionally encounter the LRA in the bush, or nomadic cattle herders enduring LRA thefts of livestock or food. This intelligence would help us learn the LRA travel routes. But in the first weeks after deployment, the intelligence picture was extremely poor, the Darth Vader sticker still unplaceable on the map I'd made the boys.

The SOG soldiers split into small teams of four or five men, and walked for days and weeks on end, tirelessly tracking in the jungle, looking for any subtle sign—grass bent down where someone had slept, the remnants of a cooking fire—that might suggest the LRA had passed there. If they found a possible trail, then came the challenge of following it, navigating the zigzags, splits, and numerous countertracking strategies the LRA employed, constantly trying to gauge how far ahead the enemy was traveling so they could call on another SOG group to try to box in the LRA. It was slow, tedious work, and even though one SOG group in particular—the one led by Lieutenant Charles—had hit the ground running, impressing the Ugandan military leadership with its drive and capability, there was no indication that the SOG's skills and ambition would actually work to stop the LRA.

There was also inadequate air support for the mission. There weren't enough helicopters and planes to get the troops in position to capture LRA leadership, gain real-time intelligence, deliver food supplies, medevac wounded victims, or transport defectors if they emerged from the bush.

The entire mission was under-resourced for air support, and only a handful of aircraft were available for troop transport. For a number of years, the US Department of State had been supplying two Mi-8 helos

to the counter-LRA mission, and they were often flown using contracted eastern European pilots—but the contract was severely limited. Negotiated years in advance, the contract had predetermined
limits on the number of flight hours, fuel amounts, and areas where
the helicopters were allowed to fly, so the air support was unable to
adapt to operational needs as they arose. The State Department helos
were stationed in South Sudan, far away from the major tracking work
in the Central African Republic and the Democratic Republic of
Congo. They could fly one run if they left early enough in the morning, but they had to fly back to South Sudan by the end of the day. On
top of that, the pilots would only use landing zones that were secured
by the Ugandan military, making the helos unsuited for remote tactical missions. The Mi-8s were also highly fuel inefficient, consuming
more than 200 gallons of fuel per hour.

If Bridgeway could contract a helo, we could choose a more fuel-
efficient aircraft and arrange for it to be stationed closer to the action
where it could accomplish more with fewer—and less expensive—air
hours. The Ugandan military could mobilize Bridgeway's assets immediately and use them to quickly adapt to new requirements such as
entering denied areas or overnighting in the jungle.

During our conversations with General Aronda the previous summer, he had insisted on the need for more air support. And I had
balked. Now we were facing the reality that General Aronda had been
trying to make us face, that the mission wasn't going to succeed without more air platforms. For the soldiers who had worked so hard to
train to be effective, the mission needed helicopters. In our eagerness
to get the training going, we had failed to take seriously the Ugandans'
top need.

Muneer and I spoke about the need for more air support—how we
had to fill the gap if we were going to end the LRA conflict. He suggested we talk to the US government about lending more support to
the mission. He was hosting an event at his home the following week

and many of the country's most powerful legislators would be present. He invited me to attend and urged me to come early so he could schedule hour-long meetings with a few senators and congressmen, including Senator Mark Kirk from Illinois. "If you can explain to them what you're doing and why, maybe they can convince the US government to back the mission in a more significant way," he advised.

This was an incredible opportunity to brief some members of Congress on the project and shore up the kind of support that could make or break the mission. But I had to think hard before I could accept. Every time we widened the circle of people who knew about the mission, we took a risk. Word could break to the media, and I feared that a story would get things wrong and sensationalize what we were doing. A story like that would only be a distraction, something that could greatly hinder our ability to push forward, so I hesitated to bring too many people into the picture. I also recognized Muneer's amazing generosity. To help fund the mission was one kind of gift. But to expend his political capital was even more extraordinary—and risky, a sign of his deep-seated trust. He was willing to risk his reputation and influence to stop a warlord. If he was willing, others might be, too.

A few days later, I sat in a room in Muneer's home on Lake Michigan. It was a muggy July day in Chicago, the air as thick as porridge, but near the water it was cooler. I watched the waves rolling over the sand and took deep breaths. For the next three hours I would tell and retell the story of Kony's atrocities and our efforts to stop them, speaking to every legislator one at a time.

Each conversation unspooled in a similar way. The men already knew about Joseph Kony and the LRA—most had signed the disarmament bill the year before. They expressed their disgust at the horrors waged on Central and East Africans for the past two and a half decades, their desire for something to be done. Senator Kirk was especially vehement. Before he knew anything about our intervention he said, coincidentally, "Someone needs to go hire Executive Outcomes"—

Eeben's former company!—"and get those guys." Muneer and I exchanged surprised glances.

By the end of my presentation, each man was pleased to learn of our training mission, and applauded our efforts. But no one saw a scenario for the US government to fund additional helicopters for the mission. Senator Kirk said, "What you're doing is important. But you're not going to get helicopters from us for something that isn't in our national security interest."

Just before he left the room he turned to me and added, "When you fail, be ready to go after Kony again. It's going to take three tries."

Senator Kirk's advice was hard to swallow, but sounded accurate. Without helos, I had to concede that it didn't seem realistic we'd succeed. I had spent the day in the company of elite wealth and political power, but the status quo hadn't changed. The US would not be able to deploy additional air assets to the mission, at least not anytime soon.

The lack of helos was another blocked path that would only prolong Kony's ability to do harm, and another frustrating recognition that even when people had the will and the means to support a cause, they weren't always able to help. And yet I felt encouraged. Everywhere we'd turned for help we hadn't faced resistance. From humanitarians, the State Department, and now the halls of Congress we'd heard again and again: "What you're doing makes sense. It's the right thing." I hadn't solved our air support deficit, and we had likely committed ourselves to many more months on the ground than we'd anticipated. But I could move forward with continued reassurance and conviction that we were doing what had to be done. I would have to trust that it wasn't just necessary—that it was possible, too. Muneer, disappointed in the outcome of the meetings, wondered if we should try to fund the helos ourselves.

CONTACT

A FEW WEEKS later, we had encouraging news from the mission: in the first month of the Special Operations Group (SOG) deployment, there had been a sharp decrease in the number of LRA attacks and civilians killed.

"We can't assume it's because of the SOG," Laren cautioned. "The LRA could be less active due to seasonal changes, or a change in their strategy."

But then, while Laren was spending some weeks at home before the launch of the second training, we heard some news we'd been anticipating: the SOG had made their first contact with the LRA.

Soon after deployment, a SOG team had tracked the LRA in the Democratic Republic of Congo, moving in the direction of a large river. There were only a few points shallow enough to cross, so the SOG troops laid an ambush on the opposite side of the river, across from the expected crossing point. The LRA sent a security party across the river that night. On their return crossing, they tripped the ambush, igniting a firefight. The confrontation ended when the LRA members scattered into the dense terrain and the SOG lost their trail. No one was captured or freed. In their hasty flight the LRA had left behind only a few pots and pans and some minor equipment, no intelligence of value. But it was contact early in the game. And it proved that as time-intensive and arduous as it was to travel the immense jungle day and night in small teams searching for signs of the LRA, the very hardest thing was possible. It was possible to track them. If the SOG could find his army, it seemed to follow that they could find Kony.

The Ugandan military already knew that Dominic Ongwen, aka White Ant—one of Kony's top three commanders and one of the International Criminal Court indictees—operated with the LRA's group in Congo. They presumed he'd been with the group that was tracked and ambushed by the SOG. Ongwen had been abducted by the LRA when he was walking to primary school one day, around twenty years ago. He'd been placed with Vincent Otti, one of Kony's senior commanders, and as Otti was promoted up the ranks of the LRA, so was Ongwen. To have already made contact with his group in particular gave me hope that we could bring Kony and his fellow war criminals to justice.

"It's working," I said to Laren over the phone, my heart beating hard.

Laren was silent on the other side of the line. "It's working," he finally agreed. "But the gaps are becoming painfully clear."

While the success of the first mission had given the SOG the invaluable confidence that they could track the LRA in the jungle, it also continued to prove the glaring deficit in air support. When Captain Kommando had called the base to request helicopter support for the ambush, he was told there was no helo available to assist for five days. It might as well have been a year for all the good it would do. With the right air support, Dominic Ongwen could already have been in custody. But he was at large again in a vast area—and now he knew he was being pursued.

COMMAND, MAN DOWN

LAREN RETURNED TO the field in September 2011 and began living with the Ugandan SOG troops working out of the forward operations base in Djemah, Central African Republic. Of the three forward counter-LRA bases, the one in Djemah was the most remote. A speck of a red-dirt village surrounded by dense, unending forest interspersed with uninhabited savanna grassland clearings, Djemah was so tiny it didn't appear on most maps. A few years later, a *National Geographic* article would describe Obo as the most inaccessible point in all of Africa, but Laren would say the writer credited Obo as most remote because you could find it on a map. "Djemah's so far out in the sticks it makes Obo look like New York City," he'd say.

Laren rotated between the forward bases as needed, to help coordinate between the three Ugandan lieutenant colonels, each commanding a different counter-LRA mission zone, and to ensure that Bridgeway was able to offer the SOG timely and appropriate assistance.

Shortly after his arrival in Djemah, Laren called to report more contact with the LRA. A SOG squad had been tracking an LRA group as it moved from the border with Congo up to northern Central African Republic. The farther north they moved, the more tracks the SOG discovered, and the Ugandan military leadership realized multiple LRA groups seemed to be converging. It had seemed likely that large, prearranged rendezvous were happening between Kony and the leaders he'd put in command of the various splinter groups. But there'd been no concrete evidence of these meetings. Now it appeared a big meeting was about to happen, one that Kony himself might attend, and the SOG had all but stumbled into it.

Captain Kommando directed the SOG team to set up a mobile command post, not much more than a radio placed in the dirt, SOG soldiers sitting around it, and an HF wire up in the trees so they could communicate with the forward base in Djemah.

Captain Kommando consulted his map, and then briefed his men. "We'll divide into three groups," he explained. "Two will flank the target location. One will operate as a pseudo group."

The men in the pseudo group would pose as LRA women. They would wear long African-print dresses and scarves on their heads, and pretend they were re-entering the camp after gathering wild yams.

"There will likely be multiple rings of security around a meeting this important," Captain Kommando continued. "God willing, the pseudo group will advance through the outer layers of security and reach the inner encampment, where the high-value targets will be."

About three miles from where the suspected meeting was taking place, the pseudo group encountered the first ring of security. The LRA fired from a distance on the pseudo team, but the pseudo group maintained their disguise and didn't return fire, confusing the LRA security who were too far away to see them clearly, and allowing the SOG to penetrate the camp. When they arrived, the meeting was already under way. Among the many gathered, the SOG team identified Okot "the Butcher" Odhiambo; Dominic Ongwen; and, against all odds, Joseph Kony.

A firefight erupted, the LRA firing rocket-propelled grenades (RPGs) and 60 mm mortars. In the deadly chaos, the LRA began to flee. Mobile command radioed back to the Djemah base—a forty-minute flight away—to call for helicopter support and ordered the two flanking forces to try to cut off and surround the LRA's escape, dropping mortars behind the camp to block the exit. The group flanking on the left-hand side got bogged down in a marsh and couldn't get into position. The group on the right, led by Lieutenant Charles, soon lost VHF radio communication with mobile command, but continued the assault.

This is when the SOG first experienced the LRA's effective tactic for retreating from a firefight: a "hasty ambush." While most of the group fled the scene, five or six combatants were left behind to fire at the attacker to slow their advance, buying more time for senior leadership to escape. Lieutenant Charles's group hit three hasty ambushes as they attempted to pursue the LRA and were pelted by fire. In the third ambush, one of the SOG soldiers took a shot right to the neck. He died almost instantly, becoming the first SOG casualty.

Lieutenant Charles's group dropped their packs, cut through the last hasty ambush, and continued to track the LRA, still without contact from mobile command. The other flanking force, stuck in the marsh, never appeared. But the gunship ordered from Djemah finally arrived overhead. If we'd known then what we know now, the gunship might have won the battle. But from the air they couldn't tell the LRA from the SOG. They didn't have enough loiter time to distinguish the good guys from the bad, so they waved off and flew home. In future operations, the SOG soldiers would put bright orange tape called Day-Glo on the top of their hats so they could be identified from the air. Lieutenant Charles's group continued to track for six hours, but after so long without contact with command, and about to run out of water, they returned.

More SOG soldiers arrived the next day to help track. By that time the LRA had split into three groups, one heading south, the other two north through the Central African Republic. Later we'd learn that Kony's group had covered their tracks and headed up to Kafia Kingi. One SOG group tracked south, but by then the LRA trail they were following was already two days old—the LRA had apparently kept walking through the night. The SOG group called for a helo to come pick them up and fly them in front of the LRA's suspected position. But there were no helicopters available.

By the end of the contact a few LRA members had been killed and some intelligence—cellphones and satellite phones—had been recovered. But we had missed the biggest opportunity in years to drop a net over the organization.

CROCODILES AND KILLER BEES

THE LRA WASN'T the only enemy in the field. The terrain itself was deadly.

The swamps, the miles of boot-high water, the constant rain—the soldiers and their belongings were always damp. The sun would peek through holes in the canopy, not nearly long enough to dry them while they were walking, and then disappear again behind the thick leaves. Or they'd hit a river and have to walk through it carrying their gear, wet from head to toe again. Some of the men developed debilitating blisters that turned into bone-deep wounds. But they had no choice. They had to keep walking. And every day they had to keep moving through hunger pains. They carried rations for two meals a day: a tin of canned corned beef (called bully beef), canned beans in tomato sauce, dry crackers, or posho and dry beans cooked over a fire.

One day, Feni, one of the SOG soldiers, wasn't looking so good. He was pale and out of sorts in the morning, and as the group broke camp he complained of aches and nausea. The other soldiers divided his belongings among them to lighten his load for his march. They progressed for a few hours, walking as they always did through the bush in a single-file line, for security reasons and for ease of movement. Suddenly the long column of men stopped. From the back of the line it was impossible to see what was happening five hundred feet ahead. The men passed hand and arm signals down the column to communicate. Finally, word reached the men at the end of the line that Feni had gone down. He was having seizures. He had malaria, they realized, a parasitic disease that struck fast. Symptoms included incredibly high fevers, vomiting, dehydration, and horrible headaches. In the best cases, it caused complete collapse. In the worst cases, the parasitic infection could enter your brain and kill you. He was cycling through fever and chills and it took constant effort to try to keep him hydrated and cool his body temperature. Ultimately, he survived. But he wasn't the last to suffer from the illness. Malaria was commonplace among the Ugandan military camps, and Laren would also get malaria close to a dozen times before the mission was through. Malaria prophylaxis medications are only 60 to 70 percent effective—and they aren't meant to be taken every day for years at a time. I would take preventive meds for my visits, but for Laren, who lived there full-time save for brief and infrequent visits home, it wasn't really an option.

The threat of snakes, tarantulas, scorpions, and poisonous centipedes was as present as the inevitable bouts of malaria. There were constrictor snakes up to forty feet long. The venom of smaller snakes—hooded cobras and black and green mambas—could be fatal, and the soldiers had little or no access to antivenom in the field. The only prevention was to wear boots at all times, especially at night.

Once, an entire SOG camp woke in the night, screaming and yelling, stripping off their clothes. The camp had been swarmed by safari ants. They move in huge colonies, sometimes twenty million strong, and pull flesh up in their strong pincers when they bite. The men discovered thousands of ants in and around each tent, and when they shone light outside there were so many ants it looked like the ground itself was moving. The colony was swarming en masse after a rain, trying to find high ground. In several places the ants had piled on top of each other, ants upon ants, forming towers three feet high. The men had to take cooking fuel and douse the ants and torch them—without accidentally torching their tents.

Even a creature as small as a bee could be fatal. Central African bees are aggressive and numerous and attracted to the salt in sweat—

and in the jungle it didn't take long for it to build up. Cooking the early evening meal could be an especially dangerous enterprise. When the posho started cooking, the bees would swarm. The men did their best to keep covered—to wear jackets, light scarves over their faces, a hat, tight sunglasses if possible so the bees couldn't get to their eyes.

One day, a group was tracking through an especially thick part of the bush. Central Africa is largely flat, but every few miles or so the land dips down to a small river and then the elevation goes up another couple hundred feet to a dry stretch, and then it drops back down into another river. Down by the rivers the bush is thickest. The point man at the front of the column, who also served as lookout and tracker, was responsible for hacking the trail for the rest of the men to follow. On this day, he managed to hack himself into a large bees' nest. The furious bees attacked. It was like being caught in an ambush. The stings were incredibly painful, and the men were stuck in a single-file line, carrying forty or fifty pounds of gear on their backs, with nowhere to run, some stung so badly they fell ill.

At night, the soldiers would string their ponchos up with sticks, elevate the makeshift tents, and put grass underneath for sleeping. Setting up near a tree added extra protection from the rain. But one night lightning struck the tree where a private from northern Uganda was sleeping. The lightning blasted through his body, coming out his legs and into the ground, killing him instantly. His fellow soldiers wrapped him in an orange body bag to prepare him to be sent home.

Another evening a different SOG squad was preparing to cross the Vovodo River and sent three soldiers to reconnaissance the other side and make sure there were no hostile forces waiting on the other shore. The three men crossed the river, found that the other side was safe, and were crossing back, when a crocodile rose up out of the water and clipped one of the men in the leg. The man escaped the clutches of the crocodile by sticking his fingers in its eyes. But the Ugandan military couldn't fly him to get medical treatment because they didn't have access to a plane or helicopter that was rated to fly at night. He had to

spend the night in the bush with a mutilated leg—yet another reminder that battle wasn't the only danger. The land and its creatures,
even the weather, could be deadly. Every close call, every terrible death,
drove home our dire need for better air support. It was more than
Bridgeway could afford, and I didn't know where else to turn for help.

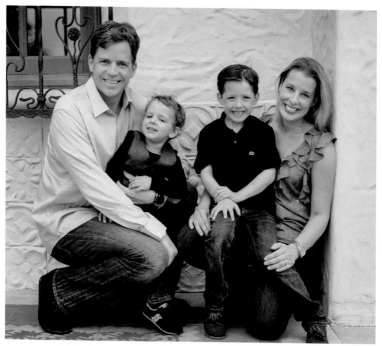

Shannon Sedgwick Davis and her husband, Sam, are pictured with their sons, Connor and Brody, near their home in San Antonio, Texas.
COURTESY SHANNON SEDGWICK DAVIS

David Ocitti escaped from warlord Joseph Kony's Lord's Resistance Army as a child, then went on to travel throughout Central Africa to help other survivors. Here he drives his field vehicle, "The Tank," in Gulu, Uganda. ADAM FINCK

Joseph Kony, notorious warlord, and founder of the Lord's Resistance Army (LRA).
GETTY IMAGES/ADAM PLETTS/CONTRIBUTOR

As part of her work with the Bridgeway Foundation, Shannon meets with an LRA survivor at a displacement camp in the Democratic Republic of Congo. (Here and throughout some faces are blurred to protect LRA escapees' identities.)
LAREN POOLE

Shannon and representatives from Invisible Children, an organization seeking to end violence in Central Africa, meet with United Nations personnel stationed in the Democratic Republic of Congo. COURTESY LAREN POOLE

A victim of LRA violence in the Democratic Republic of Congo. LAREN POOLE

A high-frequency radio is installed as part of the Early Warning Network in Bas Uele, Democratic Republic of Congo, to help villages alert one another about nearby LRA attacks. ADAM FINCK

Father Benoît Kinalegu, a community leader in the Democratic Republic of Congo and founder of the Early Warning Network that Bridgeway Foundation helped support; and Ida Sawyer, Human Rights Watch's lead researcher in Central Africa.
PATRICIA WILLIAMS

Shannon; General Katumba Wamala (*center*), commander of the Uganda People's Defense Force's (UPDF) Land Forces; and Eeben Barlow (*seated on right*), founder of Specialised Tasks, Training, Equipment, and Protection, at the Special Operations Group (SOG) graduation ceremony.
LAREN POOLE

The first SOG team graduates.
LAREN POOLE

Laren Poole and Shannon
with the SOG in Djemah,
Central African Republic.
HOWARD G. BUFFETT

Philanthropist Howard G. Buffett
and Shannon visit the SOG in
the Central African Republic.
COURTESY THE HOWARD G.
BUFFETT FOUNDATION

A SOG soldier tracks
the LRA in Djemah,
Central African
Republic.
LAREN POOLE

The SOG deploys in the Central African Republic, on the trail of the LRA.
HOWARD G. BUFFETT

A tracking dog team at work with the UPDF in the Central African Republic.
HOWARD G. BUFFETT

A soldier stands beside ivory poached by the LRA and recovered by the SOG in the Central African Republic. The LRA had been funding their operations through the illegal ivory trade.
LAREN POOLE

A UPDF soldier mourns the loss of his friend and fellow soldier, and flies with his remains that will be returned to Uganda for burial. LAREN POOLE

A recently escaped LRA captive and her newborn child, Otukene, which translates to "impossible grace," in a UPDF field hospital in South Sudan. Tragically, the mother never recovered from her infection and medical complications after giving birth in the bush. LAREN POOLE

LRA Major General Caesar
Acellam at the failed Juba
peace talks in 2006.
REUTERS/JAMES AKENA

Acellam in Djemah, Central African Republic, after capture by the SOG, who
gather with civilians to get a firsthand glimpse of the high-level rebel fighter.
Acellam will eventually gain amnesty, but here his fate is uncertain.
LAREN POOLE

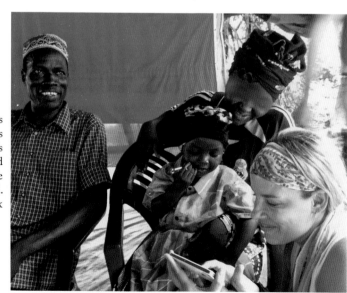

Shannon shares
photos of her sons
with Acellam's
recently liberated
forced wife
and child.
ADAM FINCK

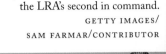

LRA Major General and Deputy Army Commander Okot Odhiambo, the LRA's second in command. GETTY IMAGES/ SAM FARMAR/CONTRIBUTOR

Odhiambo's remains are transported to Uganda for identification. Odhiambo was one of the first ever to be indicted by the International Criminal Court for crimes against humanity. GETTY IMAGES/BRENT STIRTON/STAFF

International Criminal Court indictee Dominic Ongwen during his many years as an LRA commander. COURTESY OF UPDF

Dominic Ongwen on trial at the International Criminal Court at The Hague. REUTERS/PETER DEJONG/POOL

Adam Finck on a flyer and aerial loudspeaker mission to encourage defections, in the Central African Republic. LAREN POOLE

Colonel Kabango, Laren, and Shannon in Djemah, Central African Republic, before Operation Merlin, where they hoped to finally capture Joseph Kony. LAREN POOLE

Shannon in Obo, Central African Republic, before Operation Merlin.
HOWARD G. BUFFETT

Here, Opio Sam embraces his mother for the first time after twenty-four years in the LRA, in the midst of a cleansing and reunification ceremony in his community.
DAVID OCITTI

Colonel Kabango with LRA Lieutenant Colonel Opio Sam, after he defected.
COURTESY COL. KABANGO

This heroic fourteen-year-old LRA escapee had fled alone with her baby from the Democratic Republic of Congo to the Central African Republic to reach safety.
LAREN POOLE

LRA Lieutenant Colonel Okello Okuti (*sitting, third from right*) and part of the "Zemio 19" in Obo, Central African Republic, with Laren.
COURTESY LAREN POOLE

Lapeko, part of a group of forty-six LRA returnees, in Obo, Central African Republic.
ADAM FINCK

The SOG rescues women and children from the LRA in the Central African Republic.
LAREN POOLE

David Ocitti doing family tracing and reunification in Lamwo district, northern Uganda.
COURTESY DAVID OCITTI

David Ocitti and Shannon's sons at Adam's wedding in Big Sur, California, in 2017.
SHANNON SEDGWICK DAVIS

PEACE CLUB

David Ocitti

DAVID SAT ON a hard wooden stool in front of the sparse classroom, so nervous his knees shook. He watched as groups of students passed by in the hall, some peering in at him for a moment before hurrying on. Just before his meeting was to begin, a few students, two boys and a girl about his age, ventured in the door. He took a breath to introduce himself, and a few more students trickled in, sitting anxiously on the edges of their chairs. Then a few more. The room was far from full, but it was no longer empty.

"Welcome to Peace Club," David began. "All of us in this room have one thing in common. In fact, every single person in this school shares this trait with us: all of us have been affected in some way by the LRA. Maybe we know someone who was killed. Maybe even someone in our own family was murdered or abducted. Maybe we ourselves were kidnapped by the rebels and held captive.

"And yet, this conflict that unites us, that has affected everyone in northern Uganda, divides us, too. The LRA is taboo. We are discouraged from talking openly about the conflict. And that's what motivated me to start the Peace Club. I was captured by the LRA and forced into their ranks for six months. The way that I've been treated here at school since my return has pushed me to break the silence.

To close the gap between me and you. To advocate for my fellow survivors. And to bridge the distrust and misunderstanding that separate all of us who in fact share the same pain.

"I almost dropped out of school. But I decided that I wasn't going to let the stigma define me. Instead of running away from the past or from others' judgment, I want to create awareness of what it's like to be abducted. So, tell me. Who is the LRA?"

"Rebels," a boy called out.

"Killers," someone else said.

"They say Joseph Kony is a demon, that he runs so fast that his feet leave the ground. They say his eyes glow red," the youngest student in the room said.

Those gathered began trading myths about Kony's supernatural powers. Into the noise, a single voice cut through.

"No." It was a tall, thin boy who had been sitting silently at the back of the room. "If you want to know who is the LRA, I'll tell you. The LRA is us."

By the time David graduated from high school, there were Peace Clubs all across northern Uganda. The clubs led sensitization activities on how to build trust in communities and how to treat returnees; organized debates on topics such as defection and forgiveness; performed charity work, cleaning camps for displaced persons and distributing water cans and basins; and engaged in civic education, learning about peaceful ways to bring about political change. As the Peace Club movement grew, more and more survivors came forward—others who had been abducted and managed to escape, who had been in hiding, not wanting to identify as returnees. Even the boy who had confronted David at school, blaming

David for his father's death, joined Peace Club. "We are the same," he told David. "I am lucky, I wasn't taken. But we share the same path." That was the message for hope and change rippling through communities in northern Uganda: *we are all victims of the LRA, and together, we can repair the wound of war and rebuild our communities.*

3 2

FATHER, DAUGHTER

IN OCTOBER, A month into the second SOG training, I got a text
from Ben Keesey. *Call me, good news!* he wrote.

On the phone, he told me that President Obama had decided on a
course of action in response to the LRA disarmament bill that he'd
signed over a year ago. In a letter to John Boehner, Speaker of the
House of Representatives, he had announced the deployment of approximately one hundred US Special Operations forces—including
Green Berets—to the region to "provide information, advice and assistance to select partner nation forces" and be "a significant contribution toward counter-LRA efforts."

An *L.A. Times* article soon reported that the Special Forces would
"help track the movements of the guerrillas and share intelligence
from communications intercepts and satellite imagery" and "help deliver communications gear to villagers." While emphasizing the limited scope of the intervention—Special Forces wouldn't engage in
combat with the LRA unless it was necessary for self-defense—the
article underscored the significance of the deployment, suggesting
that it could be "an exception to traditional American foreign policy of
avoiding military involvement in sub-Saharan Africa, a region where
the United States is generally thought to have humanitarian but not
strategic interests."

Not in our interests. I thought of the meetings with legislators at
Muneer's home, their support of our work but the disappointing out-

come. Now Special Forces were on the way, bringing skills, resources, technology. My mind raced with possibility: air support, satellite imagery. It felt like the tide was truly turning.

Ben later told me one of the things that had moved Obama to do something about the violence: his daughter Malia had seen an Invisible Children film about the LRA crisis on Facebook and had asked him over dinner what the United States was doing about it. I'd heard it rumored that something similar had happened with Jenna Bush and her father—that she had been the one to convince President Bush to participate in Operation Lightning Thunder. These tender stories stoked my hope for a better human future. A daughter took her father's hand and pointed to a wound in the world. Her father listened. It gave me such faith in young people, in their awareness and strong hearts, in their power to reach the older generation and build a better world.

33

JAMALED

LAREN SHARED LITTLE of my optimism about the US Special Forces deployment. He said that the buzz and excitement far exceeded the reality of what they'd likely accomplish on the ground. More than half of the hundred uniformed US military personnel would be based in Entebbe, Uganda, far from the LRA presence—with only thirty-six Special Forces split between forward bases in Congo, the Central African Republic, and South Sudan. There was no plan to embed US Special Forces into the Ugandan military tracking teams, or get them in the field in a meaningful way.

He agreed that the deployment had the potential to be a tipping point against the LRA, but he cautioned that it was going to require a lot of political noise demanding tangible results.

"If there's no heat to deliver results, we're just going to be swimming in an endless status quo bog," he said.

But I wasn't willing or able to abandon my hope that the deployment signaled a unique opportunity to share resources and efforts toward a common goal, and my high spirits continued as I prepped for a trip to Uganda: to Camp Bondo, where I would check in on Eeben's second SOG training; and to Entebbe, to meet with the first-deployed Green Berets.

Eeben had decided to expand his team for the second training. The trainers were building on lessons learned the first time around, and the new SOG soldiers were proving to be extremely proficient. But the vulnerabilities in personalities were beginning to show. The trainers frequently complained about food and conditions, and threatened to quit. Some of the trainers lost a significant amount of weight—over thirty pounds in two months—due to poor nutrition. They sometimes bought food out of their own salaries, and blamed Eeben for not insisting on better conditions. Eeben told them, "Suck it up. We're not here to waste money."

I realized on my visit that a lot of the change in morale had one simple cause: the heat. It was excruciating. Laren saw me looking miserable one afternoon, trying to take cover from the heat by scrunching as much of my body as possible under the scant shade of a tree, and he walked over to give me a pep talk. "Hey, boss," he said, "just so you know, everyone here looks forward to your visits because you always encourage and inspire them. You've got to power through and do your thing." He was right. Without my realizing it, my expression had morphed into a near-constant scowl. It was over one hundred degrees, with no reprieve.

Laren was steady and stoic through all of it—so much so that he didn't tell me about a truly dangerous incident that occurred early in the second training. Perhaps as a way to laugh their way through tough conditions, or to fight back against circumstances they found unfair, many of the South African trainers would play tricks on people in the camp, falling out of their chairs laughing when someone had been had. One day, Laren was the butt of their prank, one they had pulled on others in the past—and the joke went way too far. A few of the trainers conspired to put jamalgota seeds in Laren's beans and posho. The jamalgota seeds, dubbed "jamal beans" by the trainers, are a potent laxative, causing severe intestinal inflammation and abdominal cramps. The night Laren was "jamaled," he became violently ill. Apparently, a number of the trainers were also jamaled at one point or another during the training: one for being too slow in producing an intelligence product, another for being too grumpy. Even Eeben himself was jamaled, for being too strict. Although it was meant as a prank, an overdose of jamalgota can be lethal. I didn't realize until much later how vulnerable Laren had been.

And although I understood the weight and challenge of his responsibilities, I lacked a full understanding of what his role as the ground coordinator for the mission required of him. When he shared stories of camp life, they were most often experiences of camaraderie, not conflict. He'd been out in the field once on a training mission with Eeben and some of the Ugandan troops, and after a long and difficult day in the bush, they'd been setting up camp for the night, telling stories, shooting the breeze, when one of the Ugandan soldiers had said, "We're like brothers, but we are strangers to each other." It was true. They had completely divergent backgrounds, came from different countries and cultures and circumstances—and yet they had the same goal, believed in the same thing. As Laren said, they were bound in a strange brotherhood.

I knew the strain Laren was under, how tough and lonely it was to be in remote areas for long stretches, across the world from his wife and parents in San Diego, how challenging to be the sole person with the job of communicating between diverse organizations and personalities. And I knew how deeply Laren internalized his experience, how he tried to manage everything himself, only speaking when he had to. But I was oblivious to the danger he'd been in.

34

CALLED OUT

A MONTH BEFORE the second SOG class was to graduate, I held a sleepy Brody in my arms as we entered the inner-city mission church in downtown San Antonio for the candlelight Christmas Eve service. Connor pulled Sam ahead to get candles, alert to the privilege of holding a flame in his own hands, and I stood in the hallway near the sanctuary, nuzzling Brody, his head warm on my shoulder, his hair soft on my cheek. I savored these moments, the pure peace of being with my boys, no other thought weighing on my mind.

"I get a candle, too?" Brody lifted his head to ask.

"Yes, love." Dear boy, eager to claim his independence. He'd started in the fall at the Pineapple School, a wonderful Spanish immersion preschool, and every night at dinner when we shared our highs and lows from the day, he said his high was "apple school." It threw me sometimes, his babyhood already gone. At work, time seemed to creep by, the tedium of communication lags, the painfully slow pace through the bush. But at home there was never enough time. I'd blink and my boys would have outgrown another shoe size, their blossoming so swift they were out of a stage before I'd even gotten used to its having begun. Witnessing who they were becoming took my breath away. And every celebration of growth, the constant evolving and unfolding, was a loss, too. I swayed with Brody, breathing deeply, trying to preserve the moment in memory before it too was gone.

"It must feel so good to be home."

I opened my eyes to see that one of the church members had joined me. "It does," I said.

Time at home was especially precious because Sam's mom—the boys called her Mimi—had just been diagnosed with stage-four lung cancer. A strong, vibrant matriarch with four children and eleven grandkids, Mimi was a music teacher, an organist and pianist, who would engage me in passionate discussions of women's and international human rights. She had always been healthy and energetic—and she wasn't a smoker—but by the time she was diagnosed, the cancer had already made its way to other regions of her body and she'd been put on an aggressive course of chemo. Sam had immediately stepped in as a caregiver. We didn't know how much time was left.

"Those little ones must miss you an awful lot," the church member said.

"It's hard on us," I agreed, rubbing Brody's back, the cotton weave of his red-and-yellow polo shirt, everything about him soft, holding him extra tight.

"You're doing good in the world," she said, as the gathering crowd milled around us, looking for friends and family before heading into the sanctuary. "But don't forget your family. You have a responsibility first to your boys."

It wasn't the first time I'd been called out by a well-meaning person for the time I had to spend away from home. I was used to people implying that I wasn't being the best mom because of my job. This had been a point of tension my entire life as a mother. While I had learned to face decisions and criticisms in my work with confidence, there was nothing as daunting and challenging as being a custodian of another human being, and I was always second-guessing my parenting. It was tough when others hit me where I already felt vulnerable.

As much as my fellow church member's judgment stung, it reminded me that one of the biggest messages I spoke to my boys was my wholehearted wish for them to be whomever in the world they were created to be. Doing the work I felt called to do was the best way to show up for my boys. To model for them what it means to act on your passions, to be who you were made to be, to show up where your heart feels strong. If I didn't model these values for them, who would? And how could I expect them to live as their full selves if I was not fully being who I was created to be: a mom and an advocate? Many moms do this, and in creating and living out their passions they honor their greatest gifts: their children.

This was the truth in my heart. "Merry Christmas," I said, and carried Brody into the dark room filled with candlelight.

35

THE FARMER

I RETURNED TO Camp Bondo in January 2012 for the second SOG class graduation. For the first time in the decades of the conflict, the Ugandan military was ready to deploy a full battalion of specialized soldiers. Eeben had fulfilled his contract with us for the two rounds of training. The trainers' work was done. And the US Special Forces were beginning to deploy. Over the next few months they would build their own bases near each of the three SOG forward bases, and be dispersed into twelve-man teams. The operational detach teams were designed to be self-sufficient—each had a weapons specialist and a mechanic, and every soldier spoke at least one language in addition to English. They were essentially "diplomatic warriors" who would work with the Ugandan military and local personnel in each area of operation. And they would take over the training of the next group of Ugandan soldiers.

By then, my worry had become chronic. I couldn't sleep more than a few hours at a time before I woke up, heart racing out of my chest. But now that our training intervention was coming to a close, the tightness in my chest began to loosen.

Before leaving Uganda, I met with Laren and Eeben at Faze 3, a yellow-walled restaurant, half tandoori joint, half pub, minutes from the airport in Entebbe. It was our last meeting before Eeben and his men would pack up and leave Bondo. Our partnership was over. Laren and I expressed how grateful we were for his efforts and effectiveness, and Eeben wished us luck with the work ahead.

On paper, we had completed what we had set out to do. But our year and a half in the field had taught us how naïve we had been to believe that the training would be the silver bullet—and how much more might be possible in the fight against the LRA if we stayed. We could focus our efforts on supporting the work in the field, and trying to fill the air support gap. There'd been too much progress made to pack up now.

With Generals Wamala and Aronda, we began to plan what was next, in what ways Bridgeway could best be present and support the Ugandan SOG battalion and complement the US Special Forces team. Intelligence from informants in the north had helped the SOG pick up the LRA trail they'd lost after Kony's near capture in September 2011. It was evident that at least one LRA group had moved in that direction, but the Ugandan military didn't know if the LRA was based in one location in the north or still on the move. Then their informants reported a new commodity for sale in a market in Kafia Kingi. The new product was simsim, a small seed traditionally grown in northern Uganda and eaten by the Acholi, not a crop traditionally eaten in that region. The Ugandan military commanders believed that the LRA could have brought simsim up north to cultivate. If they were growing simsim crops, enough to sell a surplus at market, then they must have a permanent camp nearby.

There was finally a glimmer of hope that we could discover Kony's exact whereabouts. But the logistics of getting the SOG soldiers up there, supporting them and staying in communication with them while they were so far from base, and getting them back to the forward base—it was more than we could realistically take on or afford.

"US Special Forces will be forward and operational soon," I reassured Laren. "We've just got to trust and keep moving forward the best we can."

Hope came faster than I dared expect, and in an unexpected way. After our final meeting with Eeben, I traveled to Congo on business and met Howard Buffett, international philanthropist and oldest son of Warren Buffett, who was also on the same trip.

Howard was wholesome and robust, with hair gone white. It was easy to picture him on the back of a tractor. He looked like he'd have a steady, measured manner, but he acted with childlike joy. With a constant supply of junk food—black licorice, cherry Twizzlers, Tootsie Pops, Mint Milano cookies—that he passed around on the plane, he was full of boundless energy. When the rest of us were trying to nap on the flight, he would talk and talk, doing karate chops in our faces to keep us alert. He quickly discovered that I had a weak spot for purple Tootsie Pops and he'd save them for me, tossing them to me with a smile on his face.

My sense of joy was running on fumes those days. Howard's lively and joyful presence alleviated some of the heaviness. And I soon discovered, when we had the chance to talk one-on-one, how brilliantly his huge heart and wisdom shone. He had a fascinating mix of interests—an accomplished farmer and conservationist, he was also an avid photographer and he had a background in law enforcement. He'd been to 152 countries—including every country in Africa, plus Somaliland and Western Sahara, the two disputed territories there—and was rich in stories that revealed his hunger to contribute to the betterment of the world. He was more than a donor. He was an eager learner, a voracious student of the human experience.

He told me about serving as auxiliary deputy sheriff in two counties in Illinois, helping US Marshals serve warrants and canine units search for drugs; supporting victims of child and domestic abuse; farming fifteen hundred acres himself, doing all the planting and combining; providing grants to research conservation farming. "More people are recognizing the importance of taking care of soil," he said, "of using Mother Nature to break up soil compaction, increasing organic matter so you have cover on your soil year-round."

Once he was started on the farm talk I thought I'd never be able to move him back to a topic of shared experience, but then he started saying things that completely intersected with what I knew to be true in humanitarian work: "It's about technology. And knowledge. And then of course a lot of it is what you're able to pay for," he said. "And it all has to start with deep listening, with trying to understand what's really going on."

We were on a small plane, headed between remote villages. Driving would have taken us days. He waved below us at the beautiful terraced farms that rose up into the green hills. Some of the crops had been planted in lovely spiral shapes, as artistic as they were sustaining. He saw where my gaze had landed and said, "Terraces are one of the best conservation measures ever and they're the oldest known to humans. It's baffling—if you step back and look at the world, we've spent hundreds of billions, probably trillions of dollars on research for corn, soybeans, rice, wheat. And we've spent a minuscule amount of research in Africa on African solutions."

When he asked about my work in the region I started to give him a vague answer. The list of people who knew the details of our collaboration with the Ugandan military was very small. But I felt I could trust Howard, and that his insights would be a huge asset. I confidentially shared with him what we were doing to stop Kony. Every time I told the story of our involvement, I remembered how many months and years it had taken me to warm up to the idea, how crazy it would have sounded to me at the beginning, and I waited for Howard to express surprise or even admonishment. But he didn't. He got it. Instantly.

"This isn't a military operation," he said. "It's law enforcement. It's calling the police. Like if your neighbors were screaming and had a problem, you'd call the cops. And if the cops weren't there, next time you'd form a police department."

He posed great questions about logistics, intel, equipment, strategy—questions he knew to ask because of his own experience in law enforcement. When he asked what our greatest challenges had been, I told him how the lack of air support was essentially crippling any momentum that we gained.

"Why don't you just provide the air support?" he asked.

"The cost, for one." But there was another barrier, one that I hadn't articulated to Laren yet, or even fully to myself. It was the stubborn hope that another entity—a more appropriate and established entity, like the UN or a government, would step up and do the necessary thing. I had largely moved past the incredulity and anger into action, but the truth was I was still frustrated that Bridgeway's intervention was even necessary, and the more months we were in the field the more vulnerable I felt. "Even if we could afford to fly and fuel a helicopter, is it really our place to get involved in that level of military operations?" I asked.

Howard laughed. "Is it really 'your place' to train an army?"

He had a point. Here I was drawing lines everywhere, limits beyond which I wouldn't go—but essentially, we'd already gone all in.

"Look," he said. "You're absolutely not doing what private foundations usually do with charitable money. Private foundations reintegrate child soldiers, help orphans, create economic opportunity for people who have lost all their resources. Private foundations try to solve the problems that come as a result of someone like Kony. But if you just address the symptoms of problems you never get at the roots.

"Yes, you're doing something risky. And very unusual. But isn't it also the most efficient way to use charitable money? Isn't trying to actually stop a warlord—instead of just responding to the damage—the least risky solution? It's very clear to me. If you knew someone was going to start a forest fire, would you wait for him to start it and spend the next however many days or months trying to put it out? Or would you do your absolute best to stop him from starting the fire? As for the cost," he said, handing me a package of Twizzlers, "our foundation will cover it."

He offered to provide us with a helicopter and help us fund a small fixed-wing plane. With his law enforcement background and decades of humanitarian work, he also understood the tactical power a tracking dog team could add to the mission. He said that he would fund a team of Kenyan dog handlers and Belgian Malinois and Dutch shepherd dogs to assist with more targeted tracking to recover victims. And just like that we had a new partner, one of the globe's biggest philanthropists, a man who is all heart and finds a way to bring laughter in the midst of some of the hardest problems in the world.

GULU UNIVERSITY

David Ocitti

ONE JANUARY MORNING, nine years after his abduction, David was racing to school, late for his first lecture. He was two years into a business degree at Gulu University, the lucky recipient of a Gulu District NGO Forum scholarship, without which he wouldn't have been able to continue his studies past high school.

As fortunate as he was to be able to pursue a degree that would put him among the very most educated people in northern Uganda, the opportunity left David with a scar. For years he had lived and studied alongside peers who had also lost parents to the LRA. He knew he was innocent, he knew it in his head. But in his heart he felt that he was enjoying a privilege he didn't deserve.

As he ran across the red dirt road, someone shouted his name. A group of kids he knew from high school was crossing the same street. One of the young men had been orphaned by the LRA. David knew exactly when and how his parents had died. He had always felt protective of this boy as they grew up.

"I'm late!" David called to him. "I want to catch up but I can't talk now."

"I'm late for lectures, too," the young man said.

"You're at university?"

His friend nodded.

"I'm so glad for you." David knew the boy didn't have money for school, and asked how he was able to continue his studies.

"My friends and I all got scholarships from a group called Invisible Children that supports LRA victims."

If there was an organization out there repairing lives and helping his friends, David wanted to know everything about it. He decided to visit their office in Gulu that very afternoon.

After his morning classes, David found the Invisible Children office and met Jolly Okot, the country director and the person David would learn was most instrumental in creating the projects in northern Uganda.

"Is it true you offer scholarships to victims of LRA violence?" he asked.

Jolly, a middle-aged mother of young children, had short hair, full heart-shaped cheeks, and a playful twinkle in her eyes. She nodded.

"How?"

She told him that in order to give northern Ugandan survivors a chance to go to school, groups of crazy mzungu—Westerners—traveled around the United States, telling American college students about the LRA and raising money to help people affected by the conflict.

"What if people stopped giving money?" David asked. "What would happen to all of the Ugandan students' scholarships?"

Jolly said that Invisible Children had been enormously successful in engaging American youth in activism and charitable giving, but that was the only revenue stream. If Americans—in this case, mostly young American students—stopped giving, the funds would dry up and the scholarships and other rehabilitation opportunities cease.

"I want to go raise money," David said. "I have a story to tell about my captivity, and I want to help my friends go to school. Can you send me there?"

She warned him that it wasn't an easy life, that it was cold, that the food was terrible. She said it was hard sleeping in a van. That he'd get homesick.

But David already knew that the hard way was the best way, that the world didn't change unless you cut the path. "How soon can I go?" he asked.

COINED

A MONTH AFTER I had the fortune of meeting Howard Buffett, I was invited to meet Admiral Brian Losey, the former commander of SEAL Team 6 and now the special operations commander of the United States Africa Command (AFRICOM). He was responsible for all the US Special Operations Forces deployed in Africa. I was to visit his office in Stuttgart, Germany, to discuss our mission. But when I arrived on a cold February morning, I was surprised to discover that this wasn't the one-on-one meeting I'd anticipated. There were at least half a dozen other people in the room, all strangers to me, their roles unknown. I'd been prepared to have a private and specific discussion with Admiral Losey about operations in the field, but now I had a large audience of strangers. I felt nervous, my guard up. Admiral Losey, fit and polished, his face held in a constant smile, invited me to begin by describing our work.

After a few formal pleasantries, everyone except Admiral Losey and the State Department representative stood to leave. Now the meeting I'd been prepared for could begin. And it went well. As we talked, I felt Losey's polish break down a bit. I could sense the person, not just the role. We agreed to coordinate our efforts, laying the foundation for what he called "full operational cooperation," but we also set some parameters and distinctions for information sharing so as not to compromise Defense or State Department security. I was well aware of the uniqueness of the partnership that entailed unusual coordination between the State Department and Department of Defense. I anticipated there would be differences to negotiate along the way.

While the meeting highlighted yet another bridge of trust I'd need to build and navigate, I also felt optimistic that our collaboration was about to become more powerful. With Bridgeway's new air support capabilities arriving soon, and an agreed-on plan to coordinate efforts with Special Operations Forces, we seemed in a good position to follow the trail of the simsim seed and try to find Kony's suspected camp in Kafia Kingi.

At the end of the meeting Admiral Losey rose to walk me to the door. "Ms. Sedgwick Davis," he said sincerely, "we are so grateful for your efforts and I look forward to working with you." He shook my hand in both of his.

Within his firm grip I felt something hard and round against my palm. Some kind of disk, a little bigger and thicker than a silver dollar. It was cold on my skin. He was passing it to me in secret. I felt a wave of nervousness and tried to be discreet as I hid the object in my purse. What could he be sharing with me that he didn't want others to see? And would I know what to do with it or its contents?

Later, I examined what Admiral Losey had given me. It was a large coin with an engraving of the African continent on each side, surrounded by crests and seals and a ring of African nations' flags. *Presented by the Commander, Special Operations Command Africa,* the script read. *Procedimus Una.* We go together. I suddenly felt like an idiot. Admiral Losey hadn't been trying to pass me something secret. He had "coined" me, a long-standing military tradition. He only had a certain number of coins in his possession to distinguish exemplary service in the field, and he'd given me one to recognize my work and bless our mission. The collaboration with Special Forces was on solid footing, and I felt incredibly proud. I imagined giving the coin to my boys one day, a symbol of the possibility of triumph against the odds.

KONY 2012

ONE EVENING IN early March, Laren and I sat in the mess tent at the Ugandan forward base in Djemah. The US bases were always built away from the Ugandan camps, sometimes as far as twenty minutes away. The physical separation was just one facet of the distance between the forces. There were also inequities. The US Special Forces budget was close to $100 million a year. We'd been told their three bases had cost in excess of $30 million to build, with full mess halls and an abundance of equipment and modern conveniences. They spent as much as $3.5 million annually to supply the bases with reverse osmosis water filtration systems for clean bathing water and preapproved drinking water that had to be transported on contracted aircraft. The contractors flew their helos—bigger than any available to the mission—to bring in air conditioners.

Over time, some problems would emerge. The US Special Forces troops shifted every six months, pulled in and out of rotation so fast there was hardly time for them to secure familiarity or trust with the Ugandan military personnel. The relationship-building often had to start all over again every few months with each change in personnel.

Tonight we were eating dinner with Colonel Joseph, the Ugandan overall counter-LRA commander. He was a warm, jovial man with a wide mustache and deep-set brown eyes. When he wasn't commanding his forward troops, he watched Spanish-language soap operas with English subtitles from his command tent deep in the jungle. He and Laren had a fluid, friendly working relationship. I had never seen Colonel Joseph angry before.

But tonight the colonel was upset. "They've betrayed us," he said.

Invisible Children had just released a new film, *Kony 2012*. Laren and I had watched it for the first time the night before in the business center at the hotel we'd been staying at in Entebbe, the only place where the Internet was strong enough to stream video. I had expected to celebrate with Laren. Even though he no longer worked for Invisible Children, he cared deeply for the people of the organization and their success, and we were ready to applaud another installment in Invisible Children's highly effective work. But the film had made me cringe. While many the world over would find it moving and galvanizing—it would become the most viral video in the world then, garnering one million views in just one day, and more than a hundred million views in six days—I could see why the tone and content would be upsetting to Colonel Joseph and his fellow Ugandans.

To them, the film was misleading. Much of the footage used in the video was ten years old, from the time when Ugandan kids were still doing the night commutes to avoid abduction. But the Ugandan military had pushed the LRA out of Uganda in 2006. The night commutes hadn't happened for at least six years. To the Ugandans, the film paid no respect or gratitude to the significant progress the Ugandans had made against the LRA, and at least some of them felt humiliated and outraged. The Ugandans were glad that there was media attention on the LRA, but dismayed that the film spent so little time on the present realities of the conflict and on the people actually fighting the LRA.

"Why would they make a film that casts such a negative light on our country and our army?" Colonel Joseph demanded.

"Sir, I understand your anger," I said. "It isn't that they don't understand the progress made. They want to highlight the things that will cause the biggest response from Americans in order to influence US policy."

The response was indeed huge. More than one million people left comments on the film on YouTube, eleven million people shared it on

Facebook, and Joseph Kony and the LRA became a major topic of conversation around many dinner and policy-making tables. We had no idea how much publicity would come as a result of *Kony 2012*, or what the costs of that extreme public attention would be.

Invisible Children was highly unusual in the nongovernmental organization world in that it was primarily funded by high school and college kids—in its early years, 80 percent of the donations made to the organization were in amounts of twenty dollars or less. The viability of the organization relied on the leaders' ability to maintain a narrative that inspired youth to stay involved. *Kony 2012* was a product and example of Invisible Children's gifts and successes: using digital space and social media to connect and engage youth in humanitarian work; transforming the activist and donor base for large NGOs; inspiring and mobilizing young people to care about the LRA and igniting their empathy for people outside their country.

Invisible Children did a brilliant job giving American students an emotional and social connection to some of the most troubling global realities, bringing former LRA abductees to college campuses all over the country. Many of the people who ran Invisible Children were products of that life change, millennials who'd been going about their daily lives until they were suddenly moved to greater awareness and action, having a life-changing revelation about their place and responsibility in the world.

The film was created at a critical time when Congress needed to reauthorize US troop deployment to the counter-LRA mission and there was indication that this reauthorization was at risk. It garnered immediate, positive results: important doors opened in DC, increasing political strength and energy toward stopping the LRA; audiences raised more than twenty million dollars, enabling the expansion of high-frequency radio networks and other projects in Central Africa to protect communities vulnerable to LRA violence; and, as hoped, the deployment was reauthorized.

Our friend Jason Russell, who had founded Invisible Children with Laren, was the genius behind the film. He'd always been particularly drawn to activist leadership—public speaking, interaction with audiences, mentorship—and he was incredibly good at energizing and inspiring youth. With the release of *Kony 2012*, he received more significant and rightful praise for his work. He was contacted by news outlets the world over, all wanting interviews with him. He began an intense schedule of media appearances, traveling constantly, sleeping little, trying to meet the demands of the world's attention. But along with the support and praise, he also started to face criticism. When the public eye that had been such a source of validation became a source of its opposite, it was confusing for him—even toxic.

Ten days after the release of *Kony 2012*, Jason suffered a psychotic breakdown, tearing off his clothes on a suburban street near San Diego in the middle of the day, ranting about good and evil, screaming obscenities, and slamming his hands against the pavement until the police took him away. Someone recorded a video of this episode, and it, too, went viral.

Jason spent nearly two months in a psychiatric hospital before returning home to his wife and children. It was a terrible time, and my heart broke for my friend. A vibrant, charismatic, and solidly good person, a caring soul, had taken a hard turn, and now his health and well-being were on the line. Laren was especially devastated and worried. Both of us were on the phone constantly, checking in with Jason's family and speaking with Invisible Children staff, all of us deeply concerned for Jason.

Later, when he had had time to process and heal, Jason reflected on what had caused his breakdown. On top of the physical exhaustion from lack of sleep and too much travel, there was the confusing brew of massive public scrutiny. He told one news source, "On the one hand, there was Bono saying, 'Jason Russell deserves an Oscar,' and Oprah wants to fill stadiums for me, and Ryan Seacrest wants me on *Ameri-*

can Idol. And on the other, there were people saying, 'These people think they're white saviors trying to save Africa,' and, 'The money goes to corrupt places,' and, 'There is a special place in hell for you.' They were so polar opposite. So extreme. And in my head I wanted to reconcile them and I just couldn't." In an interview with Oprah about a year after his breakdown, he said, "I should have been listening to my loved ones. I should have surrendered *Kony 2012* and Invisible Children to the people at large, to my colleagues. I should have slowed down, let go. And instead I chose to keep pushing, keep pushing. Your mind is so, so powerful. It's so strong. And if you feed it with this chaotic noise, you lose who you are."

OTUKENE MEANS GRACE

LATER THAT SPRING, a SOG group stationed at the forward base in Nzara made contact with the LRA. There were no significant captures or defections in the skirmish, no intelligence gains, but as the SOG prepared to return to the base they found a woman hidden in the dense bush. She had gone into labor during the attack and the LRA had left her behind as they fled. She'd labored alone in the jungle, bringing her tiny son into the world in complete isolation. Her baby appeared healthy, a full head of dark curls, fists closed protectively over his sweet sleeping face. But his mother, terrified and weak, was still bleeding from her ordeal. She was brought to the base in Nzara where the nurse helped her into the bed in the medic tent.

Laren visited her multiple times a day, speaking through an Acholi translator, wishing her and her baby health, checking in with the nurse about their progress. The baby was nursing well and gaining weight, and when Laren visited he was always asleep, his mother curved protectively around him, the baby snug in her shelter.

On one visit Laren said, "Your baby was born on the day you got your freedom back. What are you going to name him?"

She said she hadn't chosen a name yet and asked Laren to suggest one. Laren didn't feel comfortable taking a parent's rite, but the nurse kept pressing him. "She wants you to give him a name," she said.

"Let's name him Miracle," Laren finally suggested. The translator explained that there's no exact Acholi word for miracle, no direct translation, so they settled on Otukene. Literally, it means "came on its own"—as in, everyone thought it would never happen, but all of a sudden it happened. An impossible grace.

After two days the mother was still weak. She was running a fever and she said that one of her breasts hurt. The nurse suspected that she had a plugged milk duct or the early stages of mastitis—a painful breast infection not uncommon among nursing mothers—and recommended that she be treated in a hospital. Laren arranged for her transport home to Gulu, Uganda, and two Ugandan soldiers helped her stand and slowly climb the steep stairs of the airplane.

She and the baby made it safely to the hospital, where she was diagnosed with mastitis. She was promptly put on antibiotics. But it was too late. The infection had spread. She died in the hospital from a treatable infection, and her newborn boy became another orphan of this dreaded war.

I tried to take hope in the arrival, in April, of the Bell 412 helicopter Howard Buffett was funding. The Cessna Caravan airplane had come in February and both mission-specific aircraft were stationed in the Central African Republic. The US Department of State provided fuel for both the Caravan and the Bell as part of their contract with the Ugandan military. The two aircraft had complementary capabilities. The Caravan—provided to us at cost by an aviation firm called Tempus Jets—could land on short, unimproved (i.e., dirt) runways, and was used to transport food and supplies from Entebbe or Obo to Djemah, while the Bell helo could land virtually anywhere and was used to transport troops, pick up defectors, and provide medical evacuations from the bush. Our contract was flexible, and the Bell could overnight in the jungle rather than having to return to a base. Until the United States military would bring its own choppers to Obo in about a year, the Bell 412 would perform nearly 100 percent of the mission's medevacs and defector pickups, and 70 percent of the troop movements, all at 10 percent of the cost of the two State Department helos.

Nine months after the first SOG deployment, we finally filled the mission's crucial gap in air support.

Adding the aircraft also meant we added to our team. The mess tent grew to accommodate the pilots and mechanics who now lived on the base so they could always be available for the mission. Among them: John Gianasi, a perennial handyman who'd flown for a private US company chartered to drop water and firefighters when blazes threatened the forests; and B. J. Patterson, an accomplished American bush pilot who spoke Swahili from having lived in Tanzania, and was a rare breed of pilot and mechanic, able to perform his own maintenance and repairs in the field.

When the Bell arrived, Laren and I dedicated ourselves to helping plan the operation into Kafia Kingi, the disputed area between Sudan and South Sudan, in search of the suspected LRA camp. But even with the mission's new airlift capabilities, the logistics were next to impossible. With no changes in the Special Forces helicopter assets or permissions, we were short on air support for the operation by at least half. And although more human intelligence was trickling in that confirmed Kony had taken refuge in Kafia Kingi, the Ugandan military had only a vague idea of his location, and, other than the presence of simsim for sale at market, there was no hard evidence that what the informants said was true. By the end of April, they had to concede that the operation was a no-go, for now.

BIG FISH

LESS THAN A week later, early on a Saturday morning, my ringing phone jarred me out of sleep. The first thing I saw when I opened my eyes was the pink carnation Connor had given me the day before at his school's Mother's Day concert. He'd been so proud to hand me my flower, to line up in his colorful polo shirt and sing the special songs his class had learned to honor all of the moms. I didn't usually get sentimental about the big orchestrated displays of appreciation, the Hallmark moments. I preferred the spontaneous ones, the authentic expressions of love my little ones would give that made me want to freeze us right there in time where nothing else mattered. But I'd been gone so much that spring that I got caught up in the sweetness of the ritual, almost forgetting to record him singing.

When I picked up the phone, I could barely make out what Laren was saying. He was whispering, the connection faint.

"You've got to speak up," I said.

"Come now."

"Why? What's going on?"

"I can't talk. You need to be here. Fast."

There was only one reason I could think of that would require this kind of urgency. I felt my heart quicken. "You got him?" There was only one *him* I could mean. "You really got him?"

"Just come," Laren said. "I've got to go."

Earlier that day Laren had been resting in a hammock at the base in Djemah, trying to nap through the hottest part of the day, when the radio started blowing up. "Contact, contact, contact!" the messages burst in. "We need helicopter support immediately!"

Lieutenant Colonel Jackson, the tall, wiry Ugandan commander Bridgeway worked most closely with in Djemah, ran up. He had a gravelly voice and could pivot on a dime from a steely stare to a huge smile, from delivering a thundering reprimand to celebrating a triumph with a joyful side hug. He liked to seal every discussion by going for a walk, finishing the dialogue with a low five that transformed into a handclasp, holding your hand warmly between both of his. Now, he was yelling. "Get in the helo! They've got a *samaki-makuvwa*." A big fish.

"Who is it?" Laren asked, rushing after Lieutenant Colonel Jackson to where our pilot, John, was already powering up the helo. "Is it Ongwen?"

Lieutenant Colonel Jackson shook his head.

"Kony?"

"It's a big fish, that's all we know," Lieutenant Colonel Jackson said as the chopper lifted off.

Tracking any LRA group was important for the release of the women and children who'd been taken hostage and for gathering intelligence, but to capture a high-value target could turn the tide of the entire mission. The LRA systematically protected their most crucial members. If a top commander's group was being pursued, the leader would splinter away from the main element, lying low while the rest of the group fled and led their pursuers away from the big fish. Getting the abductees home was a crucial part of our mission, but no matter how many hostages or combatants were freed, the LRA could regenerate itself again and again as long as the hard-core elements remained in the bush, able to abduct new hostages.

But their strategy had one flaw: the LRA only put Acholi Ugandans in the highest echelons of the organization. Because the LRA was no longer operating in Uganda, they weren't able to recruit or kidnap new Acholis into their ranks, so they had a finite number of top leaders. If the commanders in the field could be reduced even by one, we might see a domino effect that would ultimately cause the whole organization to topple.

Of course, Kony was the highest-value target by far, and ever since the previous year's September contact with the LRA, when the Ugandan pseudo group had penetrated the camp where the LRA's top commanders were meeting, we'd put all of our attention and efforts north where we believed Kony to be hiding. But when, at the end of April 2012, the operation to find the LRA camp in South Sudan had been called off, the Ugandan military decided to reorient the mission south where at least two LRA groups had run after the September firefight, and where recent reports had shown an uptick in LRA attacks happening in northeastern Congo and movements of the LRA back and forth across the river that formed the border between Congo and the Central African Republic. Ugandan military leadership had recently decided to throw all operational efforts and assets toward tracking the LRA group or groups that kept crossing the border.

With the new helo they'd dropped a SOG squad into the area, and after tracking for just a few days the group had found an LRA trail. They'd flown another SOG squad in and begun using the two groups in tandem, one tracking the LRA's movements, the other trying to anticipate where the LRA was headed so they could cut them off. They repeated the tactic again and again. But after nearly two weeks, despite regular signs of the LRA's presence, there'd been no actual sightings or contact. The air hours and fuel we were spending on the Congo/Central African Republic border weren't getting the mission anywhere. With no concrete evidence to support the hunch that an important LRA leader was in the area, we all worried that it had been a mistake to pivot the assets away from South Sudan.

Now the helo flew due south over endless jungle, nothing visible below except the thick green canopy.

"We can see you right above," the ground soldiers finally radioed up. "You're ninety degrees, turn right, roll out."

But they were completely obscured from the air by the triple-canopy jungle. And there was no place to land the helo. John made a few small loops, looking for a way in.

"I see a little hole," he finally said. "I'm going to try to set the bird down right there."

The helo descended into the jungle, vertically falling through trees. The dense green of the jungle surrounded them, reaching within feet of the blades.

"Are you going to be able to get out of here?" Laren asked.

"I got it, don't worry about it," John grunted as they set down in the jungle. When he cut the engine the only sound was the incessant bird-song of the forest. There wasn't a soldier in sight.

Just as Laren began to fear they were in the wrong place, SOG soldiers emerged from the trees, materializing out of the green like a mirage. Laren tried to read their faces for information. They looked exhausted as they beckoned for Lieutenant Colonel Jackson and the air team to follow them back into the trees. Laren hurried after, re-training his feet to move fast over roots and tangled vines and uneven ground, waiting for his eyes to adjust to the dim. As they turned right down a small slope, Laren saw three figures sitting on the ground, two women and a young child. The women wore baggy T-shirts and long wrap skirts made from bright African fabric, their heads bound in scarves. The ground was littered in the brass of spent cartridges. There'd been a firefight, but all was quiet now, the women's faces calm and steady. Even the young child was silent, her eyes the only active part of her body as she observed Laren with a reserved attention. Bundles of their belongings wrapped in large pieces of fabric lay tucked at the base of nearby trees.

As sedate as the scene appeared, Laren was witnessing a profound and pivotal moment: when captivity and life on the run turned to freedom. Despite the relief, it was a fraught time, full of uncertainty. As horrific as the months and years in the bush had been, the captives had learned to adapt. For the young child, it was the only life she'd ever known. Now the ordeal was finally over. But no one knew what awaited them. Kony had barraged them with false information, warned them that even if they managed to escape the LRA alive, the Ugandan military would murder them if they tried to leave the bush. And if they somehow survived and managed to find their way home, they would never be accepted back into their families and communities, he told them, if their villages still existed at all. Likely, he said, everyone they'd known and loved was already dead. The relentless propaganda had imprisoned the hostages as inescapably as the armed men standing guard around the camp each night. Now they had miraculously survived captivity and were free at last. The Ugandan military would help them return home. But it was hard for them to trust that they were really safe after having been on the run for so long. And in one respect Kony's lies were accurate: there was no old life to return to, not after what they had been through. To survive freedom they would have to find a way to make up for the lost years and education and opportunities; to grieve, to live with scars. Laren was struck again by how calm the women and child were as they met their freedom.

But where—and who—was the high-value target? Just then Laren saw him: tall, thin, sitting on the ground in the shadows, long arms loosely draped around his knees. He was dressed in a Sudanese army uniform, a red beret angled over his close-cropped graying hair, a regal tilt to his head. Laren recognized him at once from a photo of the failed Juba peace talks six years earlier, when the commander's still-black hair had been in dreads. He had aged considerably since then, but Laren identified him instantly: Major General Caesar Acellam, one of Kony's right hands, and the head of the LRA's intelligence apparatus.

"*Itye nining?*" Laren said in Acholi. Hello, how are you?

"*A tye ma ber,*" Major General Acellam replied. I'm good.

Acellam would later recount that he'd voluntarily joined the LRA as a young man—one of the few remaining commanders who had joined by choice, not through forced abduction—and had risen in rank, eventually stationed in Khartoum to maintain the relationship between the Sudan Armed Forces and the LRA. Over the years he had negotiated trainings of LRA soldiers by the Sudanese military, brokered Sudanese military contributions of weapons and ammunition to the LRA, and led a deadly attack against civilians in Djemah in 2009. He wasn't an International Criminal Court indictee, but he could and should have been. And now he'd been apprehended. He'd been rendered powerless. And he was alive, an intelligence gold mine.

Lieutenant Colonel Jackson congratulated his men, and then led an abbreviated debrief right there in the bush before flying Acellam and the others back to the base in Djemah. An on-site debrief was important because the people coming out of the LRA were often terrified, and the Ugandan military wanted to allay their fears while also gathering information during the hours when the old life and the fear of escape were still fresh. Later, when they knew they were safe, a sense of guilt or shame often made defectors more reticent to expose details about the LRA. This vulnerable time of transition between the old life and the new was a moment of truth before distance might alter what someone was willing or able to say.

Lieutenant Colonel Jackson began asking Major General Acellam basic information: Which group were you traveling with? Who was there with you? Acellam gave succinct, measured answers. Then, to everyone's surprise, he began volunteering information, such as the locations of Ongwen and Odhiambo and other top LRA commanders. His responses helped arrange the fragments and speculations about the LRA into a clearer, more cohesive picture.

Caught up in the heat of Acellam's confidences, Lieutenant Colonel Jackson asked the most important question. "Where is Joseph Kony?"

"I haven't seen Joseph Kony in some years."

"But do you know where he is now?"

Laren thought Acellam might draw a line at exposing Kony's

whereabouts, or at least hesitate before answering, but he didn't miss a beat. "Darfur."

The region where the Ugandan military informants had seen sim-sim seed for sale.

"Ask him if Sudan is still involved in supplying the LRA," Laren said to the translator.

But before the translator could pose the question to Acellam in Acholi, Acellam answered in English. "They supply medicine," he said. "Ammunition." He pointed to his dirty fatigues. "Uniforms." Then he revealed the name of his point of contact within the Sudanese intelligence, a low-level major at the nearby Sudanese Armed Forces base who traded with the LRA.

Acellam had been surrounded and then surrendered. He wasn't initially a willing defector, and this threw Lieutenant Colonel Jackson off. "Is there a reason you are being so forthcoming?" he asked.

"I believe I have fallen from Kony's favor," the general explained. "I am afraid if I stay with the LRA he might kill me." He said he would cooperate with the mission fully in helping more soldiers and captives out of the bush.

"Major General, are there many within the LRA who want to come out?" Laren asked.

"Oh yes."

"How many? What percentage?"

"I would say . . ." The general tipped his head from side to side as though balancing a scale. "Seventy-five to eighty percent."

"Want to come home?"

"Want to come home."

"They're tired?"

He nodded solemnly. "They're very, very tired."

When Acellam stood to board the helo, he leaned on a carved wooden staff. "My knees," he explained, wincing slightly as he stepped out into the tiny clearing.

On the helo, Acellam and the child, his young daughter, were very quiet, but the two women, Acellam's forced brides, pointed at the ground excitedly, especially when they had passed over the jungle and were flying above little villages and narrow roads. Laren wondered what it was like for them to have a bird's-eye view of the world, to be up in the open sky after all those years in the tangle of jungle. Through the translator, they asked Laren to name the places they passed over, to tell where each of the roads led.

40
―――――

PEANUT BUTTER AND
JELLY SANDWICH

BACK AT THE base, word had spread that a high-value target was coming in from the bush, and when the helo landed in Djemah it seemed as if every single one of the two hundred Ugandan soldiers stationed there—from cooks to mechanics to gunfighters—was waiting on the airfield, eager to see the infamous LRA commander they'd heard so much about. It was eerily quiet as Acellam and his family came down from the helo. Not a single person spoke as the LRA general walked the five hundred feet to the command tent. No one outside the mission was to know of his presence in Djemah. The secrecy was to protect any operations that might follow from his intelligence—but also for Acellam's safety. He'd been part of a brutal attack on Djemah a few years ago and it was possible survivors might seek retribution.

Despite his high-level status as one of the top five LRA commanders, and the fact that he had been an early volunteer recruit in the organization, not an abducted victim-perpetrator, Acellam had not been indicted by the International Criminal Court. He had not only committed atrocities, but he was one of the masterminds of the violence, and had negotiated the relationship with Sudan that enabled the LRA to source weapons and training from Khartoum. And yet, for some reason, he was never indicted alongside Kony and the other top commanders. And Uganda's ability to prosecute Acellam was complicated by competing domestic laws, including an Amnesty Act that allowed any nonindictees to receive legal amnesty, never facing prosecution for any crime they might have committed during their time with the LRA. Laren warned me that the Amnesty Act would likely apply. Acellam wouldn't be sent to The Hague, or any domestic court. He wouldn't face prosecution for his many brutal crimes. It didn't feel right or just. But it wasn't the first time in this conflict that a serial murderer had gone free. The same thing happened when Sam Kolo, Kony's former spokesperson, came out. And Kenneth Banya, the main military and technical brain behind the rebellion, had also received amnesty. The list goes on and on.

I'd ask Acholi men in the Ugandan army who had been personally affected by LRA violence, whose losses had motivated them to join the army, "Doesn't it upset you that the Amnesty Act applies to someone like Acellam? After they've committed so many crimes, after they've killed your loved ones, why welcome them back?" The answer was always some version of this: "We must choose peace. It is the only way to walk forward without war."

Acellam would stay in Djemah for further questioning and then return to Uganda where, at age forty-nine, he would begin his life again. The women and child would be repatriated right away, as soon as their families could be traced. This might be a lengthier process for the younger woman, who was only fifteen and from Cameroon, abducted while she was visiting relatives in the Central African Republic. She spoke fluent Acholi, testament to the five years she had spent in captivity.

For the next few hours the only agenda was to reassure and welcome Acellam and his family and help them relax. Colonel Joseph, the head of the counter-LRA mission, flew to Djemah to oversee Acellam's formal debriefing. While he went into the operations tent to send the news of Acellam's surrender up the chain of command, Acellam and his wives were served cups of tea, and basins of hot water were brought so they could bathe. They were each given a defector kit, a bundle of supplies that anyone leaving the LRA would need right away: a mattress, blankets, toiletries, civilian clothes. A meal was served: rice, beans, cabbage, a freshly slaughtered chicken.

"Is there anything else you need?" Laren asked each in turn.

Acellam sat quietly in front of his tent in his new checked button-up shirt and dark jeans and shook his head. The young woman from Cameroon asked if she could have a haircut and a soldier brought out a pair of clippers and gave her a short buzz cut. When she saw her new hairstyle in the mirror she grinned. The woman from Uganda had put her child down for a nap in their tent and now sat in a camp chair awaiting word that she could talk to her family. She spoke a little English that she'd learned in school in Uganda, but seemed hesitant to say much.

Late in the afternoon, Acellam asked if he could take a walk to work out the kink in his sore knee. He stood slowly and stepped a loose, wide circle around the ops tent, his expression reserved and meditative, leaning on his cane like a village elder making his rounds. Laren joined him for part of the stroll, chatting about different towns they both knew in Uganda, discussing the news from Acellam's native country, where he hadn't been in some years.

After their walk, Laren went to gather more supplies for the visitors' tents and in his hurry he tripped, nearly falling with his armload.

"Mot, mot ocero munu opoto," Laren said in Acholi. Slowly, slowly and the white man will fall. He was making a joke, his one Acholi party trick, reciting an old anticolonial Acholi saying that essentially meant, *Slowly, slowly we'll build ourselves up and overthrow the white man's yoke.* But when Laren, a white man, said the phrase in Acholi, at his own expense, it was too much for Acellam, who broke into an enormous smile and laughed out loud.

Late that afternoon, Laren broke away from the welcome party and snuck into the "hellhole" of the helo, the crawl space where the blades go down into the transmission, and dialed me on the sat phone.

After just one night in Djemah, Acellam was moved to Nzara, and a few days later I sat at a table in an open tent with Howard Buffett, waiting to meet Major General Acellam and his family. It was the most important surrender to date and I wanted to celebrate with the troops and help strategize a flyer drop we planned to do to encourage and help Kony's soldiers to leave the bush. Major General Acellam was so respected and famous in the LRA. Based on what he'd said about the number of LRA soldiers eager to leave, it seemed possible that a flyer with his picture, showing him safe and relaxed and free, could go a long way in reassuring and inspiring combatants to come out of the LRA.

Howard had agreed to join me to help congratulate the SOG troops, and he also accompanied me to the meeting with Acellam. I wondered what it would feel like to be in the presence of someone who was responsible for killing so many and in such horrific ways.

When Acellam and his forced wife and their child arrived and sat across from us in green plastic lawn chairs under the open-sided tent, it wasn't the general's violent history that hit me. He was reserved and distant, as though watching the proceedings from a third-person perspective, but he seemed at peace.

Perhaps the strangest thing about him was that he existed at all. His name had been so pervasive in the reports on the LRA's atrocities and so long at the top of our list of targets, his whereabouts so elusive, that he had begun to seem more like a spirit than a man. When he was finally sitting in front of me, it was as though I was meeting a ghost. To look into his long narrow face and intense eyes and hear him talk—about how hard it was to live off of wild yams and be out in the rain running all of the time, about how rested he felt now that he was free after twenty-four years in the bush—it was almost too much to take in. At one point someone asked him if he was sorry for what he'd done. His face grew introspective and he tapped the tips of his long fingers together as he reflected. When he spoke at last he wasn't defensive or regretful, just matter of fact.

"I was a young man when I was recruited into the rebellion," he said. "I was trained from a young age in the methods of war. And I learned that in the art of war, the word *sorry* does not much exist."

As the interview with Acellam continued, I made eye contact with the mother of his child. She couldn't have been more than nineteen or twenty, her cheeks still girlishly smooth and round. Acellam was sweet and deferential to her; I had to remind myself what was real, that she'd been abducted and raped, that her captor and abuser was also the father of her child. Now that she was finally free, she faced the hard road of healing from her trauma, and the stigma of returning home a single mom. Her beautiful daughter, in a bright blue-and-yellow-flowered dress and matching flip-flops, a black-and-yellow scarf tied around her head, was just a little younger than Brody. She sat contentedly in her mother's lap, smiling at me and chewing on the stick of a Tootsie Pop that Howard had given her. Trying to close a gap between us, I took out my phone to show Acellam's forced wife and her daughter pictures of my sons. For a moment the chasm between our worlds and experiences disappeared. The Ugandan mother shot me a radiant smile, a bridge between mothers.

Meanwhile, Howard had opened his backpack and, to my surprise and confusion, pulled out a small, white plastic Wonder Bread container shaped like a sandwich, and then a jar of Jif peanut butter and a jar of grape jelly. I stared at him. Was this really the time for a picnic?

"It's a peace offering," he explained. To Acellam, he said that in America we have a favorite food. He took out the two slices of bread, opened the peanut butter and jelly jars, and started spreading them on the bread. He closed the sandwich and handed it to Acellam. It was an absurd moment. And precarious. I didn't know what to make of Howard's gesture, and I couldn't anticipate how it would be received. I gave Colonel Joseph a nervous glance.

The silence stretched as Acellam looked at Howard, perhaps unsure what to do with the sandwich, or afraid that Howard was poisoning him. Howard seemed to understand Acellam's hesitation. He carefully cut the sandwich in half, leaving one half on the table for

Acellam, and taking a big bite out of his own half. Acellam hesitantly accepted the other half of the sandwich. When he tasted it, he smiled.

Howard captured Acellam's smile—his white teeth and shining eyes—in a photograph that we included on some of the flyers we promptly printed to drop over areas of suspected LRA activity. The flyers also included his personal message:

> I, Major General Acellam, have come out of the LRA, and am sending a message to my brothers in the bush. Put down your guns and stop fighting. Kony has been deceiving us all, we have nothing to fear. I am here living free, and the Ugandan army did not harm me when we met. If you come out of the bush, you will be free like me. Do not fear, the Ugandan army are our brothers and they want us to come back home. If you come out you will be granted amnesty. Let us make the war come to an end.

Twenty-six captives would leave the LRA in the next sixty days.

ROADIE

David Ocitti

THE VAN PARKED in the lot near the campus auditorium in a college town on the Upper Peninsula of Michigan, and David stepped out into the cold air. Before arriving in the Midwest for his first roadie tour, David had never seen snow. He'd been disoriented by the endless white covering the ground. Now deep mounds of snow were piled high against the edges of the parking lot.

In the coming months he would do three tours as a roadie, each in a different region of the country, eventually visiting a total of thirty states. As he moved around the country he would search for latwok in the night sky, and contemplate how far he was from home. The cultural training he'd received before his arrival in the US had prepared him for differences, but he'd been overwhelmed when he landed in San Diego for his initial orientation before deployment by the high energy of the real-life "crazy mzungus" who held up a sign and shouted his name, welcoming him, a stranger, as though he was a long-lost friend. He didn't think he would ever adapt to the winter cold or the taste of the fast food they subsisted on during tour, but he had grown used to living on the road, sleeping each night on a different couch in a different college town; to the comedy of meeting Americans who spoke to him extremely slowly as though he wasn't fluent in English. He had even grown comfortable sharing his story of abduction, escape, and reintegration.

He and the other roadies visited campus after campus to share stories about the LRA conflict, talk to students, and find ways to plug them into activism. For some students, that meant signing up for lobby days to pressure legislators to take more decisive action in ending the conflict, for others, pledging thirty-five dollars a month, which would cover one half of one person's school fees in Uganda. Tonight, David would recruit students to speak up without speaking— to stand in silence for twenty-five hours in solidarity with brothers and sisters who had suffered in the LRA war for twenty-five years. It never ceased to thrill him when young people stood up to make a difference. It was empowering to direct the pain of the past toward compassion and peace for the future, to tell his audiences, "Together, we can end the war."

Once, David had felt completely alone in his suffering. It was still a shock sometimes to realize that he was being heard, that he was helping to lead change—first in northern Uganda with the Peace Clubs, and now across the world. When he first visited the Invisible Children headquarters in San Diego, a young American man with blond hair and blue eyes had made a point of stopping in to meet him. It was Adam Finck, Invisible Children's regional program director for Central Africa. Adam had lived in northern Uganda for two years and now spent about half of each year at home in San Diego, and the other half in Congo, the Central African Republic, and Uganda.

"I'm thrilled to finally meet you," Adam had told David. "Let's definitely catch up and grab a drink when we're both back in Gulu."

Tonight, inside the auditorium, there was time for a quick microphone check and a slice of greasy pizza in the graffiti-covered backstage room before David and his fellow roadies, all in black Invisible Children T-shirts, walked out into the stage lights to begin their presentation.

"No one walks the path of life alone," David opened. "And that is why we are here today. We cannot make it alone without you joining us. We can never serve any soul unless we stand together."

TRACKING WHITE ANT

WE LOST SAM'S mom in July 2012. She'd endured aggressive chemo treatment; Sam was able to be there with her through much of her illness. And then she was put on hospice. We explained to the boys that she was dying, that cancer was taking her away too soon, that it wasn't her wish. We sat with them while they said goodbye.

Grief swallowed Sam. It was a terrible time.

"How does someone get sick?" Brody asked me once. "Will you get sick, too?"

"These are such good questions," I said. "But there aren't good answers. We just don't know."

Before I knew it, the summer had almost passed. August brought encouraging news from the field. A team from the first SOG deployment, led by Lieutenant Pauson, tracked an LRA group to their deep jungle hideout north of Dembia, Central African Republic. It was the group led by Dominic Ongwen, aka White Ant, that we'd been playing cat and mouse with for a year. Lieutenant Pauson sent a small reconnaissance team to watch the forest for signs of movement and to try to locate the LRA observation posts. When the recon team heard LRA members climbing trees in search of food, Lieutenant Pauson sent flanking squads around the camp and launched an assault. But this time, speed—not the LRA's, but the SOG's—worked against them. Impatient for results, the main assault force made contact with the encampment before the flanking squads were in position, and the LRA forces were able to escape. But the SOG troops recovered artillery, ammunition, and a notebook full of intelligence.

A few days later, Lieutenant Charles's assault team intercepted the remnants of Ongwen's group and attacked their temporary base. The LRA group scattered, but the SOG team recovered more guns and ammunition, a radio, and a captive LRA fighter who said that Ongwen had splintered from the group and was now hiding with only three women and four AK-47 rifles. It seemed just a matter of time before there would be another top commander out of the bush.

We got another boost when Colonel Michael Kabango was appointed the Ugandan military's new overall counter-LRA commander.

"I think I know what we need to do differently," Colonel Kabango told Laren one night as they sat in camp chairs.

Colonel Kabango had only been in the field a short time, but he was already bringing new vitality and strategies to the mission. He had an immediately commanding presence. His eyes were always narrowed in alert concentration, his back and broad shoulders held perfectly erect. Something in his posture and quality of attention said, "I'm the boss." At the same time, he was playful and gregarious. He often spoke with his hands, gesticulating wildly as he recounted a story or articulated a new idea. He would regale everyone with songs and stories late into the night, and he walked around camp with his headphones on, whistling and dancing along to the music.

The youngest of five children, he'd grown up in Kisoro, in western Uganda, the self-proclaimed wild child of his siblings, always in motion, often up to mischief. As a boy he'd been lucky enough to go to school and even owned a pair of shoes, but he was so embarrassed to wear shoes when others had none that he always took them off on the way to school, arriving barefoot like everyone else. He had deeply disappointed his strict father, a police officer, when he had joined Museveni's rebellion right out of school instead of pursuing a career as a doctor or lawyer or teacher as his father had wished.

Despite his family's misgivings, he had shone in the military, fighting in the original bush war that helped Museveni take over Uganda. He had been working to fight the LRA ever since, rising in rank and distinguishing himself through his leadership and commitment. He'd been tapped for command of the counter-LRA mission because he was practical above all else and had a proven ability to bring results. From day one of his command he'd been serious and systematic about getting the work done. He'd spent two weeks flying around to each and every outstation, getting to know the soldiers and seeing what they faced when they were out in the jungle.

"I see an opportunity for the squads to be more effective," Colonel Kabango told Laren that night.

By now, Laren had long since left Invisible Children to become the Bridgeway Foundation's operations officer. At first, he'd been a novice in military operations. But over the year and a half since the first training, he had proven himself capable of offering helpful insights, enough so for Colonel Kabango to respect his feedback. The two talked every day about counter-LRA strategy.

"The tracking teams hole up in the jungle and rest," Colonel Kabango continued. "They're being left in the bush too long without a break and I'm concerned that the mission's not going to get anywhere with morale this low."

The Special Operations Group—still led by Captain Kommando—had been at it for more than a year by then, and although Major General Acellam's surrender had been a huge win that buoyed the men's spirits and inspired them to keep pushing for Kony's capture, they were also exhausted.

"Most of these guys haven't been home in a year," Laren agreed. "They're out of reserves."

In the next few days, Colonel Kabango set up a rest and recreation (R & R) schedule to rotate soldiers in and out of the field—no one was to be in the bush for more than fourteen straight days—and secured an extra food allowance. Vegetables would be flown in once a month, and meat would be served at least once every two weeks. He also supplied the soldiers with new boots and got a generator for the med bay. Some leaders would have pushed the men harder, telling them that the sacrifice was its own reward, that to do something meaningful had a price. But Colonel Kabango saw that the soldiers' rest and comfort was a matter of military strategy. If they could constantly move fresh energy into the field, there was automatically a huge advantage over the LRA. As Major General Acellam had told us, the majority of LRA soldiers were exhausted and wanted to come home. Other defectors coming out of the Vovodo and Chinko river basins confirmed that the LRA was beginning to feel the pressure of the Ugandan military operations. And they were becoming disillusioned by the promises Kony had been making that he would come down from Kafia Kingi to lead them. A year after the promise, Kony still hadn't appeared.

The mission's presence alone seemed to be pushing the whole rebellion closer to collapse, and Colonel Kabango had the vision to capitalize on the LRA's vulnerability. He brought in a new intelligence officer and began stocking fuel. Acellam's surrender and the surge in defections were bringing us closer to a more exact understanding of Kony's whereabouts, and he wanted to be ready to airlift soldiers and supplies as soon as they had the intel needed to act.

With the LRA groups splintered and most on the run, it seemed an ideal time to push for more defections. Defection messaging had been successfully used all over the world to end armed conflict by encouraging perpetrators of violence to put down their weapons and come home. The UN base in Dungu, Congo, had been using aircraft to do flyer drops since at least 2010. But the UN campaign had had limitations. A long approvals process meant that it took at least one month, sometimes three, before a flyer could be green-lit and printed. Adam Finck, our friend and Invisible Children partner, and his team, had begun collaborating with the UN to make defection flyers because, without the bureaucratic red tape, Invisible Children could design, approve, print, and deliver as many as fifty thousand flyers in just three days.

In addition to providing faster turnaround, Adam and his team of Acholi and regional staff had been able to improve on the content of the flyers, collaborating with LRA defectors already home in Uganda to fine-tune the language and messaging. For example, some of the early flyers had shown drawings of defectors with their arms raised in surrender. In Acholi culture—and in particular for anyone in the LRA—this posture was seen as an act of weakness and submission. Effective defection messaging wasn't about commanding LRA members to submit to surrender. It was about empowering LRA combatants to make the choice to rejoin their families and reclaim their freedom.

The flyers now used more culturally appropriate language, and an inclusive perspective that we hoped would resonate with LRA members. The text began, *My brothers and my sisters, come home.* The photos and illustrations of the defection process, from escape to homecoming—important because many LRA members couldn't read—didn't picture defectors raising their arms above their heads, but showed them being welcomed by Ugandan soldiers and embraced by their families. It was also important to include pictures of recent defectors wearing different outfits and in a variety of situations—at home, work, social events—in order to show the passage of time and the depth of their reintegration, to help convince those still in the bush that the defector hadn't been killed after taking a single picture and that he was indeed happy and being taken care of. Sometimes a flyer would include photos of defectors drinking Coca-Colas. Since Coke was a luxury not afforded to those in the bush and a status symbol of sorts, the photos showed that defectors were not living in abject poverty but enjoying some of the pleasures in life.

Back in January, with defection efforts already seeing positive results, a US Army psychological operations (PSYOPS) team had deployed to Central Africa as part of the US counter-LRA intervention to bolster defections further. PSYOPS is a unique division of the Department of

Defense that uses nonviolent means—usually print and broadcast media—to further American objectives in conflict zones. They helped on a number of fronts, including radio messaging and flyer drops.

We brought access to defectors, strong relations with the Ugandan military, as well as unparalleled flexibility and rapid response; they brought technology, intelligence, and knowledge of how psychological defection operations had worked in other contexts.

We were grateful for the progress and success of the paper defection campaign, but we wondered if there was an even better strategy to invite the LRA soldiers home. During the Vietnam War and in other global conflicts, the US military had mounted massive loudspeakers on tactical helicopters to broadcast messages over remote areas. What if the mission could acquire tactical mounted speakers and fly a chopper around areas of known LRA activity, blaring loudspeaker messages in Acholi, telling the LRA soldiers where to surrender, and assuring them that they would not be harmed or prosecuted? The US military had access to speakers, but they didn't have the right choppers on which to mount them. The current—now the third—Special Forces commander in Entebbe helped us get the loudspeaker platform up and running on our Bell 412.

The speakers were massive and had huge batteries—each one was like a rock concert sound system squeezed into a space the size of a dorm fridge. We asked recent LRA defectors and Acholi speakers in the SOG to record short come-home messages—saying, this is so-and-so, I'm free, if you surrender you won't be harmed or prosecuted—and we played them through the speakers using the A/V jack on our iPhones. Through trial and error we discovered how long the message had to be and at what speed the helo had to fly for the entire message to be audible to someone on the ground. The messages could be heard from as far as four miles away; we could cover more than two hundred square miles in an hour of flying.

Despite our steep learning curve, the day after the first official loudspeaker mission a fifteen-year-old girl surrendered. Shortly after, the current Special Forces commander emailed me: *The other day we*

had an LRA member defect after he heard the speakers broadcast. As he was
walking out, he found a leaflet we had dropped with Acellam's picture on it
and came out of the bush waving it at a farmer to show he meant no harm.
Pretty great indicator of effectiveness, no?

And then one day in mid-October, our pilot flew the Bell 412 for
forty-five minutes over the area just south of the confluence of the
Vovodo and Chinko rivers, playing loudspeaker messages, and just
three days later two LRA sergeants—Sergeant Kidega and Sergeant
Shantel—surrendered late in the evening at Dembia. They had been in
Ongwen's group but had been separated from the rest of the LRA unit
during the August firefight with Lieutenant Charles's squad. They had
heard the loudspeaker messages and come out of the bush. In their
debriefing, they alerted us to a rendezvous of Ongwen's group set to
occur in a matter of days at the west side of the Vovodo.

Kidega's and Shantel's surrenders gave us immediate proof of concept of the loudspeaker messaging, and also confirmed the success of
our air assets in allowing the Ugandan military to act on intelligence
within hours instead of days. The aircraft played loudspeaker come-
home messages on October 15; flew Sergeants Kidega and Shantel to
Djemah for debriefing the same night they defected; inserted Kidega
with a SOG squad on October 19 to lead the way to the planned meeting point on October 29; and moved three SOG teams near the rendezvous site to ambush the meeting. A year ago, the mission had
lacked this agile capability.

The defections just kept coming. A week before the suspected October
rendezvous, another LRA soldier, Lieutenant Francis Chogme, reported to the base in Obo late in the evening and said he was ready to
go home. Like Sergeants Kidega and Shantel, he had been part of
Ongwen's group, had become separated during the firefight, and had
heard the loudspeaker messaging. When he was flown to Djemah for
debriefing he said that a meeting between Ongwen, Odhiambo, and
Kony had been scheduled for late December or early January. We kept

his surrender a secret to prevent the LRA from altering its intended meeting location, and Colonel Kabango began preparing the equipment, tactics, and personnel needed for the ambush. He wanted to be ready to move by the end of November in case the meeting was pushed earlier.

In the meantime, the assault teams moved in on the different LRA groups traveling to the October 29 rendezvous. In multiple contacts over the course of six days, the SOG teams recovered more weapons and ammunition and captured several LRA combatants. One early morning a call came into the base in Djemah—a tracking team had picked up an LRA trail crossing a river in the Central African Republic. They estimated that the LRA was about seven hours ahead. If the base could airlift troops into position, they might be able to make contact sooner. The helo lifted off into the day's first light, the air fresh, green and mist swirling below.

"Pack light," Captain Kommando, who was leading the ground team, radioed in. "You're going straight in on the target, you'll get on it and have to keep running."

He was there to greet the troops when the helo door slid open to let the soldiers out, and he flashed a peace sign as the bird lifted off.

By afternoon he radioed in again: "Contact, contact!" The helo headed back out into the bush and John found a place to land just west of the SOG troops' position. He was in the helo on the makeshift landing zone when a SOG lieutenant came out of the trees, carrying a small child in each arm. Three mothers followed him out of the bush, more little ones in their arms. The families had been trying to flee the LRA and were stuck near a river looking for a safe crossing. The SOG soldiers had helped them cross and led them out of the jungle into the grassy clearing where the helo waited to fly them home.

The youngest child, still a baby, sucked his thumb and gazed out at the big world from the safety of his mother's arms. The next oldest child, a toddler, was dressed in fatigues, an outfit his mother had fashioned out of a man's full-size camouflage uniform. He rode in the arms of a soldier who, rifle slung over his shoulder, ammo vest bulging from his chest, proudly cradled him. At the head of the group, two soldiers held the hands of a young boy who walked cautiously between them—a boy who only the day before was on a steady track to becoming a soldier within Kony's ranks. He held tightly to the soldiers' hands and eyed the helo with a mix of apprehension and wonder as he made his final steps to freedom.

OKELLO'S TEETH

EACH NEW DEFECTOR strengthened our understanding of the LRA's movements and operations. We learned that in late September, Kony had sent Okello*—one of his bodyguards and an aide-de-camp—and a group of eight fighters down to Congo to collect Lieutenant Colonel Binany, the LRA leader who had led the Makombo massacres, from Garamba National Park, a protected wildlife preserve in Congo, and bring him back to Kony's camp in Kafia Kingi (K2). Binany was in charge of the entire Congo sector and was one of the most fearsome and respected of Kony's commanders because of his battlefield prowess. In addition to supplying ivory and other goods that could be traded for medicine and GPS equipment, Binany's Congo operation—so close to the border with Uganda—was important to Kony because it validated his propaganda that the LRA's purpose was still to overthrow Museveni and return home. From our perspective, Binany was important because he led the assaults in by far the deadliest region of LRA operation.

On the way down to Garamba to get Binany, Okello's group had attacked Pasi, a village in Congo, where they had looted medical supplies, food, and an HF radio from the Early Warning Network, attacked a Congolese military base, and abducted civilians. At the beginning of November, a SOG squad laid an ambush for the LRA group on the Ouora River, trying to catch them as they headed back through the Central African Republic toward the K2 base. During contact, the SOG soldiers rescued a young boy from Congo who said that many other women and children, all recent abductees, were being marched up to Joseph Kony, forced to carry the food and ivory Binany had poached in Garamba. In the next few weeks, the SOG troops made four more contacts with Binany's group as they pushed their way on toward K2, and at least five more LRA combatants and captives defected.

Meanwhile, several Darfuri traders on their way from K2 to Obo and Mboki, moving near the South Sudan/Central African Republic border, agreed to come to Djemah for questioning. They didn't know where Kony's camp was situated, but they shared the locations of trade routes into K2 and said any of the traders traveling these routes might have information that would help finally find the central LRA camp.

Then, near Christmas, we got the luckiest break we'd had to date. In Mboki, a small town on the border between the Central African Republic and Congo, a short, quiet man in dirty fatigues stepped out of the forest and approached several residents walking on the main road to town. He was missing most of his top two front teeth—they were half shot off, nothing left but jagged stumps. He told them he had escaped from the LRA and asked if they could show him the way to a nearby Ugandan military base where he could surrender.

When he was received by the Acholi unit captain stationed near Mboki, they discovered that the defector was Okello, Kony's personal bodyguard and confidant. One of Kony's most trusted colleagues, Okello had been routinely assigned some of the LRA's most sensitive missions, including the recent one down to Garamba National Park to bring poached ivory back to Kony's K2 camp. As a tactic to prevent the spread of HIV/AIDS, Kony demanded the continual capture of virgin women to become his sex slaves, and Okello was tasked with escorting a group of captured women all the way up to K2 in addition to transporting the numerous tusks. Okello was one of the people Kony counted on to oversee the safe transit of the women and ivory.

But, under attack from Ugandan troops, one of the LRA commanders assisting with the convoy had been shot, and Okello and some of Kony's other bodyguards had split off from the group, taking the women. During the journey back to K2, Okello and the others raped some of the captive women. When they returned to the K2 camp, Kony discovered that the women delivered to him weren't all virgins, and he executed at least one of the other bodyguards. Okello learned that Kony planned to execute him, as well. He decided to escape, and fled the K2 camp late one night.

Perhaps to better hide from anyone who might pursue him, Okello opted to follow the natural topography of rivers until he found a safe place to defect. Trails used by local cattle herders also followed the water, and a few days into his flight south, he came upon a group of herders on the trail. Although some herders cooperated with the LRA, engaging in trade or helping transport supplies, many held a grudge against the LRA for stealing their cattle. Okello didn't know where the loyalties of these herders lay, and whether his status as an escapee would make him a friend or a foe. At first, they offered to protect him, and allowed him to travel in their company. But one day, they turned on him, threatening to kill him because he was LRA. He managed to flee, and kept running south. He passed Djemah, where Laren was stationed, but didn't surrender until he had traveled all the way down to Mboki. When he surrendered, he had been on the run for three weeks.

The Ugandan army transported him back up to the forward base in Djemah for debriefing. A defector of his status could have been a useful tool in encouraging other defections, but because of Okello's intimate knowledge of Kony's camp in K2, and because it was better for Kony to believe that Okello had died during his flight, they decided to keep his defection a secret.

Upon arriving at Djemah, he was warmly received by fellow Acholis in the Ugandan army, including ex-LRA, who gave him updates on other defectors. It amazed me that although mere weeks ago Okello had been in the upper echelon of the LRA, abducting and raping captives, protecting Kony, the Ugandan soldiers welcomed Okello now as though they were greeting an old friend. He wasn't an enemy. He was a brother. They didn't express any suspicion or judgment, they didn't condemn Okello for the atrocities he'd committed, or berate him for having waited so long to defect, only choosing to leave Kony's army when his life was on the line. Their conversation was warm and jovial. A common bond united them, and the fact that they could sit together and share stories and updates was a triumph.

It didn't hurt their rapport that Okello was so eager to help them stop Kony. Although he had no GPS to give us the exact coordinates of Kony's camp, he was able to draw a map—a generic-looking aerial view of a tree with some clumps around it to represent huts—and to tell us how many people were living there. It wasn't a lot to go on, but it did give us a visual footprint to look for in satellite images.

Okello also gave us the only recent stories we'd heard of Kony's actual state of mind. We knew well how tough life was in the bush. Everything out there was dangerous, and it had been a mystery how Kony had managed to live for years, and with apparent ease, in such an inhospitable environment. In the absence of real information about Kony, the mythological stories held sway, the stories that Kony used to indoctrinate impressionable children: that he could read people's minds, that he could run so fast that his feet didn't touch the ground, that he was a conduit for spirits that would possess him, offering prophecies and guidance. From Okello we learned the truth: Kony wasn't doing well. He was highly intelligent and charismatic—but he was not invulnerable. Recently, he had gotten lost in the jungle for a week, and when his soldiers finally rescued him, he was dirty, hungry, and sobbing. According to Okello, Kony was so terrified when he heard gunshots that he defecated in his pants. If the person closest to Kony could see his flaws and weaknesses, it meant others in Kony's fold might become aware of the cracks in Kony's armor and see the truth that lay under his façade of lies.

In addition to the generic map and the insight into the real Joseph Kony, Okello immediately became a tactical asset to the SOG soldiers, joining them as one of the most capable trackers. Perhaps he was motivated by a sense of guilt over the atrocities he had witnessed or committed. Maybe he was motivated by ten years of accumulated resentments toward Kony. Or maybe he was just ready to do right. Whatever his motivations, Okello's defection was a turning point, shifting the war in the SOG's favor.

One piece of intelligence is like a puzzle piece—useless all by itself. It's only in putting the pieces together that the whole picture is clear. Okello's defection yielded the first of three puzzle pieces that would soon line up to present the mission's next big opportunity. His intelligence propelled Colonel Kabango to put SOG troops on the border with K2, anticipating that Binany's group would come back that way to poach more ivory. If he hadn't, we would have missed our next lucky break.

In the months that followed, the SOG soldiers, 10 percent of whom were also ex-rebels of some kind, accepted Okello into the fold. In a gesture of goodwill and unity, they would later help him get to Entebbe for eight hundred dollars' worth of dental work to replace the two front teeth that had been shattered when he'd taken a bullet to the face fighting in Kony's rebel group.

Laren would send me a picture of the two of them after Okello's teeth had been replaced. Okello wears his Ugandan army fatigues, tipping the brim of his camouflage cap and flashing the widest possible smile, showing off his brand-new pearly whites. He and Laren stand side-by-side, arms looped across each other's shoulders, both smiling hugely. Except for the ammo vest on Okello's chest, the clothesline behind them where military uniforms have been hung to dry, the wall of jungle that rises behind them, they looked as though they might be college friends on a camping trip, happy and brotherly and carefree.

Okello challenged me, as Acellam had, to reconsider the borders between us. Before this mission, my notion of good and evil had been cut and dry. I couldn't forget what LRA members like Acellam and Okello had wreaked on innocents. The terrible past felt irredeemable. But the Ugandan soldiers were teaching me to see the world in shades other than right and wrong, to notice the fiber of humanity that bound all of us, on every side of the war.

For Christmas that year, Laren sent me the toddler's camouflage uniform that the child had been wearing when the SOG soldier had helped carry him out of the bush that fall. The uniform had been carefully cleaned and pressed, and Laren enclosed a short note: *This boy's life is different from what it was going to be.*

BINANY'S GPS

IN THE SEMIARID desert and grassland on the border between the Central African Republic and South Sudan, where, based on Okello's information, Colonel Kabango had put troops to wait for Binany, the SOG troops began questioning the large groups of nomadic cattle herders that crossed the border, within which LRA members would sometimes travel in disguise. As they moved around the outside edges of the huge herd, the SOG soldiers encountered some enraged nomads, upset because a few of their cows had just been stolen—by a Ugandan rebel, they said, who was still nearby, feasting on the meat.

When the SOG troops found Lieutenant Colonel Binany with his bodyguards, he was barefoot, roasting a hunk of stolen beef on a campfire. During the ensuing gunfight, Binany used flames from his cooking fire to start a blaze as diversion and protection. But then he became pinned, ultimately consumed by the brushfire he'd started, and burned alive. The man who had orchestrated the Makombo massacres, the second Christmas massacres that no one had known about for months, the ones that in part had led us to this riskier intervention, was now dead. And in his backpack, found at a distance from his body, the SOG soldiers retrieved a journal full of useful intelligence: ledgers of looted goods and ivory poached from Garamba National Park and gold and diamonds mined in the Central African Republic; charts of LRA units, including their locations and force strength; and a list of Binany's own command groups and operations. Most important of all, they found the second puzzle piece: a GPS device that provided a pivotal missing link that could lead to Kony's capture.

GPS units automatically check into the network multiple times every day. Of the thousands of GPS points on Binany's device, there was one point where Binany had stayed for several weeks. Because the LRA was constantly on the move to stay alive, it was unusual for the GPS data to show a single stagnant position for weeks. It seemed likely that this GPS position might reveal the location of the main LRA camp in K2. If we could obtain satellite imagery of that one point we might know, after years of mere speculation and general intelligence, exactly where Kony was hiding.

The new intelligence was sufficient for the US Special Forces—now led by Colonel Paul Korbel, the fourth commander to fill the post in Entebbe—to ask for permission to fly a surveillance drone over K2 and evaluate the situation from above.

Commander Korbel, a tall man with gray hair and broad shoulders, was somewhat of an anomaly in the Department of Defense: he sometimes brought his State counterpart to operations meetings. We had never seen anyone from State in the field before, and it was deeply reassuring to see Korbel taking measures to improve the continuity between the State decision makers in Washington, DC, and the Department of Defense troops deployed in the field in Central Africa.

US Special Forces gained approval to fly the drone over the coordinate point in Binany's GPS. At first glance, the intelligence surveillance and reconnaissance images didn't reveal anything resembling a military base. Just some grass-thatched huts arranged in little clusters, satellite homesteads in a clearing in the jungle. But its location—near water but otherwise in the middle of nowhere, deep in Darfur's no-man's-land—and the presence of significant agriculture revealed that this was more than just an average encampment. Most important, when the Ugandan army compared the aerial view of the suspected LRA camp with Okello's hand-drawn map, it was a clear match.

Okello looked at the drone images and nodded excitedly. "Yes, here's the river," he said. "Here's Kony's hut. Here's where the women stay."

The third puzzle piece fell into place. We had found Kony's elusive stronghold in K2. The mission dubbed it Camp Merlin, after the mythical wizard.

Camp Merlin, the drone images revealed, was an established LRA presence with one major camp and a couple of nearby satellite camps. An estimated 125 women and children and 40 to 60 combatants lived there. Okello showed us the exact huts to focus on to capture Kony. We had found the needle in a thousand haystacks.

That's when Laren called in the middle of the night in 2013 to tell me, "It's time to bet the farm."

4 4

OPERATION MERLIN

"THE UGANDAN MILITARY can bring two Mi-17s to help, but we'll need at least two more," Colonel Kabango said when I was in the region in early February 2013 to strategize for the assault on Camp Merlin. US Special Forces had been technically limited to an advising role—they could help train and provide intelligence for the operation, but no US military–contracted assets could go to Kafia Kingi (K2), and air support was once again proving to be a huge hurdle.

The Ugandan army needed to move troops and gather a large presence near Camp Merlin without alerting possible LRA in the area to the impending operation. The Ugandans' Mi-17 could only fly thirty soldiers at a time. Even if they'd been able to use the two Mi-8s supplied by the Department of State in the politically disputed region of K2, the helos were subject to a huge chain of command, requiring a seventy-two-hour notice to fly. In an active operation, a seventy-two-*minute* wait, let alone seventy-two hours, could be too long. We needed at least two more helos to transport troops and supplies—radios and other equipment necessary for the operation, as well as tents, bedrolls, blankets, clothes, and other "welcome-home" items for the 150 people we expected would be coming out of Camp Merlin. We would need the helos again at the end of the operation to run relays, getting the women and children and any combatant defectors back to the base in Djemah, and then to fly the SOG troops back from the field. Plus, we always needed enough air assets for the unexpected contingencies that were bound to arise. Our partners were looking at us to supply helos for the mission, and though I promised to look into it, I wasn't sure what was possible. We had spent countless months trying to secure one helicopter for the counter-LRA mission. How would we possibly find two more, and in such a short window of time?

The next day, just before I flew home to keep working on securing assets for Operation Merlin, General Katumba Wamala, the Commander of Land Forces for the Uganda People's Defense Force, asked me to take tea with him at the Lake Vic Hotel. I'd been on edge all week, worried about the operational logistics, and General Wamala's warm and cheerful presence was a balm. The image of him singing with the troops after the first SOG graduation almost two years before was still burned in my mind. I'd been impressed by his ability to kindle and inspire hope in situations where others would have given up. He'd always brought such a positive and supportive attitude to the mission, even when he'd been at the counter-LRA work long enough to have suffered many frustrations and disappointments. I wondered if today, on the eve of an assault that had been years in the making, he would express some degree of doubt or caution.

But he looked me in the eyes and said, "Shannon, it looks like we have him. It is going to happen. Please help us with some extra helicopters if you can."

He beamed at me, speaking with unbridled optimism about the mission's potential to secure peace in Central Africa. I knew that we couldn't miss this opportunity to end the war for good. I had to get the extra helos, no matter the cost.

I managed to find a contractor in Entebbe who had two Mi-17s available for charter for Operation Merlin. Funding the helos was an unforeseen and significant cost. We'd entered the mission anticipating that we'd only be involved for a short time, and the unrealistic timeline had affected how we'd used our resources. Howard stepped up again in a major way and we managed to scrape together the money for the helos. Kony's capture didn't seem like a long shot anymore. It seemed like the next possible thing.

We began to build a fuel base for the operation, and we understood that US Special Forces continued to send the drone over Camp Merlin, searching for visual confirmation of Kony's presence. Each successive flyover gave ever more detailed visuals of Merlin—the locations of agricultural fields and simsim drying racks, and the patterns of movement; where and how individuals slept; whether they used private or communal latrines—that made it possible to distinguish LRA rank and file from leadership without seeing anyone's face. But there was no sight of Kony.

Then, on February 12, while the US intelligence surveillance and reconnaissance plane was watching Merlin, Kony made a call on his satellite phone. For the first time in five years, he could be seen and heard by people on the outside of the LRA. He was threatening one of his commanders. An ivory cache had been discovered a few days before, and he blamed the commander for having trusted a subordinate to bury the ivory instead of doing it himself.

A few days later the drone feed picked up the gruesome execution of one of Kony's officers. A person believed to be Kony forced a group into a circle around the victim and then shot him point-blank. After the murder everyone dispersed, walking back to their huts, leaving the body there on the ground. We seemed to be catching up to Kony at his most vulnerable moment, at odds with his leadership, grasping for control. And he appeared to have gained significant weight, which meant he'd likely been holed up at Merlin for some time.

Operation Merlin needed to be launched immediately, while we knew Kony was there. But fuel had to be lifted into position. And it seemed prudent for the SOG troops to run a rehearsal of the assault. Intelligence put Kony's hut in the middle of Camp Merlin, which meant the SOG would have to navigate the surrounding fields and huts successfully in the early morning without raising an alarm. Recent intelligence had also revealed that there was a small Sudan Armed Forces presence within a short distance north of Merlin. We didn't know if the Sudanese forces were stationed there to protect Kony and his camp, but we had to consider that they might use their minor antiaircraft weapons to fire on the SOG soldiers during an assault on Merlin. It seemed better to be overprepared. The SOG built thatch huts in an exact replica of Camp Merlin and conducted a full rehearsal at night.

On Friday, March 1, 2013, I landed in Entebbe for the launch of Operation Merlin. I went straight to the US base to meet with Commander Korbel, and arrived just as Admiral Losey, who had been in the field ahead of the mission, was about to fly back to Stuttgart. They both seemed as optimistic as General Wamala had been three weeks before.

Admiral Losey pumped my hand, and I remembered the feel of the cold edges of the coin he had pressed into my palm almost exactly a year ago. Today his ever-present grin seemed less practiced, more genuine. "This intervention has worked well," he said. "It's a great example of the benefit of public/private partnership." He spoke as though we had already succeeded.

The next morning I met Commander Korbel for an early breakfast at Faze 3. He chattered eagerly about the recent video feed of Camp Merlin and invited me to come to the US Special Forces compound after we ate, telling me he had something he wanted to show me. The atmosphere at the base was high energy, full of smiles and thumbs-ups, an extra kick of confidence and motivation in the air. The document Colonel Korbel wanted to share with me was a plan for information dissemination and coordination with NGOs after the assault. This was a critical piece of the operation, the one that had been missing in Operation Lightning Thunder in 2008. This time the US offered clear recommendations to communicate with civilians after the attack. Civilians would be notified as soon as possible of Kony's successful capture and, most important, warned of any potential threat of reprisal killings if LRA elements managed to escape. The US plan seemed solid and I knew that Invisible Children could be on standby to get word out through the vast HF, FM, and shortwave radio networks that had been built.

Korbel was planning to fly up to Djemah the next morning to set up an operations and communications command, but I wanted to get to the forward base right away to catch Laren before he flew up to the temporary forward base that was much closer to Merlin, to be with Colonel Kabango during the assault. Just as I was heading to the airbase to fly out to the field in our Cessna Caravan, Laren called.

"The birds aren't here," he said. "We're supposed to start moving troops tomorrow, and the helos we chartered haven't arrived. The contractor's AWOL. I can't get ahold of him."

I felt my first flicker of doubt. We were cutting it close with five aircraft. There wasn't room for error or mechanical failure. If we didn't have the air support, we simply couldn't get troops into position to make the assault.

"I'll check the airfield here in Entebbe," I said.

I made a quick tour of the tarmac and saw two white Mi-17s sitting on the field. When I checked the tail numbers I discovered that they were indeed the helos we'd chartered. Two mechanics were working on them, the batteries out on the ground. I said the helos were already due in Obo and the mechanics shook their heads. They wouldn't be flying anywhere today.

I sent the Caravan on up to Djemah with some of the essential radio supplies and stayed behind in Entebbe with the Mi-17s. I hoped my presence would keep the pressure on to get them out first thing in the morning, the latest possible moment when they could leave to get the troops in position. I sat on the airfield most of the afternoon watching the mechanics do the maintenance. Finally, just before dark, they did a preflight test. The helos were ready to go, they said.

That night, I met with Adam Finck, Africa Regional Director of Invisible Children, and we took a walk along Lake Victoria. I hadn't been able to share details of the sensitive mission. Now that Operation Merlin was drawing so near, I knew I could trust Adam to help coordinate the return of the more than one hundred women and children who would likely be coming out of the LRA soon. I was springing something vital on him at the last minute, and was extremely grateful when he agreed to cancel everything else for the next few days to be completely available to assist the former captives leaving Camp Merlin.

On Sunday morning, I came back to the airfield at first light. I couldn't trust the Mi-17s were airborne unless I saw it with my own eyes. By 8:00 they lifted off, en route to Obo. I exhaled.

At 8:30 I met Commander Korbel and we boarded a US Air Force plane bound for Djemah. Recently, the Special Forces had become concerned that there wasn't enough fuel ready at the forward-most base, so they had brought the US Air Force in to drop barrels—a hundred over the last several days—using their planes that were night-rated so they could keep running relays of fuel after dark, something that had always been a limiting factor for us in the field. The US military had really gone all in on this, another sign to me that everyone anticipated a successful mission.

The troops would be dropped later that day across a mountain range from Camp Merlin. They'd bed down during the remaining daylight hours to avoid being seen by farmers or cattle herders and then start their twenty-mile march that night, walking two nights in a row to make a dawn assault on Merlin on Tuesday morning.

When we landed in Djemah, just a few hours before we were to insert the Ugandan troops, Laren was there on the red dirt airfield to greet me. His usually inscrutable face wasn't hard to read today: he beamed with enthusiasm. For more than two months now, since Okello's defection, he seemed to have been riding a resurgence of hope in the mission, and today was the happiest and most positive I'd seen him since we'd begun our work together. "We got this!" he said.

While Laren prepared to head north to the temporary forward base, Commander Korbel set up the US Special Forces operations and communications tent inside the Ugandan base so the Ugandans could be "read in" as the operation was progressing. He had also brought a ground tent so he could stay there in the Ugandan camp instead of with the other Green Berets in the US base up the road. I was truly grateful to him for this.

Early in the evening, I walked over to the US operations tent to get something to drink. They'd been handing out cold purple Gatorades all afternoon and I wanted one more to tide me through the day's last heat. Korbel looked up when I walked in. We'd been sharing easy banter all day, but now he was eerily quiet.

"We just got our eyes over Merlin," he said slowly. "It's empty."

"What? Kony's gone?"

He nodded. "The only sign of life is a couple of baboons."

It couldn't be! It didn't make any sense. We'd been told that satellite imagery of Camp Merlin was being gathered every day, for weeks. And he'd said so recently that the camp was full of life, that he'd seen smoke from the LRA's cooking fires. How could the entire population of Merlin have evacuated so quickly? And how had they known to leave? It couldn't have been a coincidence. They must have been tipped off to the impending assault. But how? And by whom?

Korbel shrugged his shoulders. "I'm sorry," he said. "The same thing happened before Operation Lightning Thunder in 2008. The intel got leaked and Kony up and left."

What were we going to do? I had to talk to Laren and Colonel Kabango. I walked to our mess tent in search of Laren, dreading what I had to say, unsure how I was going to break it to him. He eyed me quizzically when I came in. I could see him register that something was wrong.

"Sit with me," I said, pointing to one of the pilot's trunks.

He sat down stiffly, braced for whatever I had to say. Slowly, I forced out the words. "Merlin is empty."

He didn't speak. We sat together, hanging our heads. Finally he put his arm over my shoulders. "I quit," he said. "I just can't do this anymore." Tears streamed down his face.

I had never seen Laren cry, never seen him show emotion this way.

"I'm so sorry," he said. "I feel like I failed you. And the SOG guys, they are so exhausted, they are so spent from this mission, they haven't had leave in so long, and we asked them to give it their all for this last mission. One of the guys has a jacked-up heart and he's out there walking, bad heart be damned, because he's expecting to find Kony."

"We need to pray," I said. I clung to Saint Jude, still hanging around my neck all these months. I felt hopeless. *Please, God,* I prayed. *Don't let the darkness win.*

But when the SOG troops reached Camp Merlin two mornings later, they found nothing but a ghost town: empty rings of circular thatch huts and rectangular drying platforms for the simsim, a few pumpkins,

LRA Camp - K2
Code Name: Merlin

a sack of marijuana, and some opium growing in a field. The camp appeared to have been empty for at least a week. Kony was long gone. The SOG torched the camp, nothing left when they walked out but dust and smoke, the orange lick of flames glowing bright against the dun-colored grass and barren trees.

WHAT IS GOOD

WHEN WE GOT the news, I grabbed a satellite phone, and for the first and only time in the field, I called my mom and cried.

It had been a long time since I'd turned to my mom. I'd been so busy being a mom myself. But sobbing in the morning heat and humidity, I needed to hear her voice.

She answered right away when I called, even though it was the middle of the night in Texas. "I was lying awake thinking about you," she said. "Are you safe?"

"Yes, I'm safe," I told her, but I couldn't stop crying.

"Honey, what's wrong?"

I knew my devastation wasn't just about the missed best opportunity to catch Kony. It went deeper. How could something so certain have failed? I kept hearing the assurances of smoking fires. "We probably won't get another chance to get Kony," I said. "But that's not even why I'm crying. The hardest part is that doubt is taking over and I don't know who the good guys are anymore."

"Sweetie," she said. "I've been so worried for you. I can't tell you how relieved I am that you're okay."

"I don't feel okay."

My mom met my distress with a verse from the Bible, Micah 6:8, the first verse I had ever selected to memorize when I was young: *He has shown you, O mortal, what is good. And what does the Lord require of you? To act justly and to love mercy* . . . "It hurts right now, honey," she said. "But you know what is good. It's going to be okay."

Her words helped. But I was still full of outrage and sadness. It was as though the collective impact of all the awful things I'd witnessed in my humanitarian work—all of the vilest behavior toward innocents, the brothels and war zones, the jungles where mothers couldn't keep their children safe, where kids were forced to lug a gun around and serve an evil warlord—was crashing over me at once.

The light in me—my joy, my faith, my passion for life—had started out so bright. I grew up believing there was a loving, amazing God who could solve anything, and I'd come at the sorrows of the world with energetic optimism and a belief that despite all the evil, good wins. But with this failed attempt to stop the LRA, it felt like the light in me had dimmed, replaced by a terrible darkness and doubt.

God, where are you? I asked. *How are you allowing this?*

"Did you get Darth Vader, Mommy?" Brody asked excitedly when I got home. I shook my head and told him, "No, love. No."

PART THREE

There are victories of the soul and spirit.
Sometimes, even if you lose, you win.

—ELIE WIESEL

CUT THE SNAKE OFF
THE HEAD

HELLO, MY FRIEND, General Wamala wrote after Operation Merlin. *I know you must be as disappointed as I was about the empty camp. I'm yet to overcome the shock and fully understand what could have happened. Anyway, we say, the struggle continues.*

It was maddening to be in the dark. But there was no clear explanation, no one to definitively blame, no way to seek recourse. We just had to find a way to go on.

We ceased counter-LRA operations for a few weeks to regroup. My biggest priority was to check in on the SOG who'd been doing the hard work and taking all the risks. Operation Merlin was supposed to have been their last operation, the victory to end their two years of service and sacrifice. The defeat had hit them hard, and I didn't know how to express my appreciation for their dedication. I would have loved for the brave, committed men who had proved the impossible nearly possible to keep working for another opportunity to catch Kony. But they had fulfilled their two years of service, and done an incredible job.

General Wamala decided that the whole SOG unit would be reassigned to Somalia—a distinct honor for anyone serving in the Ugandan military because of the relatively high pay: about eight hundred dollars a month, thanks to a stipend from the European Union. In addition to the good pay and overall privilege of the post, life in Somalia would offer a welcome relief from the years of tracking and sleeping in the bush. In Somalia, they'd eat well and live in barracks instead of tents. I wasn't surprised when most of the men chose to be reassigned, and I was glad for them and their families.

Their departure left Laren and me with an obvious question: Was it also time for us to go? On the surface, the answer appeared to be yes. We were physically and financially running on fumes. We'd already bet the farm; we'd used the very last of our resources for the year to charter the helicopters and pilots for Merlin, and we couldn't afford to keep throwing money at bad intelligence. Then, at the end of March, a coup in the Central African Republic, the country the mission primarily operated in, threw the region into chaos, and the US Special Forces withdrew from their base in Djemah. They took everything sensitive— aircraft, ammunition, computers—but left everything else: tents, generators, and food, including a stack of dozens of unitized group rations (heat-and-serve meals) in a single flavor, turkey and gravy. All the signs seemed to be pointing for us to leave, as well.

I called John Montgomery to see if he agreed.

"I trust you to know what to do," he said. "But I like to remind people that in investing, the worst mistake we often make is to pull out when the market takes a dive. When you're at the lowest, that's when you should double down."

I remembered what Senator Kirk had said that day at Muneer's home on Lake Michigan: *When you fail, be ready to go after Kony again. It's going to take three tries.* We weren't quitters. We had set out to stop the LRA, and we hadn't done that yet. There was still so much in place on which to build success. And we'd learned a lot. We'd become more methodical and confident. We knew how to listen and adjust to help empower our partners. And now wasn't the time to walk away—now was the time to learn to walk even better beside them.

But if we stayed, we needed a new strategy. Laren and I met with Colonel Kabango in the command tent in Obo. It always struck me how little the Ugandan military had to work with technology-wise.

The space, with its long folding tables and portable whiteboards, looked low-tech. Across town, at the US Special Forces base, there were banks of computers, digitized maps and intelligence, Internet access. Here on the Ugandan base, LRA movements and Ugandan military operations were marked with Xs on the map that covered the whiteboard.

"All of this time we've been chasing Kony," Colonel Kabango said, sitting forward in his camp chair. "What if stopping the LRA isn't about catching Joseph Kony?"

By all recent accounts, Kony had become a hermit in Merlin, growing old and fat, smoking weed, handing out pumpkins to a diminishing group of abducted children who'd become adult fighters. He seemed to have become an afterthought to many of his own commanders, most of whom hadn't seen him in at least a year. Meanwhile, there were two other International Criminal Court indictees—Dominic Ongwen and Okot Odhiambo—from whom we'd diverted attention in the effort to apprehend Kony.

I saw Colonel Kabango's point. Instead of trying to take out Kony, what if we targeted Kony's key officers? Isolated him. Cut his stability out from under him.

"Kony's nobody without the people directly beneath him," Laren said. "His top-level commanders are the ones who carry out his orders and command his army. If we exploit divisions within the LRA and encourage more defections, we could topple the LRA from the inside out."

"We've been trying to cut the head off the snake," I said. "But maybe ending this war is about cutting the snake off the head."

"Exactly," Colonel Kabango said.

We had our new strategy: the Ugandan army would militarily pursue Kony's key leaders, and we would ramp up defection messaging to further erode the LRA from within. The Ugandan military tracking squads were already putting the right kind of pressure on the LRA, and creating more opportunities for people to escape. We would couple the military operations and increased targeted operations against top LRA leadership with strategic defection messaging to emphasize the reasons for LRA soldiers and commanders to *choose* a different life, to peacefully surrender and begin life anew in Uganda.

An effective defection operation had to start by acknowledging that the problem wasn't necessarily that LRA soldiers didn't want to go home; the problem was that they no longer thought they could. For years—even decades—the soldiers had been kept in the LRA by fear, lies, propaganda. "Uganda has been ravaged by AIDS," Kony told them. "Your family is dead, the defection flyers are poisoned and will kill you, if you leave you'll be prosecuted or killed by the Ugandan government, those left at home will never forgive you." They had even been told that Kony's spirits would follow them and kill them if they managed to escape.

While Kony still made hours-long speeches about his vision of rebuilding strength and returning to Uganda to overthrow Museveni, that goal was so far-flung now, the army's strength so diminished, life on the run in the bush so difficult, that it was unlikely that even Kony's most trusted leaders believed that dream anymore. They weren't staying in the LRA out of loyalty or aspiration. They stayed on because it was what they knew. And they were afraid of the alternative. Perhaps they'd made the calculation: this was a hard life, but at home, if home even still existed, it would be worse. And although there had been a steady rise in defections since the first SOG teams entered the field, we knew that each surrender had been hard-won. One defection flyer, one helo speaker broadcast, didn't typically entice a man to put down his gun and come home. It took months, even years of evidence for him to finally accept that he'd been fed a false narrative and to take the risk of leaving.

Our friends at Invisible Children had been studying defection efforts in other parts of the world. Of particular interest was what the Colombian government had done to stop the Revolutionary Armed Forces of Colombia—the FARC—the longest-running guerrilla force anywhere on the globe. The Colombian government had hired an advertising firm to help encourage the FARC's six thousand soldiers to put down their weapons and return to their families. They'd run several highly effective "come home for Christmas" campaigns, the first two in 2010 and 2011, capitalizing on the FARC fighters' homesickness around the holiday, reminding them that before they were rebels, they'd been daughters and sons.

For the first defection campaign, dubbed Operation Christmas, the Colombian ad firm loaded two Black Hawk helicopters with thousands of LED Christmas lights and decorated a seventy-five-foot-tall tree in the walking path of soldiers living in the main FARC camp. The lights were hooked up to a motion sensor, and when a soldier passed in the night, the tree burst into blue light with a sign saying: *If Christmas can come to the jungle, you can come home. Demobilize at Christmas. Everything is possible.* They'd lit nine more trees in other strategic locations, and defections had increased by 30 percent that year. More than three hundred of the defectors said that the Christmas messaging had motivated them to reclaim their freedom and the warmth of their homes.

The following year, for Operation Rivers of Light, they'd made the campaign even more personal, using the national army's radio station to invite mothers and fathers, husbands and wives to send loved ones in the FARC an individual Christmas message. Thousands wrote personal notes and gathered keepsakes, placing them in watertight, LED-lit capsules that the army set floating on the rivers near FARC bases. *Colombia and your family are waiting for you,* the rivers of light said. *Your country and your family will welcome you with open arms.*

We already knew that an LRA combatant's defection rarely had a single catalyst. It took more than one isolated message to counter years and years of indoctrination. To cut the snake off the head, we'd need to pace ourselves and be ready to play the long game. Laren and his wife, Courtney, had already moved to Uganda to live closer to Laren's work in the field. We agreed that we would both take more rotations with our families to avoid burnout. And we decided to expand our team by hiring Adam Finck, who had already partnered with us on the Early Warning Network and piloting defection campaigns. He would help us develop a more robust defection strategy.

"Taking the LRA down from the inside out is going to require better intelligence," Colonel Kabango said from across the table in the command tent. "And from here on out, I'm not going to rely on anyone else's intelligence about the LRA. I want to focus on getting our own."

More defections would thin the ranks of the LRA and also provide the Ugandan military with current intelligence on the LRA's locations, movements, tactics, and command structure. But we needed to further bolster the Ugandan military's capacity to gather and analyze intelligence. Colonel Kabango said he planned to recruit informants who traded with the LRA. Then he eyed the bulky HF radio sitting in a dark corner of the tent.

"You want to go low-tech," Laren said.

Colonel Kabango nodded. We'd thought the aerial surveillance capabilities would be a silver bullet. But they hadn't proved to be as practical or reliable as we'd hoped. So far in the mission, the intelligence that had made the most difference on the ground was from HF intercepts, GPS tracking devices, and human intelligence. Colonel Kabango suggested bringing GPS tracking devices to Ugandan military informants and tracking squads, and we agreed to help implement that technology.

LRA radio calls were being intercepted but it was impossible to decode the content. LRA communications used a complex brevity code, and the only people in the organization who knew the codes were their radio operators. A huge intelligence breakthrough would come in September 2014, a year and a half after Operation Merlin, when a radio operator defected and shared the codes.

Until then, the content of the broadcasts was impossible to discern, and it was only useful insofar as it could be interpreted to inform decisions in the field. At that time, it was difficult to collate historic and current intelligence. We hired a firm to help build an electronic mapping platform that would bring together intelligence—including radio intercepts, community reporting, and other human intelligence—and allow it to be analyzed all together.

Intelligence could now be digitized daily—sometimes even more often—and now there was the capacity to overlay present movements with historical ones, and see how the current path of movement compared with historical locations of camps or river crossings or wild yam fields, thus allowing for predictive analysis. The picture of the LRA went from static Xs on a map stuck to a whiteboard to a real-time worldview of the LRA.

47

ODHIAMBO THE BUTCHER

THE SUMMER AFTER Operation Merlin, HF-radio intercepts showed that the LRA was on the move again. Kony's group appeared to be disconnected from the other groups, and it seemed that Okot Odhiambo had been put in charge of moving between the disparate LRA groups to spread Kony's orders. If the Ugandan army could intercept a reunion rendezvous, there would be a chance of apprehending Odhiambo and Kony. Even if the high-value targets managed to escape, an assault still had the potential to decimate the LRA's morale, preventing them from fully regrouping, scheduling new rendezvous, or disseminating new radio codes.

This time, the Ugandan army tracked Odhiambo, not Kony. But despite their persistent efforts, Odhiambo and Kony managed to meet without interception, and Kony traveled back to Kafia Kingi. The decision to focus on apprehending LRA top leadership instead of Kony himself hadn't yet yielded a useful result.

Weeks passed, and the rainy season was in full force. Every stream had become a river. A crossing could hold a group—LRA or the Ugandan military—up for days as they waited for the right moment to risk the potentially fatal mix of crocs, hippos, and racing water.

"Keep ahold of Odhiambo's trail," Colonel Kabango told Captain

Charles, one of the most respected new group commanders. "Catch him at a crossing point. And for God's sake, bring a rope."

A few days later, Captain Charles's men found the trail of Odhiambo's group and began to track them through the wet forest. They were a large group, but nimble, and moving fast. Tracking is about who is more committed, the trackers or the ones being tracked. Captain Charles's men were as many as three days behind the LRA group when he found the tracks, but he pushed his team to make up ground by walking longer hours during the day, resting less, sleeping less, and maintaining a fast pace, and he ordered his men to carry as little as possible, to leave any unnecessary items behind in the interest of speed. They jettisoned rations, extra clothes, and the thick, heavy rope Colonel Kabango had provided for dicey crossings.

By the next afternoon, Captain Charles's team tracked Odhiambo's group to a wide, fast river. The LRA had already crossed, but the trail was fresh and Captain Charles thought they might still be camped on the opposite shore. He prepared his men to cross the river that night and hit the LRA camp at first light. But without a rope, in the dead dark of night, with fast water rushing by, the swim was so daunting that only eleven of his twenty men were able to get across. The two groups hunkered down in silence on opposite sides of the river to wait out the rest of the cold night.

At the first hint of dawn, Captain Charles and the members of his team who'd made it across the river were back on the trail, looking for signs of an encampment. They found Odhiambo's full camp and assaulted. The LRA fired back and a gun battle ensued, a cacophony of guns, the muddy ground littered with brass. In the chaos of fire and flight it was hard to tell who was winning, and in the thick of the fire Captain Charles got hit—not by a bullet, but by a bee, his eyelid instantly swelling. As the fight continued, the LRA fled; they ran with nothing, leaving food, tarps, and sandals in their wake. The Ugandan army tracked the LRA for five days in their rapid and scattered flight.

But the results of the assault were inconclusive, the only satisfaction being that the operation had actually come together as planned. Almost invariably in this mission, we'd been forced—by fuel deficits or bad weather or a thousand other variables—to change our plans. But this time, with the exception of the discarded rope, things had happened exactly as planned, confirming the efficacy of Colonel Kabango's strategy and the soldiers' execution of it.

We'd always thought that technology was the necessary and often missing ingredient in operations. Technology had sometimes given an advantage—helped put puzzle pieces together, or provided the confidence to take a risk. But the assault on Odhiambo's group revealed once again that the biggest asset, the truest advantage, was the sweat, persistence, and determination of the Ugandan soldiers. With or without aerial surveillance footage, whether there was complete or patchy or faulty intelligence, the whole mission rested on the shoulders of a handful of skilled and hardworking men.

Then, that afternoon, we heard the LRA on the radio talking to one another. "Big man wounded," someone said. Shortly after, Odhiambo's call sign, Two Victor, was noticeably absent from the radio. It appeared that Odhiambo had been the man hit, but we didn't know for sure; and if he had been hit, we didn't know how severely.

A week later, we learned of an encounter between Odhiambo's two bodyguards and another LRA group. Odhiambo wasn't there, but his distinctive weapon was, the unusual rifle he'd taken from one of the Guatemalan peacekeepers who had been killed by the LRA many years ago. During the meeting his bodyguards began dispersing the captive women Odhiambo had considered his wives, deciding which new groups and commanders they would join. This didn't prove that Odhiambo the Butcher was dead, but when a defector from Odhiambo's group told us that Odhiambo had been shot in the stomach during the battle and taken away from his main group, the evidence strongly suggested that the Ugandan assault by the river had pulled our mission's first International Criminal Court indictee from the field.

I felt no rejoicing at the news of Odhiambo's probable death. But I did see a certain sense of justice in the fact that the man charged with three counts of crimes against humanity and seven counts of war crimes, who had led numerous massacres and commanded attacks against displaced-person camps, burning, shooting, and hacking innocents to death, was likely no longer perpetrating crimes, and I celebrated the triumphs of the many good people who had risked their lives to make the world safe from his violence. We couldn't bring back the many whose lives Odhiambo had already destroyed. There was no redemption in his death. But he could do no more harm. We were one step closer to stopping the top leadership and preventing the cycle of destruction from repeating.

The Ugandan military couldn't announce that Odhiambo had been removed from the field unless they had hard evidence. It had been rumored once years ago that Odhiambo had been killed in battle, and we couldn't risk perpetuating false information.

One afternoon, a team of Ugandans stood in a wet stretch of forest. They could hear the rush of the river through the trees. They'd returned to the site of the battle to see if they could find any signs of Odhiambo's body or grave. By then the fight was more than a week old. Their boots sank in the mud, spent cartridges sometimes visible in the water that pooled in the holes left by their footprints.

They had no idea how far the wounded Odhiambo had run, or in which direction, if he'd been carried or if he'd fled on his own two feet. And even if they'd known where to start looking, the rain had already washed away the trail.

We had to settle for a silent and inconclusive victory. Back at the forward base in Djemah, Laren opened a box of red flyers—US military bounty flyers, picturing Odhiambo, Ongwen, and Kony, the last three remaining ICC indictees—and took one into his tent. He crossed out Odhiambo's picture with a black Sharpie.

Eighteen months later, the International Criminal Court contacted us, asking if we could prove that Odhiambo was dead so they could release his indictment. We shared with them what we knew, and that no body had been recovered. To do so would mean hiring expensive cadaver dogs—it would cost at least two hundred thousand dollars—to try to discover where Odhiambo was buried. I balked at spending the money on something that didn't directly help people living in the conflict zone, especially when finding his grave seemed like such a long shot. Before I could decide what to do, an LRA soldier walked out of the bush and defected near Obo. He happened to be one of Odhiambo's former bodyguards—one of the men who had buried Odhiambo.

But when he took Laren and some Ugandan troops to the gravesite—much farther from the battle site than we would have guessed—the grave was indiscernible. Odhiambo had been buried in the wet season, and now it was dry and the forest looked completely different. There was nothing to do but start digging holes and hope that they'd get lucky. They dug and dug most of a day. Finally, one of the Ugandan soldiers called out—he'd struck what looked like a piece of blue tarpaulin, the same color of the tarp in which Odhiambo had been buried. They finished opening the grave and loaded the remains into the helo so they could be flown to Kampala for DNA testing. Within a few months, we were able to go public with the news that Odhiambo "the Butcher" was dead.

HISTORY CHECKS IN

David Ocitti

DAVID HAD RECENTLY come home to Uganda after his last roadie tour when he heard that his former LRA commander was dead. Images flashed up—Odhiambo's strong face and intimidating eyes, the feel of the panga handle still warm from his thick hands. David tossed and turned in bed that night, his sleep disturbed by the old, bad dreams.

David had shared his story countless times, but he had never named Odhiambo as his commander, never said that Odhiambo was the one who had ordered the attack on Pabbo the night he was abducted and his father killed, the one who commanded him to take the panga and kill his friend. David would never forget the fire in Odhiambo's eyes as he raised a blade above an innocent's head. Thinking of Odhiambo, it was hard not to open the way for blame and anger. But he didn't want to live in that storm. *It has already happened,* he told himself. That was the thing about history. You couldn't undo it. You could only learn to coexist with it. And once in a while history checked up on you, as if to ask, "Hey, how's it going?"

In his heart, if he could choose, he would have had Odhiambo taken out alive. He would have had him face justice and be accountable to everybody for all the people he had captured and indoctrinated and killed. Sometimes David even imagined testifying at Odhiambo's trial, accusing him for all the world to see.

But Odhiambo was dead. And there was justice, too, in this. And hope that soon he would live in a world where there was no more LRA.

48

BLUE-EYED ACHOLI

IN EARLY DECEMBER 2013, about two months after Odhiambo was shot, a hunter near Zemio, a village in the Central African Republic, along the border with Congo, bumped into a group of rebels traveling in the forest. When he realized the rebels were LRA, the hunter tried to run away, but they called out to him in Swahili, saying they wanted to surrender. They gave him a note to deliver to the Ugandan army. It was from an LRA group subcommander. He said his group was ready to defect, and asked for villagers' help in escorting them to safety.

Locals, fearing for their lives, on rare occasions had killed defectors, so it wasn't surprising that an LRA group would ask in advance for civilians to help escort them to a safe surrender point. But so, too, had LRA groups used surrender notes as a strategy to kill community members. People living in major defection points had been alerted to bring such surrender notes to the attention of the Ugandan military stationed in the area. The army was trained to investigate and differentiate between an authentic surrender note and a ruse.

This time, the note wasn't a fake. With the assistance of local villagers, a remarkably blue-eyed LRA commander and his subcommander led their group of nineteen men, women, and children out of the bush in one day. Everyone in the group made it out, not a single person injured. It was one of the largest groups to have ever escaped the LRA.

The commander of the group was known as Lieutenant Colonel Okello Okuti, one of the most notorious brigade commanders to have operated in the Pader District of Uganda, and one of Kony's most trusted commanders. But unbeknownst to Kony, he had been considering leaving the LRA for a long time. In mid-2006, when the Juba peace talks had been initiated, in order to encourage a positive LRA response and outcome to the negotiations, the LRA was given a safe passage to move through to southern Sudan. During this period, Okuti had met some Ugandan military leaders and discussed the prospect of defection. But at that time Okuti enjoyed Kony's absolute trust and the consequent privileges of it, and he saw no need or opportunity to defect.

By early 2013, however, Okuti and Kony had suffered a falling-out. Kony had demoted Okuti two ranks, from brigadier general down to colonel, and had begun talking ill of Okuti during his speeches, using him as a case study of a good commander gone rotten. Kony even spoke of his intention to execute Okuti, and probably would have already acted on it if not for the geographic distance separating them.

Okuti had heard aerial loudspeaker messages and had also found and studied defection flyers. In addition, commanders in Okuti's group typically gathered around a handheld radio once a week to hear the come-home radio program Invisible Children broadcast over shortwave radio every Thursday at 10 p.m. It was a way to receive news from home and from defectors who had recently escaped. Although as a rule lower-level fighters and captive women could not listen to the radio, some were able to pass near to where the commanders were gathered in order to listen, and even to share what they heard with the rest of the group.

As a commander, Okuti heard the come-home messages firsthand. One night, after listening, Okuti had gone to his subcommander and said, "I'm tired of this. I want to go home." Kony always put a loyal soldier in the position of second in command. If the commander tried to escape, the second in command was supposed to kill him. Okuti expected his subcommander to execute him. But instead, the subcommander had said, "If you go, I'll go with you." They agreed to surrender together, to leave the bush with their entire group.

No LRA commander had ever before risked a mass defection. Once his group was safely at the Ugandan military camp, women smiled, children tried on new pairs of flip-flops, boys traded their camouflage fatigues for khaki trousers or loosely fitting black pants. And when he was finally home in Uganda, Okuti sat in a bright red button-up shirt and recorded a message: "We heard our brothers who previously escaped on the radio. Then we also got the defection flyers. To those who are still back in the bush: I reached safety and I am well. Nothing bad has happened to me. Each and every one of you should think about the value of your life and come back home."

FIVE-PIECE SUIT

David Ocitti

THE SPARKLING GUITAR lines and upbeat bass and horn riffs of Lucky Bosmic, one of northern Uganda's most popular musicians, blasted through the open stalls of Gulu market. David wove past the fresh produce carefully stacked on low tables and blankets. He had returned to Gulu to finish his studies and was still adjusting to the heat and pulse of home. He turned a corner, past appealing stacks of tomatoes, peppers, bananas, and carrots, and was surprised to see a blond head bobbing through the crowd. As the mzungu approached, David was even more surprised to discover that he recognized him—it was Adam, whom he'd first met in 2011 during his work with Invisible Children. They had become friends over time, and now they were meeting by chance. Adam was moving fast, running from one stall to the next, carrying armloads of clothing and supplies.

"What are you doing?" David asked as they gave each other a hug around the bundle of goods in Adam's arms. "Can I help?"

Adam explained that he was gathering supplies for LRA return-ees who had recently flown home to Uganda from the Central African Republic, where they'd defected en masse. It was Okuti's group—who became known as "The Zemio 19." They were staying in a government transit center where they would wait for their amnesty certificates to be processed, and try to find their families. Four more recent defectors, including Kony's nephew, were due to arrive in Gulu the next day.

"You're helping bring my brothers and sisters home," David said. "Let me help you welcome them."

The next morning, David was there on the landing strip in Gulu, the first person in northern Uganda to greet the newest returnees as their feet touched native soil. As the returnees carefully stepped down from the Cessna Caravan, David recognized the emotions on their faces: relief, apprehension, uncertainty. He remembered his surreal trek through Pabbo, looking for his mother, the way strangers had recoiled from his appearance, their suspicion and distance, and the crushing disappointment and fear when he discovered that his mother no longer lived there, when he'd had to face the possibility—the likelihood—that she was no longer living at all. And he'd only been away for six months. Those returning home now had been gone for years, maybe even decades. The child among them, Kony's nephew, a boy about six years old, had been born in captivity. He knew no other life.

David greeted each person in turn. *"Apwoyo,"* he said. *"Apwoyo dwogo gang."* Thank you for returning home.

David accompanied the group to the government-run transit holding center, a dingy and unwelcoming concrete structure where they would stay while arrangements were made for them to go home to their villages. He made sure each returnee had a bed and blankets, a toothbrush, and other basic necessities. Over the next few days and weeks, he would help them contact their families, a process that could be lengthy and difficult. Many LRA soldiers and captives had been abducted as young children and had spent decades in the bush. They didn't really know where home was. They would remember the name of their village, and recall a few landmarks, but they didn't know how to get there. And they had no idea if home would be at all recognizable even if they managed to return. Was anyone they'd known as a child still alive? Would they be remembered? Leaving the LRA was just the first hurdle to claiming a new life.

A few days later, he accompanied them to Gulu market to get shoes and pick out civilian clothes—each person selected two complete outfits. The group would stay while arrangements were made for them to go home to their villages.

At Gulu market, the group wound their way to the tables and blankets stacked with clothes and the stalls lined with bolts of fabric and tailored dresses, where vendors sat at sewing machines, making African print shirts and dresses. As they sifted through piles of jeans, T-shirts, blazers, and blouses, the returnees began to smile. They pressed shirts against their chests, testing for length. Kony's young nephew chose a gray five-piece suit and shiny dress shoes. He insisted on taking off his shredded clothes right there in the market and wearing his new suit back to the transit center.

LET YOUR HEART
SPEAK TO YOU

THE FIRST MASS defection involving LRA commanders was a huge victory. We were now seeing proof that the LRA could indeed be dismantled from the inside out. Odhiambo had been the commander in the LRA who moved between LRA groups, enforcing Kony's orders, and instilling fear in the rebels, ensuring they would not try to escape. In his absence, and knowing that Kony's enforcer was no longer on the battlefield and unable to come after them, people in the LRA were able to dream of leaving. We kept our strategy of pursuing the LRA day and night while simultaneously ramping up defection messaging.

And we began to address some of the gaps in our strategy that Okuti's group revealed. Yet again in this unlikely mission, the gaps became opportunities to discover unprecedented resources, alliances, and superpowers. This time, they came in the form of passionate local leader David Ocitti. I learned through Adam of David's incredible journey from LRA captive to activist and peacemaker and was again humbled and inspired by the power of individuals to respond to injustice and effect change.

One afternoon, shortly after Okuti's group had returned to Uganda, David and Adam held a meeting with Okuti and several other recent LRA defectors. They sat in a circle on folding chairs in a dark room in the government transit center. Okuti's expression changed frequently as he talked about his group's escape and their future—grinning one moment, lips parted in a smile that showed his bright teeth, and studious the next, his mouth drawn tight, brow furrowed.

International funding for rehabilitation had long dried up in Uganda, and the government was not investing enough resources either. The transit center was in terrible shape. They lacked basic supplies, the latrines were overflowing, conditions unsanitary. Returnees' stays were intended to be brief, but they often stretched to months. With a lack of personnel and funds, the family tracing and amnesty processes took a long time. David had visited the Amnesty Commission's office to learn why the amnesty process was dragging on, and found that the run-down office was locked, the windows dark. No one was there. The commission was so under-resourced that there was no money to pay the employees or process the certificates. Although the law still mandated the commission, they were unable to operate.

"I'm hearing all the time from people here that conditions are so bad they wish they never left the LRA," one of the returnees told the group.

"We can't continue to encourage surrender if life at home in Uganda is worse than life in captivity," Adam said.

David agreed. "Let's do something here first," he said. "Let's fix the latrines. Let's make it sanitary, let's bring dignity back here. Let's get funding to process the amnesty certificates so returnees can get back to their families right away." The certificates gave legal protection to defectors so they had assurances that they wouldn't be prosecuted through the Ugandan justice system. In the coming months he would receive Bridgeway grants to fund both projects.

But that was just the start. "Physical security, legal security—these are necessary for quality of life," David said. "But if we're really going to thrive after months, years, even decades in captivity, we need to be more than physically safe. We need to know that we're valued, that we have a purpose." His long face grew serious. "We have to find a way to get over the guilt from the past. We have to be able to forgive ourselves."

Okuti and the others nodded, and the room grew still.

Adam finally cut the silence. "I hear what you're saying about the importance of healing and reintegration. Are there concrete things we can do together to support that process?"

David had two ideas. He suggested that we fund the public ceremonies and celebrations in returnees' home communities to knit the community back together and spiritually cleanse everyone from the pain of the past. And he said we should focus efforts on rehabilitation and practical vocational training.

"Before captivity, each of us had a dream—to become like someone we admired, a doctor or teacher. To offer value in the community. But Kony gave us a different dream. He forced us to believe something else: I am a killer, I am a murderer, I don't belong at home anymore, this is my spot. He gave us only one dream: to rise in the ranks, to command a brigade. When we come home we need to remember: What is my dream? What pushed me to come home? What do I want to give to my family and community?"

"I know my dream," Okuti said. "I will do anything now to stop the LRA. That's my dream, to get my brothers and sisters home."

Everyone in the circle nodded and murmured agreement.

"Your courage to come out may inspire many others to do the same," Adam said. "What do you think would be most effective to influence other senior commanders and large groups to come out without bloodshed?"

Okuti's bright smile flashed. "I can tell you about other commanders who have fallen out of Kony's favor or are tired of fighting. Get messages to them, personally, that I've come out, that I'm safe."

We had seen the efficacy of broad defection messaging in encouraging people out of the bush, and we knew that high-level defectors were especially credible sources to someone still trapped in the ranks. But this was the first time we seriously considered targeting specific LRA members by name, and drawing them out with voices, not fire.

Adam helped Okuti record messages for radio broadcast and helicopter loudspeaker messaging addressed to specific individuals within the LRA—leaders like him who were primed for defection, including someone called Opio Sam. He had been abducted as a young child and had spent twenty-four years with the LRA. He'd become well respected and highly ranked in the organization, but, like Okuti, had recently fallen out of favor. He was currently in LRA "jail." Physical imprisonment wasn't possible on the move, so instead he'd been stripped of his weapons, staff, and title—a punishment that amounted to losing his identity. The advantages that might have been keeping him with the LRA didn't exist anymore. And his life was in the balance; it was well known that Kony had been killing other formerly loyal commanders. Okuti reasoned that Opio Sam might feel threatened enough to risk an uncertain fate—to end his twenty-four years in the LRA.

Okuti's suggestion to call out specific disgruntled commanders reinforced our "cut the snake off the head" strategy. Targeted messaging had the potential to further drive a wedge between Kony and his senior leadership, creating a rift that we hoped would help foster disloyalty toward their leader, while strengthening their ties to an ally who had already defected.

Okuti recorded short and long messages, some to be played over local FM radio stations in the LRA's area of operations, and some shorter and more targeted messages to be played over aerial loudspeakers in specific locations where Ugandan intelligence showed a particular leader's group might be.

"First, I want to thank the people of Acholiland and the entire people of Uganda for welcoming us back home," one of Okuti's messages began.

He went on to address Opio Sam and other commanders directly, calling them out by name:

Other people like Opio Sam, we are also friends. Remember what happened to you? Your own wife was taken and now she is with Kony himself. Just think about this and know that your life is the most important one. You were taken by force, you have been forced into all these horrible things, and *what are you fearing?* Think about your people and your home and let your heart speak to you.

A SON NEVER FORGETS

I REMEMBERED THE article Opa had shown me a few years ago at Christmas, about Kony's mother's deathbed wish for him to make peace. What if Kony had heard her plea? Could his mother's voice have been powerful enough to call him home? What if we could make the targeted defection messages even more highly personal? David had enhanced and expanded his volunteer reintegration support; he'd formed a local organization funded by Bridgeway grants, and was helping with all aspects of reunification, including tracing the families of recent defectors. What if he could help find mothers, fathers, child-hood friends of people who had not yet defected, and record the voices of their families calling them home?

David told Adam he was happy to try, but warned us that family tracing held no guarantees. He often traveled five to eight hours a day, sometimes several days in a row, to remote villages where there were no roads for cars to pass, only to find neighbors and friends and family members who had long since given the LRA captive up for dead. To hear that a loved one they'd already grieved was alive wasn't always joyful news. Families were often suspicious of David; sometimes they just didn't want to reopen a wound.

One time he'd happened upon a defector's family after they'd given up on their loved one's return and decided to fix a date to perform the last funeral rites. When he'd said he was there on behalf of their family member who'd recently returned they'd said, "No, he is dead."

David had insisted that their son had come out of the LRA, that he was safe with the Ugandan army at a base in the Central African Republic, that he was ready to come home. But the family had been so distressed and frightened that they'd smashed David's phone, taken his keys, and screamed at him to leave them in peace. David's presence wasn't a gift, it was causing them suffering. They had already let their son go, and hope was too painful for them to kindle. David had refused to leave, insisting that he was meant to be there, to help their son—who'd been abducted at age eleven and was now twenty-four—come home. He showed them a recent picture of their son—but no one, not even his own mother, recognized his face.

David had kept coming back to check in on the family, and finally, on a subsequent visit, the returnee's brother had examined the photo again and recognized him.

But now, David was on more uncertain footing. We were asking him to trace the families of individuals who had not yet left the LRA. If David managed to find their families, he had to encourage them without making any promises. To help their loved ones come home they would have to take the risk of investing hope in a reunion that might not ever occur, of falling headlong into an old loss, of rupturing whatever peace had been earned through time and healing. They would have to open their hearts to the possibility of more disappointment and pain.

David traced the family of an LRA member who seemed ripe for defection and drove long hours to the village where he hoped to interview the LRA fighter's family. The mother held her face in stiff reserve when David knocked on her door and introduced himself, but she invited him to enter her clean, simple home with its gray mud walls and dirt floor. She was much shorter than David, her back curved with age, her bony shoulders visible under her large black sweatshirt. David remembered the awe of seeing his own mother again after six months of captivity. If this woman's son came home after many years in the bush, he'd find his mother irrevocably changed. The strong back that had carried him through infancy and babyhood was now stooped, her short hair now silvery gray.

As David told her the story of his own abduction and escape and difficult homecoming, the experiences that motivated his attempt to help with the reintegration work now, she carefully nodded her head. When he described his reunion with his mother in Alero, the feeling of her hands on his head as she cleaned his wounds, tears gathered in her eyes.

"Does my son even remember me?" she asked.

"Take it from me," David told her, "a son never forgets."

Her message for her son was as poignant as it was simple: *"Dwag paco."* Come home. "I have never stopped waiting for you."

BROTHER, YOU ARE HOME

WE CONSTANTLY PLAYED Okello Okuti's message over the area where we knew Opio Sam's group was operating, and waited to see if the targeted defection approach would work. But for week upon week there was only silence on the other end.

Then, on May 17, 2014, an LRA HF radio communication was intercepted. The signaler said, in brevity code, "As we talk right now, Opio Sam has escaped." For many months he had been hearing defection messages and contemplating leaving the LRA. He had reputedly split away from his group, but had kept with him the forced wives of other men. His "hands passed onto them"—he raped them. He feared there would be consequences for his transgression. This was the tipping point that pushed him to finally act on his long-standing desire to leave the LRA.

Two other HF radio intercepts confirmed that Opio Sam had left the ranks. We waited to see if and when Opio Sam would surrender. Weeks passed, but he didn't appear.

In late June, Laren and Adam came to San Antonio for an operations meeting. We were sitting at my kitchen table, reviewing defection efforts, when Colonel Kabango sent us a text on WhatsApp, followed by an email: *Lt. Col. Opio Sam is out*, the subject line read. The body of the email said, *Go to my drop box for photos!* On June 24, Opio Sam had walked out of the bush near Nzako. He wore dirty military fatigues. His head was wrapped in a black-and-white checked bandana. He'd made the decision to end two and a half decades of captivity. And he'd made it out alive.

He was brought to Obo, and Colonel Kabango was the first to greet him with a big smile and a warm handshake, an arm around his back. Then the Ugandan troops stationed at the base there greeted him one by one. In the photos Colonel Kabango shared with us, Opio Sam looked thin from years on the run. His camouflage jacket was buttoned high, his belt cinched tight. But in every photo, he was beaming.

"His smile says it all," Laren said.

Opio Sam's defection was a huge triumph—the first time in the mission that we'd experienced such a successful convergence of military pressure, intelligence, and defection tactics. It was also incredibly poignant. I'd been privileged to see the Ugandan army welcome defectors throughout the mission. "Brother, you are home," each Ugandan soldier would say, some respectfully shaking the returnee's hand, others enveloping him in a huge hug.

I still wanted Kony and his warlords to stand trial at The Hague. But I was seeing a different version of justice, the peace that came from deep forgiveness and restoration.

Opio Sam was offered food and a shower and civilian clothes, but before he would attend to any of these creature comforts, he wanted to make sure his ambitions were clear. "I want to help the others come out," he said eagerly. "I heard those voices in the jungle—now I want them to hear my voice calling them home." Sam volunteered to pose for a defection flyer photo before he'd even been invited. His smile in the photo is infectious.

After the debriefing, he went back out into the bush with the Ugandan military squad to chase the same satellite group he'd once commanded. He led them to a weapons cache he'd helped bury. And he initiated meetings with community leaders. In one village, a diamond-mining town where some had traded and met with the LRA, Sam held meetings with the same villagers he'd met with when he was an LRA commander. He insisted on wearing a Ugandan military uniform to these meetings to send a signal, essentially saying, *The LRA has lied to us. We've all been lied to. I'm out by choice, and I'm working with the Ugandan military now to get these guys out.*

Opio Sam also recorded loudspeaker messages with Adam, and flew with him several times over the jungle in the Bell 412 for hours on end during four straight days of message dissemination, playing his message: "I, Opio Sam, am urging you to have the courage to come back home, so you can start a new life." When they flew over areas where certain commanders were known to be operating, he called them out by name.

THE BITTER ROOT
David Ocitti

WHEN IT WAS time for Opio Sam to return to Uganda to begin his new life, David was the one to drive him to his home village several hundred miles outside of Gulu. David steered his aging Land Cruiser—he affectionately called it "The Tank"—over uneven ground, turning the music up, trying to make Opio Sam as relaxed as possible, and also trying not to dwell on the mixed emotions of being in the presence of an older, high-ranking former LRA commander, someone who had participated in the brutality for twenty-four years. David had been held captive by men like Opio Sam; they'd forced him to take orders, to witness unconscionable acts. Opio Sam had left the bush, but many abductees were still in the ranks. Ending the cycle of violence required so much more than one person's defection. And helping get someone like Opio Sam home was only the beginning of the pivot from violence to peace.

To remove a combatant from the battlefield was one thing; the battlefield also had to be removed from the man. He needed an ox-plow and seeds so he could farm and eat. He needed psychosocial support so he could learn to trust others and build healthy relationships. Many defectors suffered from PTSD and were prone to erratic behavior. They needed a way to make a living and a life, when in many cases the LRA was the only life they'd ever known—or at least the only life they remembered.

"Man, you're back," David said to Opio Sam now, navigating The Tank over a pothole. "You fought the first battle."

"Yeah, and I'm done fighting for a madman," Opio Sam said. "I'm through with all that." Opio Sam had worked for Odhiambo and still bore the scar on his lower back from a caning for an unnamed offense. His body held many scars.

"Coming out is just the beginning," David cautioned. "Going home seems like the end of the struggle, but it's not going to be easy."

Opio Sam looked away from David, staring steadily ahead as if trying to see through the cloud of dust rising up on the road.

"It's a battle where you won't be following anyone's command. It's your choice how it ends up—whether it's positive or negative."

David knew that Opio Sam had already applied to join the Ugandan army, the chosen path of many defectors. A military career didn't appeal to David, and it was important to him that LRA defectors have choices in the life they made. But he could understand why joining the Ugandan military would be appealing to some. They were already proficient soldiers, and they wanted to make a positive contribution with those skills. In addition, the military paid better than many other trades. It was a way to make enough money to give back to their families. Moreover, the highly structured military life helped many make sense of freedom. Though Opio Sam had wished to join, he was in his mid-thirties, and had been deemed too old to begin a military career with the UPDF.

"I worked with small motors in the LRA," Opio Sam said. "I think I could be a good mechanic."

"If that is your dream, that's good, we can help you get some training," David said. "When we get to your village, you'll see that the community is going to welcome you. But don't think they're going to forget the past. No one ever forgets. Once it's written, it's written. It will never disappear."

David thought of the terrible look on the boy's face when he had confronted David in the schoolyard, the ragged edge in his voice as he yelled, "It was you!" The pain and confusion and guilt had been so intense, he had barely endured. But now he saw that moment as a blessing. It had prompted him to choose a path to peace and to discover a life purpose.

"They lost everything," David continued. "They lost limbs, they lost loved ones. And now that you're here, what are you going to do to reassure them that yes, it was you, but you didn't intend to? It's your job now to show your community that you feel their pain and you're here for the good."

David had been to many reunification ceremonies, and he was well-versed in the traditional reconciliation mechanisms built within Acholi culture. When they arrived in Opio Sam's village, a local leader would help facilitate two traditional ceremonies that worked hand in hand with Uganda's policy of legal amnesty to enable victims and perpetrators to live together in peace. The dissonance had to be acknowledged—even accepted—before it could be transcended. The community reunification ceremonies helped clear the air.

They arrived in Opio Sam's village under a gunmetal sky, the earth still soft from recent rain. The entire community, about one hundred people, had assembled. As The Tank drove up, they rushed toward the vehicle, encircling it. David slowed The Tank to a crawl as they gathered. Some were barefoot, some in sandals or flip-flops, others in dress shoes, the men wearing collared shirts under sweaters or jackets, the women in brightly printed dresses with high pointed shoulders and long full skirts—turquoise, gold, magenta—

some with matching scarves wrapped around their heads. The elders
held carved wooden staffs. The community members shook their
hands above their heads, ululating joy and reverence, running
alongside the car as though pushing it in their current. David cut the
engine and Opio Sam opened his door, flashing his gigantic grin.
Before he stepped out, David put a hand on his shoulder.

"*Gang dong en,*" he said. This is home. Home is here now. Home: a
place and a moment in time. This is it, and here we are.

Opio Sam waved at those gathered, gazing everywhere, as though
drinking them in, searching for a familiar face. He would not be allowed to see his mother until the first ceremony was complete. She
waited for him now inside her hut. Community members called his
name, reaching out to touch him, hug him, bless him as he stood
among them for the first time as a man. Their ululations rose into a
song of welcome. An elder led them, dancing, to the doorstep of
Opio Sam's mother's home. The elder signaled that he was ready to
begin the ceremony by holding up a small brown egg.

"When our sons and daughters are taken away by the LRA," the
elder said, "we believe that because of the atrocities they've done, their
feet became bloodied in the jungle. Opio Sam, you did not choose to
be taken away, but now you walk on dirty feet. You are like this egg. Its
shell is dirty, we don't know what it has touched, where it has been.
But inside the egg, nothing dirty has touched it. Inside, it is pure."

He laid the egg on the ground at the threshold of the hut. "Opio
Sam, our brother, our son, you have come home. You will now step
on this egg, you will break its shell to show that you have intentionally broken the old path, that you are walking a new path now."

Opio Sam lifted his foot and smashed it down on the egg in the
doorway of his mother's house. The bright yolk, the iridescent white
spread over the ground, coating the mud, covering his foot.

"The purity inside of the egg has washed the dirtiness away. You no longer walk a dirty path. This is your new beginning."

The celebratory cries took on a heady pitch. The air reverberated. Now Opio Sam was cleansed from everything in the past. Now he could go inside and be welcomed by his mother.

He stepped through the door. It was dim inside her house. David stood behind him in the doorway, also searching the dark for the mother's face, her high cheeks and kind eyes. She moved out of the shadows. She cried her son's name. She drew his body close and he bent to embrace her. She was delicate and small. She gripped him with force.

David came into the house, followed by the elders. Wooden folding chairs had been gathered in a circle for *mato oput,* the second ceremony, a communal cleansing. Mato oput was usually performed only when a combatant had committed violence against his own community or family. In this case, the community had requested mato oput because of Opio Sam's status and duration in the LRA. He had been a high-ranking commander. He hadn't attacked his own community, but he'd been a man of power in the LRA and they needed a way to forgive him for that. Why hadn't he chosen to release his captives? Why hadn't he left a long time ago?

A woman brought a wooden bowl filled with a brown liquid, a tea made from a bitter root. Opio Sam would drink the tea, and so would any in his community whom the LRA had harmed. They would swallow the bitterness together. Victim or perpetrator, they shared the same pain, and in sharing the harsh bitterness of the tea together they would become free of guilt and blame. They would be cleansed and ready to feast together on the goats killed and cooked for the occasion, and to face each future moment—joyful or bitter—together.

5 2

GRACE'S SUN

IN SEPTEMBER, ADAM called from Obo. "Laren's sick again with malaria," he said, "but I'm going to tell you what I'm seeing right now so you can see it, too." He was out on the landing zone, about to welcome the single largest return of LRA members since the mission began. As part of a multi-day release of captives, dozens of women and children had been cut loose by their commander and come out of the bush unscathed. It was the first time such a large group of women and children had come out on their own, without any men.

I could hear the spin of the chopper's blades in the background. Adam began narrating everything he saw. "The helo doors are opening," he said. "Women and children are pouring out. There are so many people, over forty I'm counting." One woman had a one-week-old baby in her arms. She had given birth on the run, eating roots to keep herself and the baby alive during their flight. As the mother's feet touched the ground, Adam described a piercing ray of sunlight that burst over her and her tiny newborn, over everyone gathered to welcome the group home. I could picture it exactly as he described it, and feel the warmth of that bright sun. It felt like a blessing. The message was getting through to people stuck in captivity that there would be a life for them back in Uganda, that these kids could go to school, that there were opportunities to rejoin their families and get jobs. The combination of pursuit and messaging was wearing down the LRA command and devastating morale. In this case, a large LRA group in

Congo had been ordered by Kony to release half of their women and children so they had a better chance of outrunning the UPDF's pursuit.

There were so many young ones in the group—babies, kids in fatigues who took off their uniforms and gum boots and put on tennis shoes. We had stockpiled dozens of defector kits in the event of a mass defection like this one. We had nine dome tents at the base chock-full of supplies: new clothes, toys, radios, pots and pans. Adam helped open up the tents and distribute the goods and called David in Gulu so he could begin preparing to welcome the returnees and help them get home.

One young boy stood out from the others. He was about two years old. He wore a zippered army fatigue vest and fatigue shorts. He was tiny, with a broad forehead and gently sloping eyes. His hair had an orange tint and his belly was distended, signs that he might be malnourished. While the babies and other toddlers his age were safe with their mothers, sitting in laps, held against hips, this boy didn't appear to have a mother. He wandered the group, receiving brief attention from one mother before being passed to the next. He circled among the women, and then back to Adam, raising his arms in the universal gesture of a child wishing to be picked up and held. He clearly wanted connection and comfort. But he didn't speak a single word to anybody. His name was Lapeko. He was the only child in the group to have come out of the bush without his biological mother.

His father, a low-ranking Ugandan LRA fighter, had two captive wives, one Ugandan and one Congolese. Lapeko was the son of the Congolese forced bride. She had not been released with the group of forty-six. Lapeko needed a caregiver.

And then there was the matter of his silence. It seemed less that he was unwilling and more that he was unable to speak. David promised to do his best to find the child's father's family in Uganda, and to see that he received care and treatment in the meantime.

More than a year after Merlin, our change in strategy and its results were coming into focus. We had removed Odhiambo, an International Criminal Court indictee, and Binany, the orchestrator of the Makombo massacres, from the battlefield; convinced Okuti and his entire group to defect; and now we were pressuring the LRA to release its captives en masse. What if Kony did live out the rest of his days commanding a diminishing army from his hiding place in Kafia Kingi? He was scared, in poor health, grasping for control. His fate seemed less significant than surmounting the challenges and embracing the possibilities that were now available to so many others: Lapeko; the newborn baby whose mother had given birth on the run; the former combatants, afraid to face their communities after the atrocities they'd committed, being embraced by their families; the mothers reaching to welcome them home. The mission had taken us further than we ever anticipated going. And we were still out here for the compelling reasons that had put us on the ground in the first place.

Viewed through that prism, we had to measure our success not only by the number of indictees removed from the battlefield—which, so far, was one—but also by the number of children and mothers and combatants we helped out of the bush, and their quality of life once they reached freedom. Since the start of our mission to stop a warlord, more than seven hundred of Kony's captives had been liberated. Better all of them than one Kony.

53

HE CALLS HIMSELF ALI

ONLY ONE MORE International Criminal Court indictee, besides Kony, remained in the bush: Dominic Ongwen, aka White Ant, who had ordered the attacks in the second Christmas massacres in 2009. We might not apprehend Kony. But there was another opportunity for justice to be served.

Ongwen eluded capture throughout the rest of 2014, but during this same period of massive defections, intercepted communications between LRA groups revealed that morale was at an all-time low and that there'd been a major disruption of command and control structures within the organization. At least 14 percent of the LRA's core fighting force had defected or been captured since Operation Merlin, and defections of long-term LRA members had gone up by 81 percent since Odhiambo's death. With constant pressure from the Ugandan military and fewer fighters in the field, the LRA's capacity for violence had dropped significantly. We wanted Kony to be captured and brought to justice. But with nearly all of his top commanders gone, he had lost effectiveness.

In January 2015, almost two years after Operation Merlin, a chief in a community near Kafia Kingi contacted the Ugandan army about an LRA defector who was traveling in disguise—he called himself Ali, and was dressed as a nomadic cattle herder. US Special Forces went to pick him up and bring him back to Obo. On the flight back to their base, they realized who was in their custody. The man called Ali was none other than Dominic Ongwen.

Popular among the rank and file of the LRA for standing up to Kony and his violent brutality, Ongwen had become a threat to Kony and had been marginalized within the organization as Opio Sam had been, stripped of his title and weapon. He had escaped weeks later with the help of LRA members sympathetic to his plight.

He was the first indictee to come out alive, the first LRA warlord who would face a global court and be held accountable for his crimes, the first time the mission could fulfill the goal of bringing a perpetrator of mass atrocities to The Hague. It had been six years since I'd read Ida Sawyer's report on the first Christmas massacres—violence that Ongwen himself, as senior commander of the LRA forces in Congo, had led—and convinced John Montgomery and the Bridgeway Foundation board to redefine and narrow our priorities to stopping the LRA. My heart pounded when I called John to tell him the news. I felt joy, an overwhelming sense of victory. I also realized that I was holding my breath. There had been so many close calls and near wins, surprises and betrayals over the years that I couldn't quite trust that this outcome was real.

We began flying our Cessna Caravan, dropping flyers that pictured Ongwen in an ivory-colored T-shirt, his black hair in a crisp buzz cut, a circle of yellow beads around one wrist. His message read in part:

> I am Dominic Ongwen. You all know me. I spent a very long time in the LRA; I know everything there is to know about the LRA. I have decided to come out from the bush. For those of you who are still there, you should know that Kony now has no plan that can push the LRA higher. He only wants to be the chief and you to work for him and his family like a slave. You are not the one who started the LRA, so why do you want to remain there? All your brave commanders have been killed or defected.

Kony is planning to kill all of you. I am Dominic Ongwen, former LRA brigadier commander, but I don't want to be in the LRA. Thank you.

The last remaining International Criminal Court indictee other than Kony had left the battlefield. A week later, Ongwen was sent to The Hague.

His defection was further proof that Kony was grasping for control, demoting and executing senior officers, promoting junior officers, shaking up the command structure in desperate attempts to keep his power. Kony was frustrated and morale throughout the organization was at an all-time low. For all intents and purposes, the snake of the LRA had been cut off its head.

Bringing Ongwen to justice signaled a clear victory for the mission. His story also embodied the complexities of the war: a child victim could become the world's worst mass murderer; and the perpetrator who on the surface seemed unredeemable came out with a kernel of humanity intact. Ongwen had left the LRA to protect his own life, but he also took action to help others come home.

Not long after Ongwen's defection, seven LRA combatants living in Kafia Kingi planned what is believed to be the first-ever assassination attempt of Kony from within the organization. Since Odhiambo's death, there had been a power struggle within the LRA to see who Kony would choose to fill the number two spot in the command structure. Alex Aliciri, one of Kony's chief bodyguards, was angry that junior members of the LRA were being promoted to senior positions, and troubled by the wave of beatings and executions Kony was committing against his inner circle. He did the unthinkable. He led the rebels in his direct command in an uprising, attempting to kill Kony in his own hut late at night. Kony's bodyguards managed to defend Kony in the gunfight, and the would-be assassins fled. It took them a month to trek to Obo, where they surrendered in June. Their defections brought the number of combatants in Kony's personal group to a new low: sixteen.

SO IT CAN END

David Ocitti

DAVID LAY ON a cot in a military tent in Obo. It was past ten o'clock at night. The generators were off and the camp was dark. Alex Aliciri and some of the others who had attempted the rebellion against Kony rested nearby in the tent. They'd been out of the bush for a few months, had gone home to process their amnesty certificates and perform reunification ceremonies, and then asked what more they could do to stop Kony. David had accompanied them back to the Central African Republic to help them with a defection messaging campaign.

It was late, but David couldn't sleep. He could hear the others moving around and chatting in the dark.

"What do you think Kony's up to right now?" someone asked.

"That man was like a dad to me once," another replied.

"Yeah, a dad who ruined your life. Now he should pay for all the time he wasted that you won't ever get back," Aliciri said.

Sometimes David found it hard to be around others who had left the LRA. It forced him to relive the past, to remember the fierce look in the commander's eyes when he'd demanded, "Who do you love the most?" To see the fathers grouped together. To hear the thud of the rebels' sticks. Sometimes the memories pushed him down the path of rage and desperation, or futility. Sometimes he searched for information about his brothers, trying to uncover any tiny clue that could reveal something about their fate. Always, the fall was steep when he realized there would be no miracle, no surprise reunion, not even a piece of information that could help bring closure to the loss.

And yet, there was a comfort, too, in trading stories with the only other people on the planet who knew the world he knew. Around him, the other men began sharing stories in the dark, of abductions and beatings and battles. Among these men, nothing was secret. Nothing was too much to share or to hear. They had seen it all, lived through it all. You could speak openly with people whom nothing you said could shock or terrify.

The air in the tent was still. Aliciri spoke. "This one night we got into a heavy gunfight with the UPDF," he said. "They shot my gun from my hand. I had to leave it there when I ran."

A few of the men murmured, acknowledging the gravity of their own stories, of the countless similar attacks they'd been forced to participate in.

"Where was that?" David asked.

Aliciri thought a moment. "Pabbo," he said.

David's heart pounded. His whole body tensed. He felt that a door stood before him. He tried to keep his voice from shaking. "I'm from Pabbo," he said. "It's where I was abducted."

A silence grew between them, thick like smoke.

"Man," Aliciri said.

David stared up into the dark. His chest felt tight. *It has already happened*, he told himself. *It's not happening now.* They were the words he used to repeat to himself. *It happened. Now what?* Once, he had longed to hold his captors accountable. To stand before the world and name the wrongs that the perpetrators had committed against him and countless others. But that wish had changed form.

A laugh burst out of him. "Damn," he said into the night. "Full circle."

A tight place within him, something he'd kept so long, released. The others laughed, too, their chuckles growing longer, softer, changing cadence. Then they were quiet again in the dark.

"Can I ask you something?" Aliciri asked out of the silence. "Why are you trying to help us?"

"So you can help someone else," David told him. "So it can end."

54

EVIL HAS TAUGHT ME
THE MOST

KONY WAS STILL at large. I wanted desperately for him to stand trial before the International Criminal Court. But the mission had changed me. I'd seen so many different versions of justice: Acellam, Okello, Okuti, Opio Sam, and so many others coming out of the bush and starting new lives; Odhiambo's death; Ongwen's imminent trial. Each instance of amnesty and retribution had forced me to grapple with the humanity of the perpetrators—and with my own. I still believed in the necessity and significance of the International Criminal Court, and I was proud to have supported the effort, risk, and sacrifice that brought one of their first-ever indictees to stand trial. But I no longer thought that retributive justice worked on its own. I also had faith in the restorative kind.

I decided it was time to tell Laren and my team that our work on the LRA was for the most part done, and it was time to move on. I knew Laren would see things differently: that we hadn't yet finished what we started, that the outcome wasn't the one we'd hoped to accomplish. But it didn't make sense to me to continue to commit more and more resources to the hunt for a ghost who was no longer causing the same level of harm. It was neither sustainable nor practical.

Laren flew to San Antonio and we sat at my kitchen table. He seemed to know what I was about to say.

"We're going to live in a world where a mass murderer goes free," he said, his voice full of steady conviction. "We didn't capture Kony. I can't say we won."

"We tried everything," I said, "and we won on so many fronts. There were close to eight hundred civilians killed by the LRA the year before the SOG deployed. Last year, only thirteen people died. It's devastating that any lives were lost. We want that number to be zero. We want no one to be killed by the LRA ever again. But the mission has had huge successes securing the region, protecting children and families. That's what the mission was always about. Protecting lives. Now we can take our resources, take what we've learned, and apply them in other contexts and conflicts. We can keep pursuing better ways to stop atrocities."

Laren was quiet. Finally he said, "I always imagined the day when Kony would come out in custody. How all of us from such different walks of life—Colonel Kabango, the Ugandan soldiers, David, the US Special Forces, the Central Africans running the HF radios in Obo—how all of us who'd been there together in a hostile environment trying to stop this vicious group would exchange hugs. How we'd celebrate. We got so close to that dream."

"We did," I said. "And this time, it's as close as we're going to get."

I always thought that the goodness in the world would awaken me to my highest spiritual self. But it's evil that has taught me the most, that has brought me to advocate for innocents so fiercely. It isn't comfortable, it's an unsavory concession, to give so much credit to the power of evil. But it brought me and many others to see our human interconnectedness more clearly, and to take action that didn't seem possible. If the mission has taught me anything, it's that we can't eradicate the shadows. But we can hold our share of the night. For those of us whose lives have been largely protected from horrors, for those of us who have been fortunate to grow up in peace instead of war, we have a responsibility to share in the efforts to end human suffering. To stand together, to live in service to others' lives, to find our own way to make a difference.

recently deployed to Somalia with the African Union mission to stabilize the country from the terrorist group al-Shabaab.

General Katumba Wamala was promoted to Chief of Defense Forces of Uganda, assuming the highest military rank in the Uganda People's Defense Force. He now holds a government post as Minister of State for Works in the cabinet of Uganda.

Howard G. Buffett, as chairman and CEO of the Howard G. Buffett Foundation, continues to invest rare risk capital to support food security, conflict mitigation, and public safety. In September 2017, he was sworn in as sheriff of Macon County, Illinois.

Colonel Michael Kabango is now a brigadier general in the Uganda People's Defense Force. He has served as a defense attaché to Somalia, the leader of the quick reaction force to Burundi in 2016, and the overall commander of the Ugandan military force protecting Uganda from the terrorist group the Allied Democratic Forces. He is now the commander of Uganda's 5th Infantry Division and the Ugandan Contingent Commander to the African Union Mission in Somalia (AMISOM). He and his wife have three children.

Opio Sam, having been rejected by the Ugandan army when he first came home to Uganda, earned his mechanic's certificate in December 2015. Shortly after his graduation, the UPDF made an exception on age limits for new recruits for soldiers leaving the LRA, and he completed basic training. He is now deployed with the UPDF, and fulfilling his dream of helping his family members attend school.

Lapeko, the only child among the forty-six captives who were part of the multi-day release in early fall 2014 to come out without his biological mother, spent two years at St. Jude Children's Home in Uganda while David Ocitti tried to find members of his extended family. It was especially challenging to find them because Lapeko's father was a low-ranking Ugandan LRA fighter who had been abducted from a large camp and about whom few details were known, and because Lapeko couldn't talk or communicate (his caregivers eventually discovered that he is deaf). David began screening people who were abducted around the same time as his father and finally discovered someone who could help locate his family. St. Jude arranged for La-peko's reunification with his grandmother and extended family. He is now six years old, and will begin school soon. To date, Lapeko's father has not returned from the LRA.

Dominic Ongwen is still in the custody of the International Criminal Court, awaiting the completion of his trial, which began in December 2016. The prosecutor has charged him with seventy criminal counts, including attacks against the civilian population, inhumane acts, enslavement, outrages upon personal dignity, forced marriage, rape, torture, sexual slavery, and the conscription and use of children to participate actively in hostilities.

ACKNOWLEDGMENTS

This book was an extraordinarily challenging project. There are so many people without whom it would never have happened. While I am only able to thank a few here, I am grateful for each and every person who made this book possible—and who made the mission it describes a reality.

First, to our inspiring Ugandan and Central African partners, and individuals and communities affected by the LRA, who allowed us to join you on this journey: I learned more about humanity and myself in these years than I ever could have imagined. Your strength and protection of innocents have compelled me to be a better mom and a better person each and every day. Thank you for teaching me what true forgiveness and reconciliation look like.

David Ocitti, of all the choices you could have made after your terrifying experiences, you chose the hardest path: radical forgiveness and dedication of your life to serving those who are looked upon as perpetrators. You doubled down and gave all of yourself back to the cause to help your brothers and sisters. You are a giant of humanity and I literally pinch myself every day that I get to call you friend.

For Abbé Benoît, you fought for the country you knew and so many are standing on your shoulders today and are safer because of your courage and your dedication.

General Wamala, thank you for being an honest and open partner in this endeavor. Thank you for your heart.

Colonel Kabango, thanks for always bringing the men home safe. Thanks for being an incredible collaborator on the mission.

To the SOG, thanks for pushing to the end. Godspeed. May the wind always be at your back and the sun on your face.

Laren Poole, finding the words to thank you is the hardest part of this book to write. Words are wholly inadequate to express the depth of my gratitude and awe. Long ago, as a sophomore in college, you took a risk and went to a faraway place where you saw terrible things. Instead of coming home to your comfortable college student life, you allowed what you'd seen to transform you—and even quit college just a few credit hours shy of graduating so you could fully commit yourself to stopping the atrocities you'd seen. You introduced me and countless others to the LRA, rejecting the injustice that a mass murderer went free solely because he perpetrated atrocities on people who "didn't matter." It was your righteous anger that propelled us on this journey, and your commitment to never give up until innocents were free from terror that made this mission a reality. That ferocious spirit is the only thing that carried us at times. You've worked tirelessly from that point through today, walking together with me through a decade—through the highs and the lows, and the lows, and the lows. Your sacrifices are numerous: malaria a dozen times over the course of this mission—including cerebral malaria, which could have taken your life, but you were back out there weeks later; and more that brought us to the brink, but through which you were unswervingly relentless. There is simply no one else with whom I could have done this. All of it is because of you. Thank you.

Courtney Poole, you surprise me at every turn with your flexibility. Thank you for moving to Uganda, for the sacrifice of being away from your husband so many weeks and months on end, and for displacing yourself and supporting your husband through this mission.

Mama Poole, thank you for offering to buy that camera for Laren back when he was in college, and for always encouraging his passions. Thank you for raising a son without whom this mission would not have been possible.

Adam Finck, thank you for making the sacrifices and taking the personal risk when few others would. You made us better, more powerful, and taught us so much. This was never a job for you but rather an act of love and friendship.

Jen Tallon, thank you for making it all work. We never could have done this without your fierce heart, organizational skills, and dedication to the mission.

John and Ann Montgomery, thank you for founding a company to stop horrific tragedies on the globe and thank you for entrusting me with that mission.

To my partners at Bridgeway Capital Management, thank you for doing the everyday work that made this mission and so many others possible. Thank you to the partners who showed up at the right time to give support in just the right way. Tammira Philippe and Tony Ledergerber, thank you for your help, especially as we brought this book across the finish line.

Ida Sawyer and Ken Roth, your work is never-ending and often thankless. Thank you for shining a spotlight on this tragedy and doing the deep work of fighting for change.

Greg Joachim, thank you for your tireless efforts on behalf of this cause. Your help took many forms, and your guidance was a superpower for us.

Muneer Satter, our first partner in this mission, thank you for your persistence and counsel. Whenever we got stuck you were there and it made all the difference.

Howard G. Buffett, you brought laughter and joy to this work. It was the only thing that sustained me many times.

Ann Kelly Bolten, I met you and within hours you purchased boots and jumped on a plane to go with us. You never left us. Your presence has been a constant in this journey and made us better at each turn.

Mark Rigel and all the dog handlers, thanks for the incredible job in the field.

To our friends and alumni at Wellspring Philanthropic Fund—

Myles, John, Mike, Sadia, and Caroline—thank you for your continued partnership and support, and for being a strategic thought partner.

To Scott Terry, thank you for taking a risk on us and donating such a significant portion of the cost of your air platforms to us and for sending the greatest pilots on the planet to work with us on this mission: B.J., John, Guil, and the other fearless bush pilots who joined us along the way.

Eeben Barlow and the trainers, your sweat and sacrifice translated to lives saved, thank you.

Dan Pickard, thank you for your wise counsel during this unorthodox mission.

Sam, when I left home each time I never doubted that I was leaving our boys with the only person in the world whose love for them matched mine. That is the greatest gift I could have received. Thank you for loving us so well.

To my boys, Connor and Brody, you are and will remain my constant inspiration. You are my heart.

Mom and Dad, what a tremendous privilege it was to be parented by you. Thank you for showing me with your actions every day that a life spent investing in others is truly a life fully lived.

To my dearest Opa, who died in the final days of finishing this book, thank you for loving me unconditionally. I was never alone.

To our local human rights partners operating in hostile environments, risking your lives in order to defend the rights of others—your bravery inspires me beyond measure, and your work is making the world a more secure place.

To the International Criminal Court staff, thank you for the great collaboration and for working so diligently on these cases.

Jason Russell, thank you for selflessly sharing your extraordinary gift for storytelling and using it to highlight the plight of those affected by the LRA. Ben Keesey, thank you for building a compassionate and proactive organization to serve those suffering the most.

Jolly and Emmy, thank you for all the hard work and connections you made to help with the mission, and all you continue to do.

Paul Ronan, thank you for giving over a decade of your life to this cause, for seeking truth even when it involved weeks of travel in uncomfortable circumstances. Thank you for helping us with the details of this book. And Michael Poffenberger, thank you for founding one of the most effective and dedicated grassroots advocacy organizations I have ever witnessed.

Admiral Losey, thanks for the unprecedented collaboration on this mission. One day I will give the coin to my boys.

To those who are still active members of different parts of the US government and need to remain unnamed, thank you for taking a risk on us. For not letting the red tape or the conventional way of doing things get in the way.

Archbishop Tutu—Arch—thank you for loving me. Thank you for all the ways your life has been an extraordinary example to humanity.

Gary Haugen, it all started with you. Thank you for the inspiration, trust, and incredible example you set for me.

Gi Morales, a friend in the truest sense of the word, you pitched in with carpools, food runs, and homework help for my boys while I was away and loved them like your own. This never would have been possible without you. And to all the others in my mama tribe, thank you for loving on my family so that this was possible. Melinda Tucker, Estelle Ybarra, Asia Ciaravino, and countless others—thank you.

Pam Omidyar, my soul sister, when the words wouldn't form you were there to listen to my silence, and you heard me. You powerfully set me back on the path over and over, and called me to my better self. I am grateful to you and to this work, as it brought you into my life.

Bill Townsend, thank you for always and unequivocally having my back. Everyone needs a Bill in their life. Thank you for being mine.

Richard Branson, thank you for never failing to ask me how the mission was going or encourage me every time we spoke.

Jean Oelwang, thank you for your friendship, constant encouragement, and solidarity in striving for a better world.

Dan Cooper, thank you for being there on the ground with us after we failed to help pick up the pieces. Failing is hard, failing alone is impossibly hard—thank you for not letting us fail alone.

Fred Smith, when the evil I encountered caused my faith to shake, you were there to remind me that deep sadness and regret for the state of our world is not only consistent with my faith, but part of the journey.

Esmé Schwall Weigand, I've lost count of the number of times I wanted to give up on this book. Thank you for keeping me "in it" and bringing my heart to its words and pages.

Kathy Robbins, it wasn't easy, and at times it was insanely hard, but you were always there by my side to make it easier.

Doug Abrams, I told you this story at a time when I believed it wasn't going to be possible to put it on paper. You assured me it could be done and then graciously came alongside me to ensure it was. Thank you, friend.

Spiegel & Grau at Random House, thank you for giving this book a home. For Julie Grau and Gina Centrello, thank you for that meeting so many years ago where you gave me confidence that this book could come to life. For Emi Ikkanda, thank you for living this book with us, and for your incredible contributions along the way.

To those whose names I had to change in this book, you know who you are. Your sacrifices were immeasurable and your names are left out here because you continue to make those sacrifices. Thank you.

Many people prayed for me all along this journey. I am certain that prayer sustained us. Thank you all for that investment, and for keeping us covered in prayers every minute: Deborah Amini, Scott and Shannon Austin, Julie Baldwin, Michele Camp, Sarah Canfield, Mark Carvajal, Elsabeth Cooper, Sam Davis, Mike and Joanie Davis, Will and Cara Davis, Tynan Davis, Shantel Davis, David Dixon, Kenny and Karen Fargason, Steve and Polly Friess, Jana and Jeff Galt, Emily Gambino, Susan Gay, Rob Harrell, Steve Hearne, Monika Henderson, Les Hollon, Rachel Hollon, Shawn and Xochitl Hughes, Miriam Keesey, Jeff Kemp, Kevin and Kelli Mainz, Jesse and Sue Minor, Kristen Minor, Luann Mire, John and Ann Montgomery, Gi Morales,

Mike Mulcahy, Opa (Melvin Sueltenfuss), Carey Peek, Vicki Petty, Leslie Popiel, Kourtney and Matt Price, Tiffany Scott Soliz, Abigail Sedgwick, Perry and Dee Dee Sedgwick, Chris and Jill Sedgwick, Dan and Katherine Sedgwick, Richard and Debbie Sedgwick, Joanie Sedgwick, Brian Stone, Alyssa Stone Dixon, Missie Swayze, Jen Tallon, Danielle Voss, Janet Weatherson, Stan and Theresa Whitney, John and Linda Wright, and Summer Wright.

TIMELINE

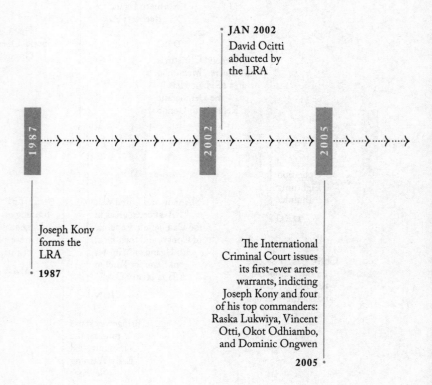

JAN 2002
David Ocitti
abducted by
the LRA

Joseph Kony
forms the
LRA
1987

The International
Criminal Court issues
its first-ever arrest
warrants, indicting
Joseph Kony and four
of his top commanders:
Raska Lukwiya, Vincent
Otti, Okot Odhiambo,
and Dominic Ongwen

2005

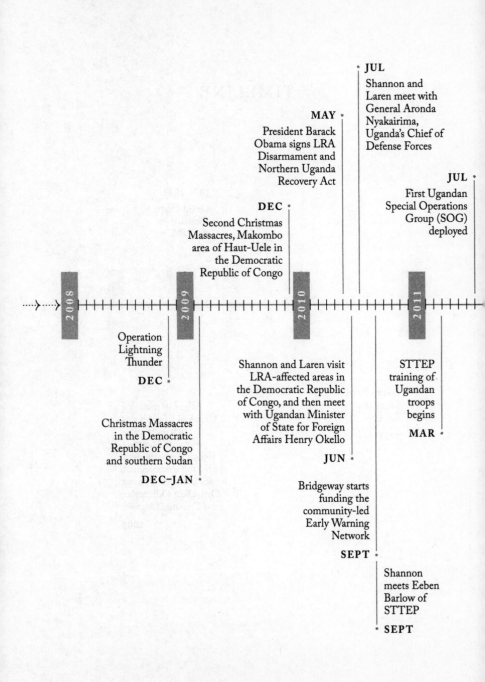

JUL
Shannon and Laren meet with General Aronda Nyakairima, Uganda's Chief of Defense Forces

MAY
President Barack Obama signs LRA Disarmament and Northern Uganda Recovery Act

JUL
First Ugandan Special Operations Group (SOG) deployed

DEC
Second Christmas Massacres, Makombo area of Haut-Uele in the Democratic Republic of Congo

2008   2009   2010   2011

Operation Lightning Thunder
DEC

Shannon and Laren visit LRA-affected areas in the Democratic Republic of Congo, and then meet with Ugandan Minister of State for Foreign Affairs Henry Okello
JUN

STTEP training of Ugandan troops begins
MAR

Christmas Massacres in the Democratic Republic of Congo and southern Sudan
DEC–JAN

Bridgeway starts funding the community-led Early Warning Network
SEPT

Shannon meets Eeben Barlow of STTEP
SEPT

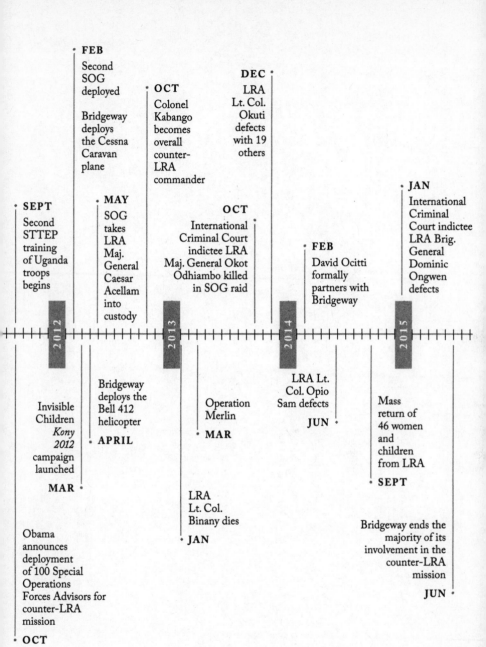

FEB
Second SOG deployed

Bridgeway deploys the Cessna Caravan plane

OCT
Colonel Kabango becomes overall counter-LRA commander

DEC
LRA Lt. Col. Okuti defects with 19 others

JAN
International Criminal Court indictee LRA Brig. General Dominic Ongwen defects

SEPT
Second STTEP training of Uganda troops begins

MAY
SOG takes LRA Maj. General Caesar Acellam into custody

OCT
International Criminal Court indictee LRA Maj. General Okot Odhiambo killed in SOG raid

FEB
David Ocitti formally partners with Bridgeway

2012   2013   2014   2015

Invisible Children *Kony 2012* campaign launched

MAR

Bridgeway deploys the Bell 412 helicopter

APRIL

Operation Merlin

MAR

LRA Lt. Col. Opio Sam defects

JUN

Mass return of 46 women and children from LRA

SEPT

Obama announces deployment of 100 Special Operations Forces Advisors for counter-LRA mission

OCT

LRA Lt. Col. Binany dies

JAN

Bridgeway ends the majority of its involvement in the counter-LRA mission

JUN

GLOSSARY OF TERMS

Acholi An ethnic group from northern Uganda. The LRA's founders were Acholi and later it was the Acholi population that suffered the most at the hands of the LRA.

AFRICOM United States Africa Command, the US Defense Department entity responsible for military relations with African nations, the African Union, and African regional security organizations, and overseeing all US Department of Defense operations, exercises, and security cooperation on the African continent since 2008.

Bridgeway Foundation The philanthropic arm of Bridgeway Capital Management that gives away half its annual after-tax profits.

DRC The Democratic Republic of Congo, also called DR Congo or Congo, and formerly called Zaire; the second-largest country in Africa and the eleventh-largest in the world; bordered by Zambia, Angola, Republic of the Congo, the Atlantic Ocean, the Central African Republic, South Sudan, Uganda, Rwanda, Burundi, and Tanzania.

Garamba National Park One of Africa's oldest national parks, located in the northeast corner of Congo, and home to chronic poaching, which contributed to the imminent extinction of northern white rhinos. The LRA established its base near Garamba after leaving Uganda in 2006, and continues to exploit the park for ivory.

Holy Spirit Movement A Ugandan rebel group led by Alice Auma (later called Alice Lakwena), an Acholi and spirit-medium who attempted to topple Yoweri Museveni's government in 1987. The LRA was formed from the remnants of Alice Lakwena's army.

Human Rights Watch A nongovernmental organization that exposes human rights abuses like torture, violence against women, and child exploitation, helping protect rights and save lives in more than ninety countries worldwide.

The International Criminal Court (ICC) Based at The Hague, an intergovernmental organization and international tribunal established in 2002 under the Rome Statute, with jurisdiction to prosecute individuals for crimes of genocide, crimes against humanity, and war crimes in situations where national courts are unwilling or unable to prosecute criminals, or when the United Nations Security Council or individual states refer situations to the court.

Kafia Kingi A disputed territory on the border between Sudan, South Sudan, and the Central African Republic where Joseph Kony is still believed to be hiding; also called **K2**.

LRA The Lord's Resistance Army, the rebel group Joseph Kony established in Uganda in 1987 to defeat President Yoweri Museveni; accused of committing vast human rights violations, and still led by Joseph Kony, the LRA continues to operate in Kafia King, the Central African Republic, and the Democratic Republic of Congo.

The LRA Disarmament and Northern Uganda Recovery Act A 2010 US act of Congress signed into law by President Obama that made it

American policy to dismantle the LRA and promote recovery efforts in war-affected northern Uganda.

MONUC The United Nations Organization Mission in the Democratic Republic of the Congo, the UN mission in Congo established in 1999. The acronym is based on its name in French. The organization was renamed **MONUSCO** in 2010.

Operation Lightning Thunder A failed military attack on the LRA base near Garamba National Park that began in December 2008, a joint offensive by the Ugandan, Congolese, and South Sudanese armies, with logistical support from US military advisers. The botched mission furthered death and displacement in the region when in response to the attack, the LRA conducted a wave of bloody reprisal killings against civilians in northeastern Congo and southern Sudan.

SOG Special Operations Group, the soldiers within the Ugandan army who received specialized training in counter-LRA tactics by Eeben Barlow's team, and went on to see many successes in the counter-LRA mission.

STTEP Specialised Tasks, Training, Equipment, and Protection International, a privately owned military, intelligence, and law enforcement training and advisory company supporting primarily African governments, led by Eeben Barlow.

The Elders Founded by Nelson Mandela, an independent group of global leaders working together for peace and human rights.

UPDF Uganda People's Defense Force, the national military of Uganda.

US Special Forces Specialized members of the United States military, in this book referring to those deployed on the United States Department of Defense's counter-LRA mission in Central Africa.

Yoweri Museveni President of Uganda since 1986, Museveni helped lead the rebellions that toppled two previous leaders, Idi Amin and Milton Obote. His early political marginalization of the Acholi fueled the formation of various northern rebel groups, including the Holy Spirit Movement and the LRA.

HOW YOU CAN HELP

At the time of this book's publication, the LRA's capacity to commit atrocities has been severely diminished, and members of Kony's rank-and-file continue to defect from Central Africa. Through David Ocitti's incredible leadership, and alongside dedicated partners on the ground, we are continuing to develop and distribute defection messaging, encouraging combatants to lay down their arms and surrender peacefully. We are committed to carrying out family tracing and reunification for Ugandan men, women, and children coming out of the LRA and to supporting this vital work for years to come.

Becoming aware of atrocities in the world and confronting our increasingly interconnected reality is an important step in the process of creating change. Sometimes, the greatest gift we can give others is presence. Other times, it is to speak out—to use our voice, our art, or our influence to amplify the voices of others. And sometimes, it's to be generous with our skills and resources, and to get behind local leaders living and working on the frontlines.

To ensure that David's critical work is sustained, and to carry out and support other impactful protection initiatives in the region, we have a non-profit fund called The Resolve dedicated to ensuring that every person who escapes or chooses to surrender can be reunited with their loved ones and go through a meaningful reintegration program that gives opportunities for healing and economic empowerment. Beyond the LRA, we are working to apply best practices for locally led

322 HOW YOU CAN HELP

communication and reintegration initiatives into other neighboring conflicts in Central Africa. We believe in the power of peace messaging to stop conflict and in meaningful reintegration to end it for good.

To see this work in action and get updates from the ground, or to make a tax-deductible donation to help promote peace in Central Africa, visit theresolve.org.

SHANNON SEDGWICK DAVIS is the CEO of Bridgeway Foundation, a philanthropic organization dedicated to ending and preventing mass atrocities around the world. As an attorney, activist, and passionate advocate for social justice, she has guided Bridgeway Foundation in pioneering solutions to these seemingly intractable issues. Before joining Bridgeway Foundation in 2007, Sedgwick Davis served as Vice President of Geneva Global and was the Director of Public Affairs at the International Justice Mission (IJM). She is an honors graduate of McMurry University and Baylor Law School. Sedgwick Davis currently serves on the Advisory Council of The Elders and is a board member of several organizations, including Virunga Fund Inc. (chair), Humanity United, charity: water, This Bar Saves Lives, Verdant Frontiers, and, formerly, TOMS LLC.

ABOUT THE TYPE

This book was set in Caslon, a typeface first designed in 1722 by William Caslon (1692–1766). Its widespread use by most English printers in the early eighteenth century soon supplanted the Dutch typefaces that had formerly prevailed. The roman is considered a "workhorse" typeface due to its pleasant, open appearance, while the italic is exceedingly decorative.